Special Thanks to:
Joani Blank
Michael Burns
Rachelle Goodfriend
Ruth Gottstein
Michael Graves
Liz Hudgin
Steve Mehalko
Phillip Mitchell
Tom Moon
Don Polkinghorn
Don Propstra
Wendell Rickets

Anal
Pleasure
& Health

SECOND EDITION

a guide for men and women

Jack Morin, Ph.D.

illustrations by
Jen-Ann Kirchmeier
Tom Till

Copyright © 1981 by Jack Morin
Second Revised Edition © 1986

ISBN 0-940208-083

Yes Press
An imprint of Down There Press
P.O. Box 2086
Burlingame, California 94011-2086

See back of book for ordering information.

Yes Press participates in the Cataloging in Publication Program of the Library of Congress. However,
in our opinion, the data provided us for this book
by CIP does not adequately nor accurately reflect
its scope and content. Therefore, we are offering
our librarian/users the choice between LC's treatment and an Alternative CIP prepared by Sanford
Berman, Head Cataloger at Hennepin County
Library, Edina, Minnesota.

Library of Congress Cataloging in Publication Data

Morin, Jack. 1946-
    Anal Pleasure and Health.

    Bibliography: p. 237
        1. Anal intercourse. 2. Anus (Psychology). 3.
    Sex customs — United States. I. Title.
    HQ72.U53M74   613.9′6   81-9789   AACR2

Alternative Cataloging in Publication Data

Morin, Jack.
    Anal Pleasure and Health: a guide for men and
women. Burlingame, CA, Yes Press, copyright
1981, 1986.

    PARTIAL CONTENTS: Anal pleasure and the
anal taboo. —Looking and touching. —Beneath the
skin: locating and exercising anal pelvic muscles.
—Anal eroticism: including the anus in self-
pleasuring and masturbation. —Attitudes toward
rectal stimulation. —Mutual exploration. —Anal intercourse. —Power and anal pleasure. —Common
medical problems of the anus and rectum.
        1. Anal sex. 2. Sex manuals. 3. Masturbation.
4. Sex and health. 5. Body awareness. 6. Anus. 7.
Rectum. 8. Sexual exercise. I. Down There Press.
II. Title. III. Title: Health and anal pleasure.
        612.6

TABLE OF CONTENTS

LIST OF FIGURES AND GRAPHS

PREFACE TO
THE SECOND EDITION

It has been more than four years since the first edition of *Anal Pleasure and Health* was published — plenty of time to observe public reaction to the first book on this hidden subject. The biggest surprise to me is the intensity, pervasiveness and persistence of the "anal taboo." The first dramatic evidence of this came when the bindery took one look at the book and promptly shipped it back to the printer, unbound. And the bindery that eventually took the job now refuses this second edition. Then came the unwillingness of some important review media to publish reviews and the refusal of the vast majority of bookstores to have anything to do with such a book.

One bookstore in Texas, asked by a customer to order the book, couldn't even *hear* the correct title, so the order came in for *Ain't No Pleasure In Health*. Is is it a coincidence that this distortion is completely contradictory to the central idea behind the book?

Of course, even when the book is available in a bookstore, most people are too embarrassed to buy it openly or to be "caught" reading it in public. Therefore, we decided to present this second edition with a removable jacket over a plain cover. Now you can read about anal pleasure on the bus without creating an uproar.

As always, however, there's another side to the story. In spite of (partly *because* of) the anal taboo, there is a very strong current of curiosity about anal sexuality, and a hunger for accurate information. Overcoming many obstacles, thousands of men and women have found ways to obtain and read the book. As we were preparing the second edition, there had to be three additional printings to keep up with the demand. Among those who have read and used the book, the response has been almost totally positive.

This second edition has been completely re-edited to make it clearer and more accessible. A number of important citations have been added and material has been expanded in many areas. For example, this edition addresses more completely the concerns of "insertors" in anal intercourse. And responding to readers' requests, we've added an index to help you more easily locate specific information.

Appendix A on anal medical problems has been given special attention, including the addition of current information on Acquired Immune Deficiency Syndrome (AIDS). AIDS was making its unwelcome appearance in the U.S. just after the first edition was published. Now it's even more crucial that those who wish to enjoy anal sex become well-informed and sufficiently comfortable with the subject to discuss it openly with a partner. This is the best way to make health-promoting decisions about sexual behavior.

I'm recommending, as I always have, that anal intercourse be de-emphasized and more attention given to other, less risky forms of anal sensuality. In fact, until a vaccine becomes available that is effective against the AIDS virus, intercourse should be practiced selectively. And if there is any chance that either partner might have been exposed to the AIDS virus, a condom should always be used. The chapter on anal intercourse has been expanded to help readers face the challenges of AIDS in a self-affirming manner.

It is important that necessary behavioral changes be made without reverting to old, anti-anal attitudes. Unfortunately, it is abundantly clear that AIDS is intensifying the anal taboo. Nonetheless, AIDS need not ruin the sensual/sexual enjoyment of the anus, as many people think. Rather, this health crisis requires that we become even more conscious about all aspects of our sexuality. There is no better time to reject the silence, discomfort and misinformation perpetuated by the anal taboo. Now, more than ever, this is the best road to anal pleasure and health.

Jack Morin, Ph.D.
October, 1985
San Francisco, California

1

ANAL PLEASURE AND THE ANAL TABOO

This book is unusual because it concerns a part of the body that very few people discuss openly: the anus. In fact, many, perhaps most, men and women are deeply alienated from this part of the body. For these people, the anus is a hidden, dirty, uncomfortable or numb area; it functions outside of their consciousness except, of course, when pain erupts. The anal area is either a source of too much sensation (pain) or none at all (numbness).

It's different when we are infants and small children. Then we take delight in all parts of the body. But something happens in the course of growing up; most of us learn to take much less delight in our bodies. We may mistrust or ignore our physical selves, perhaps viewing the mind or spirit as more important than and separate from our bodies. We are taught to view sensual play and self-exploration as immature and self-indulgent if not kept within strict limits.

This process of physical self-alienation is especially pronounced in the anal area, which often is the bodily symbol of all that is unclean and disgusting. It is understandably confusing that a part of the body that is supposed to be so unsavory is also extremely sensitive and potentially among the most enjoyable. Especially for children, the discovery that the anus is considered bad and repulsive must be confusing, because that idea directly contradicts their pleasurable experience.

People learn to cope with this contradiction in a variety of ways. Some make only the concessions necessary to meet social standards of appropriateness, and go on enjoying anal sensations in every way they can. Such people will find the information and suggestions in this book helpful in reinforcing and enhancing anal pleasure. Others have accepted cultural attitudes and are emotionally and sensually separated from their anuses. Some of these men and women prefer *not* to become more familiar with this part of their bodies. They will probably have little interest in reading this book.

Another group of men and women are trying to overcome a long history of misinformation and negative attitudes. They are discovering—or at least beginning to consider the possibility—that they have been missing something to be found between the extremes of pain and numbness: pleasure. This book is primarily for these people. It is a practical guide, based on the experiences of dozens of men and women who have actively sought to rediscover the anal area as a positive part of themselves—a part to be known intimately and enjoyed.

Yet another group of people have much to gain from reading on, even though they have no particular interest in anal *pleasure*. These are the millions who live with annoying, often very painful, anal medical problems. Diseases like hemorrhoids, fissures (tears or scrapes) and constipation are among the most common medical problems in our society. And those who suffer from these conditions will find useful information and practical tools in this book, including suggestions for self-exploration that can lead to permanent relief. Once freed from anal problems, many people are delighted to discover that the same nerve endings that once transmitted pain are available for transmitting pleasure.

Anal pleasure means different things to different people. Usually it is a private experience. At the least, most men and women have occasionally experienced anal pleasure during bowel movements. Others may have noticed spontaneous pleasant sensations in the anal area in the course of walking, dancing, sitting or other activities. These sensations emanate mostly from nerve endings called proprioceptors, which transmit stimuli generated by muscles and organs within the body.

It is possible to provide oneself with pleasant external stimulation, as when wiping after a bowel movement, bathing or simply touching oneself for the pure pleasure of it. External anal stimulation is sometimes erotic, a part of deliberate self-pleasuring or masturbation. Self-stimulation may also be internal as when a finger or object, such as a vibrator or dildo, is inserted into the anal canal or rectum.

Anal pleasure can be shared as part of sensual or sexual play with a partner. This may involve stimulation only of the anal opening with fingers or mouth. Oral-anal stimulation is called analingus and the popular slang term is "rimming." In other instances, depending on personal preference and comfort, internal stimulation may be desired with a soft object or with another person's finger or penis. Rectal stimulation with a penis has been called by a variety of names such as anal coitus, sodomy, buggery or the slang expressions "butt fucking" or "ass fucking." In this book, the descriptive term *anal intercourse* will be used. The term *anal sex* will refer to *any* erotic anal play, not necessarily intercourse.

Certainly this book will be of special interest to those who want to explore anal intercourse as something to be enjoyed. Others, because of sexual orientation or personal preference, may have little or no interest in anal intercourse. This book is of potential value for these people, too, because *anal pleasure, with or without intercourse, can be a comfortable part of the sensual and sexual experience of any man or woman who wants it, regardless of sexual orientation.*

ANAL PLEASURE
IN THE UNITED STATES

Very little is really known about how people experience anal pleasure. What is known focuses almost exclusively on anal intercourse. This is not surprising given the tendency in our culture to consider intercourse the only "real" sex and to label everything else "foreplay."

In their pioneering studies of human sexual behavior done in the forties, Alfred Kinsey (Kinsey et al., 1948; 1953) and his associates recognized the erotic potential of the anal area with regard to nerve distribution, proximity to the genitals, muscular relationship to other pelvic muscles and anal contractions during sexual activity. Of the men in their sample who had experienced homosexual sex play as preadolescents (which, incidentally, was reported more commonly than heterosexual play), 17% recalled trying anal intercourse. Kinsey also noted that anal erotic activity was sometimes reported as part of masturbation and adult heterosexual and homosexual encounters. In addition, he found that a few people could be brought to orgasm by anal stimulation alone. Kinsey concluded that the anus had erotic significance for about half of the population, although no specific sexual activities involving the anus were reported frequently enough to be included in his statistics. Kinsey felt that social prohibitions against anal sex probably resulted in considerable reticence among his subjects to discuss these behaviors.

In the early seventies, Morton Hunt and his associates analyzed questionnaires completed by over 2000 American men and women. Hunt was looking for changes in attitudes and behavior that might have occurred in the more than 30 years since the Kinsey studies. He reported a "remarkable" relaxation in attitudes toward anal intercourse. Well over half of the men and women surveyed *disagreed* with the statement: "Anal intercourse between men and women is wrong" (Hunt, 1974).

As for behavior, he found a substantial increase in anal sexual experimentation or, at least, a greater willingness to respond to questions about anal sexuality. He reported the following:

> While we do not know how many people respond strongly to such (anal) stimulation or employ anal foreplay regularly, we did find that such techniques as fingering, kissing, and even tonguing of the anus have been used, at least experimentally, by anywhere from a sizable minority to a majority of younger Americans and by a small but measurable minority of older ones, and that about a quarter of the married couples under 35 use anal intercourse now and then

(p. 36) . . . Well over half of the under-35 males and females in our sample have at least experimented with manual-anal foreplay at some time or another, and over a quarter have experienced oral-anal foreplay (p. 200).

This increasing openness to anal experimentation appears to be continuing, especially among younger sexual sophisticates. In the latest *Playboy* survey of 100,000 readers (80% predominantly heterosexual men), 47% of men and 61% of the women had tried anal intercourse. Thirteen percent of the married couples reported engaging in anal intercourse more than once a month. Sixty three percent had tried other forms of anal stimulation. For example, nearly 36% of the men and 39% of the women had experienced oral-anal contact (Peterson, 1983).

These findings refer to anal-erotic behavior between males and females. Just as some people might be surprised that so *many* heterosexuals appear to be experimenting with anal stimulation, others might be even more surprised to find that *so few* homosexual men use anal intercourse. Hunt reports:

Anal intercourse, commonly thought to be universal among homosexual males, has been experienced as insertor by only 20% of all males with any homosexual experience, and by 18% as insertee; and even in the currently active adult group, only about half had experienced it either actively or passively, or both, within the past year (p. 318).

That anal intercourse is not the major sexual activity of homosexual American males is supported by other studies in which sexual activities such as oral-genital stimulation and mutual masturbation were found to be practiced more frequently than anal intercourse (Bell and Weinberg, 1978; Henry, 1941). It is probably true that gay men who are open about their sexual orientation are far more likely to experiment with anal intercourse than those who are "in the closet."* It also appears that younger gay men tend to experiment more sexually (Bell and Weinberg, 1978).

* For example, among over 1,000 gay-identified men who responded to a questionnaire by Spada (1979), 76% said they enjoyed anal intercourse (well over half as both giver and receiver). Yet anal sex was still not as frequently practiced as oral sex.

Two large surveys focusing on women's sexual behavior have included some interesting findings on anal sex. Responding to a questionnaire in *Redbook* (Tavris and Sadd, 1977) magazine, 43% of the women (most of them married) had tried anal intercourse at least once. Of these, about 40% described the experience as enjoyable, while 42% found it unpleasant and 7.5% found it "repulsive." Younger women were more likely to have tried anal intercourse. In a *Cosmopolitan* (Wolfe, 1980) questionnaire, 15% of the 106,000 female respondents — the magazine calls them "Cosmo girls" — said they "regularly" (not defined) had anal intercourse. No questions were asked in either study about other forms of anal stimulation.*

OTHER TIMES AND PLACES

Information is even more scanty about the role of anal erotic behavior in other societies and throughout history. Just as data about anal eroticism among Americans center on anal intercourse, this tendency to ignore other forms of anal pleasure is even more pronounced in the data available from other cultures. Throughout the world, cultural attitudes toward anal intercourse have ranged from harshly negative — sometimes with death prescribed as punishment — to apparently very permissive. In other cultures, however, as in our own, a split often exists between proclaimed standards and the actual behavior of at least some members of that society.

A culture's level of acceptance of anal intercourse is closely related to its acceptance of male homosexuality. This connection is probably due to the fact that in most times and places, anal intercourse appears to be, or is at least presumed to be, the preferred form of sexual expression among homosexual men. **

* An interesting doctoral dissertation exploring anal eroticism among women was done by Barbara Mercer, R.N., Ph.D., at the Institute for the Advanced Study of Human Sexuality in San Francisco in 1983. The study is concerned with the relationship between a variety of anal sexual behaviors and fantasies, sexual orientation and attitudes.

** The apparent differences between American gays and homosexuals in other times and places with regard to the importance of anal intercourse probably has several sources. First, in our culture there is a tendency—increasing with education—for both heterosexuals and homosexuals to

Historically, most attention has been given to the occurrence of anal intercourse in ancient Greece. It appears that many ancient Greeks, especially members of the upper classes, ascribed special significance to anal intercourse between men and boys. Often romantically praised for its unmatched purity, this form of anal eroticism was also thought to have educational value when practiced by teachers and their students. By receiving anal intercourse from his teacher, a young man's education was highly personalized, which many Greeks considered essential for learning, no matter what the subject. Then, too, the act of receiving intercourse was believed to impart wisdom and masculinity (Dawson, 1963).

Even though this type of encounter was unmistakably homosexual, involving two males, the young partner—always the receiver of intercourse—was seen as soft, passive and not yet a man. There were also elements of dominance and submission involved in the encounter, with the receiver always in a submissive role. The ancient Greeks had a similar perspective on male-female sex. The man's role was to dominate, the woman's was to submit.

Oddly enough, at the same time that anal intercourse between men and boys received a fair degree of social approval, the ancient Greeks tended to be anti-homosexual. In some segments of society, homosexual expression among adult males was viewed as "abnormal and impure" (Marrou, 1956). As the young man grew up, developing appearance and characteristics considered more manly, he probably became less sought after by adult men. Most likely, as the youthful receiver of intercourse aged, he would begin taking a dominant role with other boys or with women. This type of arrangement was certainly not the only form of homosexuality in ancient Greece. But mainly, the ancient Greeks accepted both homosexuality and anal intercourse in the context of a large age discrepancy between the part-

be somewhat more experimental and less rigidly tied to intercourse. In addition, strongly negative attitudes toward the anal area no doubt divert many Americans—including gays—from the enjoyment of anal sex. Finally, anthropological and historical reporters have no doubt missed much of the subtle variety of homosexual behavior because of their own anti-gay biases and assumptions.

ners, with the younger partner being viewed as sexually submissive.

Of course, there is nothing unusual about a commitment to sex roles that are defined in terms of dominance and submission. Throughout much of the world, including our own society, this attitude prevails. For example, in Mediterranean cultures, acceptance or toleration of anal intercourse among males usually requires that one partner be viewed as "womanly" (usually a younger man or boy).* Similarly, in Central and South America, men frequently have anal intercourse with other men, in spite of strong religious prohibitions. The "insertor" retains his heterosexual identity. The receiver is seen as homosexual and suffers a loss of social status. American men often express the same attitude—i.e., it is the receiver of anal intercourse who is *really* homosexual.

Some societies have developed a clearly-defined and accepted role which the French, and now all anthropologists, call the *berdache*. A transvestite of sorts, such a man would typically adopt the dress and mannerisms considered feminine in his culture. Some cultures have offered a similar opportunity for role-reversal for women, although not as frequently. The institution of the *berdache*, though not, of course, a matter simply of sexual preference, included the opportunity for a male to engage as a "passive" partner (e.g., to receive anal intercourse) with a minimum of social disapproval. *Berdaches* were especially common in societies that demanded tremendous aggressive abilities from men (hunting, fighting, etc.). Perhaps one function of the *berdache* was to provide a role for the many men who, emotionally or physically, could not or did not want to fulfill these obligations.

Other societies, while not having any specific role like the *berdache*, nonetheless had many men whose special function was to receive anal intercourse. In China, in contrast to current restrictive attitudes toward homosexuality and anal sexuality (Chinese officials now claim there is no

---

* Karlan (1971) contains a wealth of information about homosexuality— and attitudes toward it—in other times and places. The information in this section, unless otherwise noted, comes from this source. Unfortunately, many of Karlan's conclusions are of limited value because of a pervasive anti-homosexual bias.

homosexuality in their society), there was a long tradition of institutionalized homosexuality. This tradition included male prostitutes trained from a young age to receive anal intercourse. There are similar reports about Japan from the 17th to 19th centuries. In the revolution of 1868, Japan banned all homosexual acts along with other sexual variations.

Throughout the Middle East, homosexuality and anal intercourse have flourished, at least at certain times. From the Moslem world have come many reports of widespread homosexuality and male-male anal intercourse, in spite of vehement restrictions against both, restrictions which are as explicit in Islam as they are in Christianity. In Persia (Iran today) during the Middle Ages, heterosexuals were encouraged to engage in anal intercourse by theological codes designed to limit rampant population growth (Edwardes, 1965). Like Persia, Turkey and North Africa were centers of homosexual activity. As in China, male prostitutes existed throughout much of the Arab world and Moslem Asia.

Ford and Beach compiled anthropological data about more recent sexual behavior patterns in two hundred societies around the world (Ford and Beach, 1951). In 64% of these societies other than our own, some form of homosexuality among males is considered acceptable, at least for certain members of the community. Once again, anal intercourse is reported to be the preferred form of sexual expression. Among the Siwan of Africa, all men and boys engage in anal intercourse. Apparently both partners retain a masculine identity and neither partner loses status. Those who do not participate are considered peculiar. The Kiraki of New Guinea universally practice anal intercourse as a part of initiation rites. They believe—like the Ancient Greeks—that receiving intercourse from older men helps young men become strong. Similarly, among many Australian aborigines, anal intercourse is a custom between unmarried men and uninitiated boys. Among the Melanesians, homosexuality (with anal intercourse being the primary sexual activity), is condoned and openly discussed. Men do not even object to their sons receiving anal intercourse from their adult male friends, as long as their friends are kind and generous (Davenport, 1965).

Very little is known about the role of anal intercourse in heterosexual relationships in other societies. Among the Manganians of the South Pacific, anal intercourse is frequently practiced during menstruation when vaginal intercourse is considered unclean (Marshall and Suggs, 1971). It may well be that investigators have not adequately inquired about anal sex in heterosexual encounters. If not, this may be due to the tendency of some investigators to view all forms of heterosexual sex, other than vaginal intercourse, as "foreplay" and therefore of secondary importance. Anthropological observation and reporting may also have been influenced by the common assumption, already noted, that anal intercourse is an activity engaged in only by homosexual men. In spite of its limitations, historical and cross-cultural research on sexual behavior does provide a clear picture of the incredible diversity of human sexual expression.*

WHAT IS NOT KNOWN

This brief overview represents virtually all that is known about anal sexuality in the United States, and also indicates the limited scope of research into other times and societies. Although this information is interesting, perhaps even provocative, when we compare it with the depth and detail of materials available about other sensual/sexual behaviors, especially in studies of Americans, it is clear that we are faced with a striking "information gap." For example, we know next to nothing about people's *feelings* toward anal pleasure. We do not know how many people want to enjoy anal intercourse but find it painful or uncomfortable. Neither do we know how many think about trying it but are afraid or embarrassed. We also don't know how many people explore their own anuses during masturbation or how many want their anuses touched but are afraid to ask. Many, no doubt, do not want to "go all the way" to anal intercourse and feel that a request for anal touching would be misconstrued as an invitation for intercourse. Among

* For a fascinating and entertaining selection of poetic expression about anal intercourse for other times and places, see Walker (1977).

couples who try anal erotic stimulation, we don't know if they actually discuss their fantasies, desires and fears or if they just act in the heat of passion, never to talk about the experience openly with one another. Finally, we don't know how many people receive little or no conscious sensation from the anal area.

By far the greatest block to gathering accurate information about anal pleasure is the deeply ingrained idea that verbal communication about such things is not polite or appropriate. It is one thing to fill out an anonymous questionnaire about anal sex, but quite another to discuss it openly with a friend or lover. Many people complain that if they do try to discuss anal pleasure, their comments or requests are seen as funny no matter how they are intended. The same phenomenon occurs in groups when anal pleasure is mentioned—an unusual amount of nervous laughter. This is not to say that the anus cannot be a subject for humor. But when any subject retains the aura of the forbidden (as the anus seems to in spite of the "sexual revolution") people have trouble making that subject the focus of authentic humor without a certain amount of nervousness being triggered simultaneously. With all these factors working against frank discussion of anal pleasure, the man or woman who wishes to feel better about this part of the body will probably have to confront strong external and internal forces saying, in effect, "Don't feel good about *that* part of your body!"

The pressures against anal enjoyment are complex. Looking at the law provides only a partial clue. Legal codes in our country address only one form of anal pleasure—anal intercourse. Strong sanctions have been imposed against anal intercourse since the days of the colonies, when harsh penalties (including some executions) were enforced for anal intercourse, especially when practiced by two men.* Most states still have "sodomy laws" on the books which strongly condemn anal intercourse, as well as a variety of other commonly practiced sexual activities, often referred to as "crimes against nature." These laws have been only

* For a comprehensive look at the history of America's attitudes toward and punishments of gays and their sexual behavior, see Katz (1976).

sporadically enforced. Today, enforcement is rare, although there is strong pressure to keep the laws on the books as deterrents or as statements of moral principle, even though they have little or no influence on people's actual behavior. It is doubtful that negative attitudes toward the anal area and anal pleasure—especially reluctance to talk about it— are being maintained any longer by the law.

Ethical values and moral principles are still potent behavior shapers. In spite of the free-wheeling attitudes about sexual experimentation advocated by today's sexual liberationists, people still look to some moral code or ethical system to guide their behavior. The current trend, which may or may not continue, is increasingly to allow individual interpretation and preference. It is quite legitimate for a person to decide not to participate in certain sexual behaviors or situations on the basis of an internal or external sense of "rightness" or "wrongness." Usually, however, ethical or moral value systems do not themselves deter open discussion. Nor do they turn faces red with embarrassment or cause nervous laughter. These reactions reflect the force of taboo.

THE ANAL TABOO

In this era of sexual exploration, attitudes toward the anus and anal pleasure are still, to a large extent, governed by the processes of taboo. Taboo is a form of psycho-social control more potent than even the most rigid moral code. Modern societies are in the habit of believing that the scientific method has eradicated taboos and that only "primitive" peoples are still affected by them.

This is not altogether true. While science has been instrumental in freeing us from many irrational ideas and fears, our culture, like all others, nonetheless still has its taboos. A taboo is a prohibition collectively shared by a society, with a force so strong that it is rarely questioned or even discussed. *It just is.* Every society has rules, laws or principles intended to guide or control behavior. These grow out of general systems of values shared by most members of the culture. Taboos are different. Sigmund Freud made this important distinction:

The taboo restrictions are different from religious or moral prohibitions; they are differentiated from moral prohibitions by failing to be included in a system which declares abstinence in general to be necessary and gives reasons for this necessity. The taboo prohibitions lack all justification and are of unknown origin . . . (They) are taken as a matter of course by those under their dominance (Freud, 1913).

Taboos, then, have an all-encompassing quality—like the air we breathe—which makes them highly resistant to logic, scientific inquiry or even experience. Although taboos obviously do develop from within a culture, it is as if they are imposed from beyond it. For instance, in the Judeo-Christian tradition, the taboo against anal intercourse is seen as coming from God. In the Old Testament story, God completely destroys the city of Sodom, presumably as punishment for rampant sodomy among its people. Many scholars now believe that the punishment was for Sodom's violation of hospitality rules, and had little, if anything, to do with sex. The sodomy interpretation, however, is still the one generally accepted. Among believers, condemnation of anal sex is not based on any discernible principle except the desire to avoid the wrath of God.

Some taboos are readily taken for granted by virtually everyone in the culture with little or no ambivalence or emotional charge. The taboo against eating the meat of dogs or cats is of this type. We are socialized to feel that this would be distasteful and the issue never arises again. If, however, we were to find ourselves in a situation where no other food was available except a dog or cat, we would be thrown into deep ambivalence. Some people would probably come close to death before violating the taboo.

Other taboos tend to be accompanied by strong ambivalence and a high emotional charge. The incest taboo is the best example of this type. Because everyone at some time has sexual feelings toward their parents, and vice versa, the taboo against acting upon or even feeling these desires has even greater psychological significance. Early sexual feelings toward mother, father, sisters or brothers are almost certainly pleasurable. The feeling of pleasure versus the taboo throws the person into a state of ambivalence, until the ambivalence is itself repressed with varying degrees of success.

Both types of taboos have a chilling effect upon behavior and thought. However, taboos of the second type never really eliminate the behaviors and feelings they forbid. Instead, these desires go "underground," both individually and collectively, where they take on a bigger-than-life, almost cosmic significance. In this way, a taboo gives the forbidden feeling or behavior an inflated significance. In turn, the ambivalence and guilt which a person feels are intensified even further.* Freud pointed out that in Polynesian the root meaning of taboo is *both* sacred *and* forbidden or unclean. The opposite of taboo is simply ordinary, common or readily accessible.

All of this applies to the feelings of most people in our culture toward the anal area and anal pleasure. There is no other way to understand the frequent responses of rational men and women, even scientists, when asked straightforward questions about the anus and anal pleasure, especially anal sex. More often than not they are unwilling to discuss the subject in any detail or are repulsed by the very idea. Often the effects of the anal taboo are hidden under a few simple rational-sounding arguments (e.g., anal intercourse is medically dangerous), which fail to meet even minimal standards of logic or scientific investigation. If anal pleasure and eroticism were simply a bad idea, objections (whether moral, legal or physiological) could be discussed without embarrassment. In actuality, it seems that most people can more comfortably discuss murder and rape than anal pleasure.

Like the incest taboo, the anal taboo tends to be highly charged, though usually not as strong. This is true because the sensitivity of the anal area assures that beginning early in life virtually everyone will receive pleasurable sensations from the anus. To some degree, then, negative messages about the anus are bound to contradict actual experience. Because of the strength of the pleasurable sensations and

---

* This was a central issue in the theoretical conflict between Sigmund Freud and Carl Jung. Freud thought that strong incestuous desires were an inevitable psychic occurrence. Jung, on the other hand, thought that the incest taboo itself, in combination with guilt about sexual desires, intensified incestuous feelings.

the strength of the negative messages, some degree of ambivalence is inevitable. For some, the discomfort of mixed feelings can be partially avoided by suppressing all thoughts and feelings related to anal pleasure. This is the most common reaction. Others are clearly interested *and* repulsed, fascinated *and* guilty about anal pleasure, especially anal eroticism.

Charged by the excitement of the forbidden, a few people become anal enthusiasts, ascribing tremendous importance to anal sex. This can be a problem for those who feel that the more forbidden or "naughty" a sexual behavior or fantasy is, the more important it becomes, as a matter of principle, to do it. Such men and women often engage in anal sex as a symbol of open-mindedness, whether they actually like it or not. This is an example of how a taboo—and subsequent reactions to it—tend to exaggerate or distort the significance of the forbidden behaviors and feelings. Taboo behaviors and thoughts, whatever they happen to be, then assume a looming importance that both expresses and perpetuates the taboo.

In the context of taboo, clouded by the crossfire of conflicting extremes, it becomes very difficult clearly to recognize the forbidden object or behavior or to make a decision as to whether the forbidden object or behavior has anything of value to offer. The emotions generated by a violation of the taboo become the focus of attention. The behavior behind the taboo is likely to be all but ignored in the struggle.

SOCIAL FUNCTIONS
OF THE ANAL TABOO

Taboos are not just psychological phenomena. They have social significance as well. The incest taboo, for example, functions to help reduce severe conflict among family members and between generations. The taboo against eating dog and cat meat functions to maintain the special feelings people wish to have about their pets. The functions of a taboo are not always clearly discernible. They become blurred as the taboo is passed from generation to generation. As a taboo becomes intricately woven into the collective psyche, its original significance may be lost. The anal taboo has never been systematically studied by social scientists. Nonetheless, it is possible to speculate about its social functions. Cross-cultural data about sexual mores and behavior strongly point to four likely functions.

First, negative attitudes toward the anal area appear to be universally tied to concerns about cleanliness. All societies encourage cleanliness, though ideas about what is required vary widely. Relatively few cultures are as compulsive about these matters as Americans tend to be. Yet the idea that cleanliness is necessary for spiritual purity (i.e., "next to godliness") is not unusual. Often, symbols of cleanliness, or dirtiness, serve as focal points of intense significance. Specific substances like certain foods, mud, urine, mucus, and feces trigger strong feelings of revulsion, thereby symbolizing the much broader concern about cleanliness. The anal taboo functions in this way. By becoming symbolic of all that is unclean, and fostering the emotion of disgust, the anus and feces serve to focus and intensify the value placed on being clean.

Second, the idea that an inherent conflict exists between the spirit and the body is prevalent. This notion is certainly strong in all Judeo-Christian societies. By intensifying negative emotions about one area of the body, the anal taboo expresses and perpetuates a more general mistrust of the body. It makes concrete the conflict between spirit and body, increases guilt, and thereby reinforces religious doctrine.

Third, almost all cultures associate receiving anal intercourse with femininity, probably because of its physiological similarity to vaginal intercourse. With few exceptions, a man who receives anal intercourse is viewed as less manly. Therefore, another possible function of the anal taboo is the maintenance of strict sex-role differentiation. Sexual receptivity—and all that it symbolizes—is expected of women and strongly discouraged in men. If anal pleasure is prohibited, then, the chances of men receiving anal intercourse decrease considerably.

Finally, acceptance of anal sexual behavior is virtually always correlated with acceptance of some forms of homosexuality. It therefore seems reasonable to conclude that another function of the anal taboo is to bolster sanctions against homosexual behavior, particularly among men.

From these perspectives, this time in history is ripe for challenging the anal taboo. Scientific advances in the study of health and disease make it more possible for decisions about cleanliness to be rational rather than emotional, although emotions still do and probably always will play an important part. The split between mind/body is being directly challenged in philosophy, psychology and even medicine. Similarly, the value of strict sex-role differentiation is being questioned by both women and men. At the same time, negative attitudes toward homosexuality are beginning slowly to change. For all these reasons, the functions the anal taboo once served may no longer hold such significance.

Those who wish to counter the long, complex effects of the anal taboo must focus on two central questions: One, what can the role of the anal area be in healthy, self-affirming, sensual and sexual activity when freed from the stranglehold of taboo? Two, how can people go about freeing themselves from the taboo? This book is intended to help you investigate these questions and find your own answers.

2

THE ANAL TABOO
AND THE
HELPING PROFESSIONS

Every culture has its experts—those believed to possess special knowledge or wisdom. Traditionally, such guidance has come mainly from spiritual leaders. In our society, we have increasingly turned to medical and mental health professionals. We hope that their research and experience will shed light on behaviors conducive to or incompatible with health and well-being. Unfortunately, helping professionals are not immune to the influences of taboo. Scientific inquiry is inherently slow, incomplete and subject to personal interpretation and bias. Also, the tendency of taboos to function outside of consciousness assures that the perspective on reality inherent in the taboo will be taken for granted, and therefore not questioned. With few exceptions, the anal taboo has had just this kind of influence on helping professionals.

THE ANAL TABOO IN MEDICINE

The most prestigious professional helpers in our society are physicians. The medical community has always been profoundly influenced by the anal taboo. In proctology, the branch of medicine specifically concerned with the anus and rectum, there has been an almost universal reluctance to acknowledge that the anus and rectum have potential sexual or even sensual significance. In 1954, the first proctologic study related to the medical aspects of anal intercourse was published under the title, "Proctologic Disorders of Sex Deviates" (Feisen, 1954). This judgmental title was necessary for publication at that time. Even so, the article was rejected by several respected medical journals. While the article was a breakthrough for its day, it essentially confirmed the prevailing belief that anal intercourse is physically dangerous. It reported the anal and rectal medical problems of men who received anal intercourse regularly. The sample was highly unrepresentative. It consisted entirely of men who sought medical help, or those incarcerated in penal institutions where anal rape is often a ritual expression of an aggressive, sometimes violent "pecking order." The situation has improved slightly since then. Today, many proctologists acknowledge anal sexual activities as something of which they ought to be aware, but these activities, especially intercourse, are virtually always viewed as problematic.

That so few proctologists have been able to transcend the anal taboo is understandable in light of the fact that they have had to treat, usually without discussing it with their patients, problems caused by uninformed, painful and often reckless anal experimentation. So it is not surprising that proctologists, especially those who have no personal experience with anal sex, would tend to view it as dangerous. In addition, proctologists are unlikely to be aware of the experiences of those who enjoy anal stimulation comfortably and safely. Even after a lifetime of clinical practice, it is quite possible for a doctor never to meet (or know that he/she has met) such a person. Of course, acquiring a distorted view of human experience is a danger inherent in all the helping professions, and is not exclusively the result of taboo influences. After all, people rarely consult professionals to tell them how good they feel or how much fun they are having.

For these reasons, the medical community, which could be a valuable source of information, experience and expertise about the anus, has had little to say except "Don't touch it!" It is not unusual for people who enjoy anal intercourse and who seek help for anal medical problems to be told that they must give up this form of pleasure in order to have a healthy anus. If they were freed of the anal taboo, physicians could better hear the concerns of their patients and offer constructive suggestions on how the anus can be experienced pleasurably with a *minimum of risk.*

Of equal importance, they could become much more effective in helping their patients overcome anal medical problems. Almost all common anal problems, especially if they are persistent, are exacerbated, perpetuated and often *caused* by negative attitudes toward the anal area, lack of anal awareness and chronic muscle tension—the same factors that limit anal pleasure. Nothing can help a person develop and maintain anal health more than a comfortable, relaxed sensitivity to the anal area—including a willingness to explore it. There's no doubt about it; *the anal taboo is dangerous to your health!*

THE ANAL TABOO IN PSYCHOLOGY AND COUNSELING

Just as the anal taboo has inhibited the medical community from offering any more than incidental information and support to those who want to explore anal pleasure, similar pressures have blocked any substantial positive contributions from the field of psychology. Freud at least discussed the erogenous qualities of the anus. In fact, he saw it as the strongest focus of pleasure throughout one period of each person's life. He called this period the "anal phase" and he ascribed to it power to shape human personality. Although his complex theories brought the "anal phase" and other phrases such as "anal retentive" and "anal fixation" into popular parlance, the overall impact of his theories has been to legitimize anal pleasure as a developmental necessity for small children while labeling it "infantile" for adults.

Freud viewed all "mature" sexual activity as having reproductive potential as its aim. As a result, he oriented his theories toward penis/vagina intercourse and male orgasm. He tended to view all sensual "lingering" at nongenital body zones as "perverted" if such lingering did not further the aim of reproduction. Thus, he believed that most human erotic activities such as masturbation, clitoral stimulation, general body stimulation, and oral stimulation were "immature," if they did not lead to vaginal intercourse. So, while Freud introduced anal eroticism into psychology (and was sometimes considered scandalous for doing so), his theories may now be more influential than moral doctrine in convincing grownups that they may enjoy their anuses only at the risk of being negatively labeled (e.g., neurotic or fixated). With this ironic twist, Freudian theory has tended to bolster the anal taboo.

Hundreds of theoretical variations have been offered since Freud. Many have toned down the emphasis on sexuality as the central driving force of human personality. In addition, many psychotherapists take a far less dogmatic view of sexual behavior and accept a much wider range of sexual activities as potentially healthy and mature. The movement toward greater acceptance of variation in sexual preferences can probably be seen most consistently among the rapidly-expanding ranks of sexual specialists—sex educators, counselors and therapists—as well as among those studying sexuality from sociological or anthropological points of view.

Professionals within these disciplines are producing much of the current literature about human sexuality. For example, in virtually every modern college text on the subject of human sexuality, anal stimulation is briefly and nonjudgmentally mentioned as an option that can be chosen by men and women for their personal or shared pleasure. One popular text, after quoting the Hunt statistics on anal intercouse, offers this representative statement:

> For most people anal intercourse is an experimental or occasional variant rather than a mainstay of their sexual lives. It is enthusiastically endorsed by some and thought to be unspeakably vulgar and offensive by others. Apart from matters of personal preference and legality ("sodomy" penalties are horrendous . . .), anal intercourse entails certain health considerations. First, it often entails some

discomfort even when adequate lubricants are used. Second, there is serious risk of infection if vaginal intercourse follows without washing first. Finally, repeated experience may result in a variety of chronic ailments (Katchadourian and Lynde, 1980).

To be sure, a statement like this is morally neutral, but of little value to a person who would like to learn more about his/her anus and how it can be enjoyed. In addition, it tends to confirm widespread fears that discomfort and health problems are to be expected.

Written in a more practical, less academic style, Alex Comfort's enormously popular *Joy of Sex* has no doubt helped to shape current attitudes toward anal pleasure:

> This [anal intercourse] is something which nearly every couple tries once. A few stay with it usually because the woman finds that it gives her intenser feelings than the normal route and it is pleasantly tight for the man. . . The anus is sensitive in most people and the sensitivity can be cultivated. Unless you find it very rewarding and are free from the feeling that it's unesthetic, we doubt that it's worth doing more than satisfying curiosity and the occasional impulse this way, however (Comfort, 1972).

Many readers have doubtless found support for experimentation with anal pleasure in Comfort's book. However, it is difficult to imagine how anyone could find support here for integrating anal stimulation on an ongoing basis into sensual or erotic behavior.

In the current sexual literature, the only publications that express overtly positive attitudes toward anal eroticism are those specifically directed toward gay males (Freedman and Mayes, 1976; Silverstein and White, 1977; Walker, 1977). These publications have helped to meet the needs of many people for more information about the anus; both straight and bisexual men and women have sought out these publications for this purpose. More important, these authors have been lonely voices of reassurance that the desire for anal pleasure is a natural and healthy one. Unfortunately, whatever the sexual orientation of the writers, they have had to do their work within the larger context of the anal taboo. Consequently, they have often had to make up for the lack of detailed information and research by offering somewhat overgeneralized personal or anecdotal material.

Most of the current literature contains an implicit message which, loosely translated, goes something like this: "Many people try various forms of anal stimulation and apparently sometimes enjoy it. It is probably within the realm of normalcy if you try it too as long as you are cautious." The gay publications go further, suggesting, again loosely paraphrased: "Anal stimulation can be very enjoyable. Relax. Take your time and everything will be all right."

Anyone who has had the opportunity to discuss sexual feelings and behavior with a variety of people is probably aware that many men and women—nobody knows *how* many—have been able to learn or *re*learn their inborn capacity to enjoy anal stimulation under a broad range of conditions. Some have easily discovered the possibilities of anal sensuality. Others have needed considerable experimentation and practice by themselves or with a sexual partner. A few have undoubtedly benefited from the information and support contained in the available literature.

Others have found themselves partially or totally blocked from anal pleasure. Negative emotional reactions and physical discomfort continue to render anal stimulation *un*pleasant no matter what they do. Some people in this position quickly abandon anal exploration as soon as it does not work out comfortably. Others, because of a strong personal desire, perhaps in combination with pressure from a partner, keep right on trying in spite of the discomfort. Increasingly, people are not willing to accept either alternative; they do not want to give up, nor do they want to endure discomfort. Some are now consulting psychotherapists and counselors, especially those specializing in human sexuality, hoping to find the same kind of help that is now available for other sexual problems.

SEX THERAPY
AND ANAL CONCERNS

Sparked by the publication of Masters and Johnson's works on sexual problems, a new field of research and therapy has grown rapidly. With the expansion of the field of sex therapy has come greater awareness that sexual difficulties, far from being rare, actually affect large numbers of people. The most common problems for which people seek help are those in which a person feels unable to experience some desired sexual behavior (Kanfer and Saslow, 1969). Men seeking sex therapy are usually concerned about getting or maintaining erections under various conditions, or else they are concerned that they ejaculate too fast (premature ejaculation) or that they take too long (inhibited ejaculation). Some men are unable to ejaculate at all or in certain situations (e.g., during intercourse). Women seeking sex therapy are usually concerned about lack of arousal or not being able to experience orgasm. Both men and women who have little or no interest in sex are increasingly likely to consider this a problem (Kaplan, 1979).

Although theories and techniques for dealing with these problems vary widely, all sex therapists view sexual behavior, whether positive or problematic, as *learned* phenomena. This means that sexual values, preferences and difficulties are shaped far more by psycho-social processes than by biochemistry or other inborn forces (traditionally called "instincts"). Seeing sexual behavior as learned implies some capacity for *un*learning and *re*learning. But just how much sexual change is possible and how changes occur is still, and probably always will be, a subject of intense debate.

Almost certainly, aspects of a person's sexuality that are learned early in life and are effective at generating arousal are quite resistant to change. And fundamental elements of sexual self-image such as core gender identity (the inner sense of being male or female) and sexual orientation (gay, straight, bisexual) are usually so thoroughly woven into a person's entire psyche that substantial change is virtually always impossible. In other words, basic sexual learning is not like learning to roller skate. It's infinitely deeper and more complex.

In general, sex therapists are *most* successful at helping clients to learn new sexual behaviors and to expand their preferences somewhat (but usually not dramatically). If these new behaviors turn out to be better (more pleasurable and fulfilling, less anxiety-provoking or uncomfortable), then they will gradually supplement or supplant older behavior patterns (unless the old patterns produce stronger rewards of their own—which is sometimes the case, even with problematic behavior). Sex therapists are *least* successful at helping clients get rid of behavior or alter preferences that bring them excitement or pleasure, regardless of whether the client expresses a desire to change.

Modern sex therapists try to help their clients develop more satisfying sexual behavior through *direct intervention in the present*. This kind of direct focus on changing behavior is usually called ''behavior therapy'' to distinguish it from ''evocative psychotherapy.''* In evocative psychotherapy, the focus is on the psychodynamics affecting behavior (e.g., unconscious conflicts from childhood). In the evocative psychotherapies, behavior is expected to change as the inner psychodynamics change. This process can be very time-consuming and has been found not to be very effective when used by itself.

Currently, many therapists feel that the behavioral and evocative therapies need not be at odds (Sloane, 1969). There are no convincing reasons—other than theoretical chauvinism—why behavioral intervention cannot be used in conjunction with most evocative psychotherapeutic approaches (e.g., Transactional Analysis, Gestalt Therapy, Client-Centered Therapy, Rational-Emotive Therapy or even Psychoanalysis).

In combining behavioral and evocative approaches to sexual problems, a therapist is concerned with 1) providing the client with accurate sexual information, 2) suggesting experiential exercises (sometimes called ''homework'') free of pressures to perform, 3) teaching practical techniques for coping with and reducing anxiety and tension and 4) helping the client to improve or expand interpersonal skills, especially the ability to discuss sex openly and to be more assertive in asking for what feels good. Usually, the development of new behaviors—or resistance to the new

* This terminology is proposed by Ullman and Krasner (1969).

behaviors—will evoke emotional reactions and sometimes insights into how past experiences have contributed to the difficulties with sex. As these awarenesses sharpen, they are explored and new behavioral suggestions are offered to provide additional opportunities for both learning and self-awareness (Annon, 1974; Barbach, 1975; Belliveau and Richter, 1970; Kaplan, 1974; Masters and Johnson, 1970).

Generally speaking, sex therapists base their work on the assumption that sensual and sexual pleasure is a positive human experience as long as it is accompanied by a sensitivity to the rights of others. Furthermore, there are few, if any, sex therapists who consider sexual activities to be primarily the servants of reproduction. Rather, sexual pleasure is seen as having the potential to enhance a person's self-esteem as well as his/her relationships with others. Of course, different therapists have different emphases. For example, Masters and Johnson are particularly oriented toward the interpersonal aspects of sex. Others, like Lonnie Barbach, for example, place more emphasis on the self-pleasuring aspects of sex. Finally, sex therapists with a humanistic point of view tend to assume that, if given supportive conditions and accurate information, people are capable of developing the sexual lifestyle most suited to their needs. Cognizant of the tremendous range and variety of sexual behavior among human beings, these therapists usually feel less compelled than traditional psychotherapists to formulate universal ideals of how people "should" behave. These basic assumptions are primarily responsible for the advances of modern sex therapy, probably more so even than the specific techniques that have received so much publicity.

Notwithstanding the overall atmosphere of openness that permeates much of the field of sex therapy today, sex therapists have been affected by the anal taboo, and therefore are rarely as open about anal sexuality as they are about other sexual activities. Some therapists are quite willing to discuss anal pleasure with their clients. However, few know how to deal with the concerns of clients who would like to enjoy anal stimulation but whose attempts have resulted in pain and discomfort rather than pleasure. Most therapists have not had the opportunity to learn about or discuss anal pleasure with their colleagues—or anybody else, for that matter.

Some therapists view the ability to enjoy anal pleasure, especially anal intercourse, as a special talent, which, because of anatomical or psychological factors, is available only to a relatively small number of people. The usual understanding of these therapists that sexual behavior is learned, and therefore subject to change, gives way to a far less flexible perspective than they would ever apply to other sexual behaviors. Sometimes therapists who generally express negative attitudes toward Freud's theories of sexuality will begin speaking of "anal personalities" and "anal fixation" without the slightest reservation. Given the atmosphere of mystery and misinformation associated with the anal taboo, this is understandable.

That sex therapists have not made any systematic attempts to apply their skills and techniques to the problems of blocked anal pleasure is due, at least in part, to the fact that such problems have not traditionally been *defined* as specific concerns worthy of therapeutic intervention. My clinical experience and research suggest that difficulties in enjoying anal-erotic stimulation, including but not limited to anal intercourse, can and should be defined as a specific sexual "dysfunction."* To a person who desires anal pleasure, the inability to relax the anal muscles is as much a problem as a man's concerns about his erections or ejaculations or a woman's concerns about her arousal or orgasms. When anal pleasure is inhibited, it can have the same

---

* I am somewhat reluctant to name and define a "new" sexual dysfuncton. Afer all, the *last* thing we need is another sexual ideal to live up to, another condition to feel inadequate about. In fact, any time we explicitly define a problem, especially in the sexual realm, we create trouble for some people. Not only can the new label be used for self-deprecation and criticism, but it can also be employed in interpersonal power struggles. For example, some men will undoubtedly use the concept of anal sexual dysfunction to pressure a partner into accepting anal intercourse, with little regard for the actual desire of the partner. But since defining sexual problems also has many benefits, about the best we can do is to be aware of the potential negative consequences and conscientiously try to avoid them.

negative effects on a person's behavior and self-esteem as any other sexual concern.

I have named the concern *anal spasm*, reflecting my personal observations and reports from clients that spasm (involuntary contraction) of the anal sphincter muscles (and, to some degree, rectal muscles as well) is the primary physiological mechanism getting in the way of anal pleasure, especially the pleasure that can be derived from internal stimulation of the anus and rectum. Physiologically, anal spasm is similar to *vaginismus*, which involves an involuntary spasm of the muscles surrounding the outer vagina, making insertion of a penis, gynecologist's speculum or sometimes even a finger painful, difficult or impossible (Ellison, 1972). Vaginismus, like anal spasm, not only prevents insertion; in time, it also tends to reduce all pleasurable sensations—or at least the ability to enjoy them—in the surrounding area.

In order to define anal spasm in more detail, and to explore ways in which anal tension could be reduced—thereby enhancing the capacity for pleasure—I began an informal pilot study in 1975. Twenty-nine men worked with me in three small therapy groups, each of which met weekly for two months. The men had previously consulted me with concerns about anal tension after hearing me lecture on the subject of anal awareness, relaxation and sexuality. No women participated in these pilot groups, although many women did become a part of my later research.

Men in the pilot study learned to make careful observations of their anal tension under a variety of conditions, both sexual and nonsexual, when relaxed and under stress. They also tried many experiences at home, regularly sharing their feelings and observations in the groups. Their reports taught me a lot about anal tension and pleasure. Their feedback and suggestions were invaluable in helping me to develop the therapy process upon which this book is based.

REDUCING ANAL TENSION

During the pilot study, it became apparent that anal tension can be reduced and that the capacity to enjoy anal stimulation can be learned even by those with a long history of chronic anal muscular spasm. To test this more carefully, I began a formal study in which 143 people (114 men and 29 women) participated in an eight-week therapy process developed and refined during the pilot study. They ranged in age from 21 to 62. Represented among the participants were men and women of all sexual orientations and a variety of backgrounds and lifestyles. All wanted to experience less pain and more pleasure from anal erotic stimulation. Eighty percent wished specifically to be able to enjoy anal intercourse. A detailed description of the participants, the research methodology and the findings can be found in Appendix B. This will be of special interest to professional researchers and therapists.

For the lay reader desiring to enchance the capacity for anal pleasure, it is only important to be aware that this is not an impossible or even difficult goal. Among the 143 participants in the research, 71% learned to enjoy anal stimulation in the ways they desired by the time the eight weeks of therapy had ended. An additional 12% were able to do this within four months after therapy. For the total of 83% who reached their goals, many factors contributed to their success. Most important of these was the willingness to devote regular time and attention to anal exploration, and to carry it out with calm persistence.

Virtually anyone, regardless of sex or sexual orientation, can become more aware of the anal area, learn to relax anal/rectal muscles and expand the capacity to enjoy whichever types of anal stimulation may be desired. Required, however, is sufficient motivation, a little patience and a clear idea of how to proceed. It is usually also necessary to become aware of and to challenge the effects of anal taboo. Almost everyone with whom I have worked has found that the rewards—anal pleasure and health—are well worth the effort.

3

HOW TO USE THIS BOOK

This book is designed not only to be read, but also to be *experienced*. It is not intended for passive consumption, but for active use. As you move through each chapter, you will be following essentially the same process of anal exploration that my clients have found most effective.

I have communicated with several people who live in other parts of the country, guiding them in their anal exploration processes via letter or with one or two visits to my office. Their reports indicate that most of them are able to make significant and welcome changes without the regular involvement of a therapist. A therapist offers clients opportunities to clarify their feelings and needs, and gives support and guidance in working through any "rough spots." These therapeutic functions cannot be replaced by a book. It is possible, however, to provide yourself with support and feedback by taking the risk of honestly discussing your feelings and activities with one or more close friends. With adequate motivation and persistence, most people are capable of initiating and directing their own self-exploration, using this book as a guide.

HOW THE BOOK IS STRUCTURED

Anal awareness has two dimensions. First, there is the individual process of self-exploration. The second dimension involves sharing anal exploration and stimulation with a partner. The first part of this book deals with the more private aspects of anal exploration. Other people participate only through your memory, imagination or fantasies. The latter part deals with how to include the anal area comfortably and safely in sensual and sexual experiences with others.

Each chapter first presents relevant information from the fields of anatomy and physiology, medicine, psychology and sexology. Then, a section entitled *experience* presents simple "things to do." This section is intended to help you to apply new information, in a concrete and practical way, to your own behavior. The *response* section should help you integrate new information and experience into your life. In this section, I discuss *feelings* you might have as a result of your experiences, *blocks* that might get in your way and *possibilities for positive change*.

When I discuss the experiences or quote the actual words of my clients, it is important to keep in mind that these are *not* offered as "norms" or "standards" for what you should experience or feel. Instead, consider them to see if they are helpful in understanding yourself. If some of these statements are not relevant to you, do not hesitate to move on. Before dismissing anything as irrelevant to you, however, take a moment to ask yourself if possibly the material is, in fact, *very* relevant, and thus somewhat threatening. If you have a particularly strong negative reaction to something you read, it is a good indication that you could benefit from spending more time with that section.

WORKING WITH A PARTNER

Some people want to work with a partner right from the start. If you want to do that, be sure to spend at least as much time exploring by yourself as you spend with your partner(s). If possible, your partner(s) should spend time exploring alone, too. If you do not have an appropriate partner right now or you do not feel comfortable talking with him/her about anal pleasure, you can still proceed on your own. Later, when you feel more comfortable, you can think about your best options for including a partner.

SETTING ASIDE TIME

How much you get out of this book will depend on your motivation, which is, to a great extent, reflected in how much time and energy you are willing to devote to exploring your anus. Most people find they need to set aside three or four quiet, private exploratory periods, of one-half to one hour each, during the week. These periods should be during "prime time"—whatever time of day is best *for you*— not when you are tired, preoccupied or in a hurry. If you are like most people, you will have to guard your chosen, private time militantly against encroachment by other pressures and demands. In order to avoid becoming too rigid with yourself—which is not conducive to relaxation— allow yourself the option of skipping one of your exploratory periods during the week. Avoid turning anal exploration into a conflict-generating drama. If you do not feel like doing it, then don't. However, sometimes a *gentle* push is necessary to overcome one's discomfort with the unfamiliar.

KEEPING A JOURNAL

Your process will be greatly enhanced if you keep a journal. This is a notebook in which you can write about your experiences, thoughts, and feelings as you progress through the book. For many people, this is difficult to do. But I have yet to find a person who kept a journal who did not report that it was tremendously valuable.

GOALS AND EXPECTATIONS

Perhaps you are reading this book without any particular ideas about what you would like to get out of it; you're just browsing to see if there's anything useful for you here. On the other hand, you may, like most of my clients, already have specific ideas about how you would like to change. If you do have goals or expectations in mind, even if they're not very clear, it is worthwhile to state them explicitly to yourself or a friend or lover. (And write them down in your journal.)

My research has shown unmistakably that the way a person approaches anal exploration is significantly related to how positive the process turns out to be. Those who hope to be able to *perform* better as a result of therapy (that is, their main motivation is to please someone else) are far less likely to reach their goals than those who wish to develop new options for pleasure. (Their main desire is to please themselves.*) Therefore, if you already have performance-oriented goals (e.g., "I want to satisfy my lover(s) by being able to receive anal intercourse"), see if you can begin now to develop more pleasure-oriented expectations (e.g., "I'm going to explore how *I* can enjoy my anus sexually").

Unfortunately, clients with all types of sexual problems frequently have trouble distinguishing between these two types of goals. Many people become so performance-oriented that their partner's pleasure is seen as synonymous with their own. If the importance of this distinction is not clear to you now, keep thinking about it as you move through this book. Changing your attitudes may not be so easy, especially if you're used to putting a partner's needs and desires ahead of your own. So it's a good idea to start now.

Your goals may have little or nothing to do with enjoying the anus sensually or erotically. You may simply want to restore or maintain anal health. Perhaps you are seeking to resolve a chronic medical problem that has not responded to traditional treatment. If so, be as clear as you can about what you hope to accomplish. Doing so will help you get the most out of this book. Feel free to skim over material which seems irrelevant to your concerns. But keep in mind that most of the information and suggestions are potentially useful to you.

---

* Among "pleasure-oriented" research participants, 89% reached their goals, whereas 67% of the "performance-oriented" group reached their goals. See Appendix B for a description of how this distinction was made.

A FUNDAMENTAL AGREEMENT

Whether or not you have specific goals, the positive results of any anal exploration you decide to do will be greatly enhanced if you make one fundamental agreement with yourself: *From now on, I will do everything within my power to protect my anus from any pain or discomfort whatsoever.* Without this agreement, your anal stimulation will be overshadowed by uncertainty. You probably won't feel safe enough for your anal muscles to relax.

Do not make this agreement flippantly. If it is a "cheap" agreement, it will do no good. Understand that honoring this agreement may require you to place the comfort of your anus ahead of the desire of a sex partner. To say "yes" to your own body, you may have to say "no" to somebody else. If you are currently "grinning and bearing" anal pain in the interest of your partner, or in the hope you will learn to like anal sex, you may find this agreement a difficult one to make. It is better to admit that you are not ready to make this agreement than it is to make it and then break it. But the vast majority of people seem to be more than happy to remove pain from their repertoire of anal experience.

TIMING AND RHYTHM

Among my clients it is unmistakably clear that each person has an individual pace for self-discovery and change. Some people find that things move smoothly and quickly from the moment they start. Others need much more time to explore themselves gradually. Eight weeks or longer with fairly regular practice is not too long.

There is even more diversity with regard to people's *styles* of changing and growing. Some progress step-by-step. Most, however, experience spurts of self-exploration activities, out of which they may report "breakthroughs," followed by periods when nothing at all appears to be happening for them. For some, these ups and downs are dramatic and charged with emotion; others take their rhythm more in stride.

Expecting yourself to grow according to an ideal schedule and style is just another way of putting pressure on yourself and thereby inhibiting relaxation and pleasure. In fact, those who have the most difficulty with sensual/sexual enhancement of any kind are usually those who constantly compare themselves to others. The more you can honor your personal timing and rhythm, the more you will accept yourself and, consequently, the more good things will happen.

4

LOOKING AND TOUCHING

Beginning Anal Exploration

Learning about your anus is best begun by exploring your anal area with the senses of sight and touch. Growing up, for most of us, involved strong prohibitions against any more than incidental body exploration. In spite of these prohibitions, the readily accessible parts of our bodies get a fair amount of attention. It is easy to look at and touch ourselves in the course of acceptable activities such as bathing and grooming.

On the other hand, people don't just happen to bend over, rear side toward the light, mirror in hand, to sneak a peek at their anuses. All but the most haphazard anal exploration happens only when motivated by *conscious intention*. Consequently, it is quite possible for a person to reach adulthood with an almost total absence of sensual information about his/her anus. Most people have looked closely at their anuses only when motivated by pain or discomfort and have touched the anal area only in the course of getting clean.

To the extent that this describes your situation, a lack of firsthand experience may have left you susceptible to a wide range of negative ideas and feelings about your anus, many of which might have been quite different if you had been allowed free visual and tactile exploration of this hidden body zone.

THE ANAL OPENING

The anus is the external opening into the short anal canal and the larger rectum. The anal opening, hidden by the buttocks, is formed by folds of soft tissue which give it a "puckered" appearance. Anal tissue is pink-red in color unless it is irritated, in which case it may appear bright red. Within the anal tissue is a vast array of tiny blood vessels and nerve endings that make it one of the body's most sensitive areas. These same nerve endings also let you know, in no uncertain terms, if your anus is hurting. Except for the tissue that forms the anal opening, the anal area contains many hair follicles. The hairs growing in this area may be almost too light and too fine to see, or they may be coarser and darker, but *everybody* has hair growing in this area.

To a large extent, the appearance of the anus reflects something of your past and current experiences, though you may not realize it. Some look comfortable and relaxed. Others look irritated, abused, drawn and tense.

There is nothing inherently dirty about the anal opening. Regular and careful washing can leave your anal area fresh and clean. Feces do contain bacteria that are not found on the surface of the body, but most of these organisms are harmless. A few troublesome parasites can be picked up from infected sexual partners, usually through oral-anal contact. Unless you are already infected with intestinal parasites (in which case you could reinfect yourself) there is absolutely no risk in exploring your own anus. Concern about anal germs is far more the result of unrealistic fears than of rational understanding.

Most sex therapists and gynecologists recommend that women *not* insert a finger, penis or anything else in the vagina after direct contact with the anus, because the vagina is an unusually hospitable environment for a variety of infections. It is important to realize, however, that the danger of vaginal infection, even after direct contact with a finger, penis, or object that has been in or near the anus, is by no means automatic or even probable. It is just possible. Precautions should be understood in this light.

EXPERIENCE

Begin by taking a leisurely bath or shower, whichever is more relaxing and enjoyable for you. See if you can feel as if you are doing something nice for yourself—not just getting clean. It may help to reflect this mood in your environment by turning off bright lights and using candles, playing music and, perhaps, using bubble bath or bath oil.

Feel the warm water against your skin. As you wash, make each stroke slow and sensuous. Gently wash your anus, giving it a little extra attention. Take as long as you want. There is no rush. But stop *before* you get bored. Dry yourself in this same slow, sensual way.

At this point you might want to take a break, lounging around the house naked for a while. When you are ready, turn up the lights again and look at yourself overall in your full length mirror. Then moving in closer, look at each part of your body in detail, one at a time. You might start with your hair, forehead, ear, eyes, etc. Using your hand mirror, do the same with the back parts of your body.

Some parts of your body will look better to you than others. When you come across something you do not like, acknowledge your feelings and how you would like it to be different, and *then move on.* Do not suppress your negative feelings, but do not get caught up in them either. When you come across something you like, see if you can let yourself enjoy that area. Talking to yourself about your likes and dislikes sometimes helps.

Using your hand mirror and plenty of light, take a close look at your anus. Find a comfortable position in which to do this. Figure 1 illustrates a variety of positions for anal self-examination. Try them all. Find a position you can maintain without discomfort or fatigue. Remember you are not just sneaking a quick peek. Really examine your anus— overall at first, then moving in for details.

As you look at your anus, note any feelings you have. Do not expect these feelings to seem logical. See if you can just

44

Figure 1

POSITIONS FOR ANAL SELF-EXAMINATION

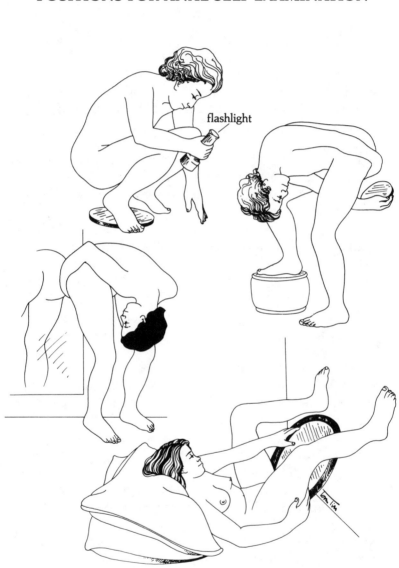

be aware of and accept them, whatever they are.

Now take a break and find a comfortable spot to sit quietly and relax. Imagine how mom and dad might feel if they knew what you were doing. If this fantasy triggers a strong reaction within you, you can write in your journal an *imaginary* letter to one or both of your parents, telling them exactly what you are doing and how you feel about it. Do not censor or tone down anything. Write it the way you would if you were *completely* open with them. Remember, no one is going to read the letter.

Also in your journal, consider using a pencil, crayons, or colored pencils to draw a picture of your anus. You might want to take another look in the mirror while doing so. This is not a test of artistic ability, but a chance to let your visual impressions take some form. It is not a mechanical drawing, but a work of self-expression.

If you do most or all of these things, they can take a lot of time. When you feel like stopping, by all means do. You can continue another time or day. On the other hand, you may be energized by what you are doing and want to continue. Either way is fine.

Whenever you decide to continue, go back to your full length mirror again and begin another detailed exploration of your body. Only this time, *touch each part* as you look. Touch yourself in different ways to see which feels the most pleasant, relaxing, sensual, or erotic. Find a position in which you can easily touch your anus. Begin gently stroking your anus and the surrounding areas. Notice how your anal tissue feels in relation to nearby tissue. At least part of the time, see if you can look at and touch your anus simultaneously. Can you see any response in the anal area as you touch it? Does it seem to get more tense or less tense, or stay the same? *Do not insert your finger in your anus at this point,* even if you have done it before. Right now, just explore the surface.

Again, pay attention to your feelings. Try not to avoid or judge them. Just notice what you feel. When you are finished looking and touching for the moment, write your reactions in your journal, or simply sit back and think about them.

RESPONSE

Doing these things is likely to be a new experience for you. Though you have no doubt seen and touched your anus before, you probably have not done it in such a slow, deliberate way. Some people get a sense of liberation from past restrictions and a feeling of intimacy with the body. Some people find the experience to be immediately sensual or even erotic. Others approach it almost as if conducting a scientific experiment. Still others find themselves turned off, bored, or even repulsed. Any of these reactions, or a combination of all, is fine. As far as possible, see if you can avoid predetermined ideas of what you should or should not feel. For example, some people who want to enjoy anal sex become dissatisfied when their own touch is not immediately experienced as erotic. If this is true for you, see if you can relax without trying to force yourself in any particular direction.

Some "negative" feelings commonly accompany sensual exploration of the anus. You will get the most out of your experience if these feelings are *not* avoided or suppressed. Acknowledging negative as well as positive reactions provides opportunities for self-awareness and change, though you may have to tolerate some uneasiness in the process.

One of the first things you may have to confront is the extent to which prohibitions against body exploration in general and anal exploration in particular have affected you. Some women readers will have already dealt with similar prohibitions in learning to examine their genitals. The vagina, like the anus, simply cannot be explored without intending to do so. On the other hand, penis and scrotum require persistent effort to ignore. In general, women who have overcome early injunctions against genital exploration tend to have gained a deeper awareness of how prohibitions against self-knowledge and pleasure have affected them. Consequently, these women usually can look at and touch their anuses with greater ease.

On the other hand, women who have not yet extensively explored their genitals tend to find the whole process more threatening. While most men report having explored their genitals quite a bit, this experience does not appear to transfer to the anal area. Those men who have learned to thoroughly enjoy slow masturbation sessions do seem more open to anal exploration and many have already experimented with it.

In the course of becoming more aware of the effects of prohibitions against self-exploration, most people discover that the prohibitions often were not stated directly by parents and other grown-ups; rather, they were more subtly communicated through body language (e.g., "Hold your body rigid like me so you won't feel as much") or indirect parental messages (e.g., "Stop running around without your clothes. You're too old for that!"). In my work as a psychotherapist, I regularly see powerful examples of how such messages are communicated "underground." For example, relatively few clients ever remember actually being told not to masturbate. Yet virtually all knew that they should not talk about their masturbation or do it where they could be seen. Indirect parental injunctions can be far more potent than direct orders because they operate largely out of one's conscious awareness. There is no doubt that each of us is affected every day by lessons we learned this way without ever knowing it.*

Prohibitions against body awareness and pleasure are most likely to enter consciousness when they are violated. But just *thinking* about doing forbidden things sometimes triggers strong avoidance reactions. It is not unusual for people to find endless reasons why they cannot take time to look at and touch their anuses. Rarely are any direct internal "voices" saying "Don't do that!" Such thoughts would be relatively easy to deal with. It is more common for there to be vague feelings of guilt or naughtiness. One woman, Dorothea, expressed her feelings this way: "Why is it that

---

* Transactional Analysis describes two different communication processes through which prohibitions are passed on within the family: *injunction* and *attribution*. Injunctions are direct orders, e.g., "Don't play with yourself." Attributions are more tricky. They tell you *who you are* instead of what you should (or should not) do, e.g., "You're a good boy/girl; good boys/girls don't play with themselves." (Of course, the last part of the sentence is usually not stated but *implied*). Whether transmitted via injunction or attribution, such prohibitions replace spontaneous self-exploration with more "scripted" behavior (1974).

I feel like a bad girl when I look at my anus? It's the same way I feel when I play with my genitals.''

Dorothea had discovered something very important about herself that she did not even know was there: While she did not remember the actual prohibitions passed along to her by her parents, she was able to see the *effects* that they were having on her. George tried to deal with his feelings in a different way: ''Well, you know, I don't get all this talk about guilt and all that. I look at and touch my anus and it just *bores* me. That's all!'' It took George several weeks to admit, even to himself, that he was being affected by messages he had received as a child. Feeling bored is often preferable to feeling anxious.

Writing the imaginary letter to mom and dad can be very useful to you in uncovering feelings that may *seem* to belong to the distant past but which, in reality, are still very much with you. It is one thing to do something that mom and dad would not like—in this case, exploring your anus. It is quite another thing to state your intentions openly and without apology. To do so, even if only in make believe, can reduce guilt and build self-esteem and autonomy. The impact of this exercise is probably greater if shared, perhaps ''role played,'' with a friend (your friend plays mom and dad and responds to what you say).

Some people protect themselves from all these messy dealings with a more tricky strategy. They are quick to agree with *everything* (e.g., ''*Yes,* I feel guilty. *Yes,* I'm responding to prohibitions from childhood,'' etc.). But they are simply unwilling to explore it further, side-stepping every suggestion with ''I already know that!'' Such people have a very hard time getting anywhere at all. They are intellectually committed to change but are unwilling to *do* anything about it.

Another response that restricts anal awareness is the strong feeling of dirtiness or even revulsion that is often associated with the anus. These feelings may accompany looking or touching or both. Of course, such feelings are not limited to the anus, but often include areas such as armpits, genitals, etc. Often these feelings are subtle and carefully concealed. You may, for instance, be quite willing to touch your anus for a moment without discomfort, but you may be unable to take your time to *experience* the touch fully.

It is sometimes difficult to separate legitimate hygienic concerns from unrealistic feelings of revulsion. Generally speaking, legitimate cleanliness needs are dealt with easily and with little or no *emotional charge*. When issues of cleanliness are highly charged with feelings, it is clear that irrational fears are at work that need to be challenged by accurate information and new experience. Initially, all anal contact can occur right after bathing so that cleanliness is assured.

Other less common reactions are feelings of *frustration, resentment* and *anger*. Russ expressed this perfectly: "When I looked at my asshole, I thought it looked pretty good. But then I found myself getting mad. At first this surprised me and I even was kind of embarrassed. I said to myself, 'Now, what did your anus ever do to you?' You know, it's done *a lot* to me. It hurt me. It's embarrassed me! Right in the middle of sex when I wanted to have a good time it made me shiver with pain. My anus has been a pain in the ass!"

Jean expressed her frustration differently: "Why do I have to go through all these exercises and spend all this money? It's not fair! All I want is a little pleasure and some of my friends seem to get it naturally. So what the hell's wrong with me?"

Russ and Jean's feelings are completely understandable. When each got support for feeling anger and frustration, they soon were able to see that there was nothing wrong with them. They had simply neglected the self-exploration necessary for anal relaxation and enjoyment. They also realized that people are different. What one person takes for granted can be quite a test for someone else.

Sometimes anger that is at first directed toward the anal area can be redirected toward its real objects, e.g., parents, teachers, social mores and institutions which have encouraged you to dislike or mistrust your body, especially your anus. Don't be surprised if it comes out initially as bitchiness. In groups, we often have a "bitch session" in which participants get mad at nearly everyone and everything. Of course, such complaining does not change anything, but it can be very helpful in releasing a lot of old emotional "garbage." It can also be a lot of fun even if you do it alone in front of the mirror. Going through this can help open the way to more productive self-assertive behavior.

Your drawing of your anus can help you give expression to feelings toward your anus. Draw as many pictures as you wish as you progress through this book. You may be surprised by the differences. Often it is helpful to ask a close friend what he/she sees in your drawing. The responses can be quite illuminating.

Dialogue with and support from others can be a useful means of exploring your feelings and experiences. If you have a friend with whom you feel trust and rapport, particularly if he/she has been doing anal exploration too, you may want to begin talking together, giving each other suggestions, feedback and encouragement. If, however, you do not know such a person, or you feel uncomfortable about raising the subject, continue to explore on your own. Later, we will focus on comfortable ways to include others when you feel ready.

PERSONIFYING THE ANUS

Many of my clients have found it helpful to imagine that the anus has a personality of its own. If you are unaware of your anus, and it feels numb—as if it isn't there—you can picture you and your anus as strangers who need to get to know each other. If your anus has been the source of pain and frustration, then your "relationship" has been one of conflict.

Although this technique may sound silly at first, it is a useful tool. The goal initially is for you and your anus to become acquainted. This involves listening to what your anus is trying to "communicate" to you through muscle tension, uncomfortable sensations, irritated appearance, etc. It also involves treating your anus as you would a friend— protecting it from pain and discomfort, discovering what it needs to be healthy and being willing to change any behavior to which your anus responds negatively.

People who try this usually find that a sense of friendship with the anus is associated with relaxation, comfort, and an increase in pleasurable sensations. Once you establish an intimate friendship with your anus, you can abandon the idea that you and your anus have separate personalities. Bill put it this way: "Since I have started paying attention to my anus, I have developed a 'buddy, buddy' feeling about it. It's the last part of my body I have gotten to know. My sense of myself is more complete."

5

BENEATH THE SKIN

Locating and Exercising
Anal and Pelvic Muscles

As you continue looking and touching, you will gradually become more familiar with your anal area, learning more about it and liking it better. But this is just a beginning. Below the surface lies a complex system of muscles and nerves. Your sense of intimate contact with these is crucial to anal discovery and pleasure. Next, you will locate important pelvic muscles and start a program of exercise to restore or enhance their tone, elasticity and sensitivity.

ANATOMY OF ANAL MUSCLES

A full and detailed description of the pelvic muscles relevant to anal pleasure would be very complex. In fact, *nobody* fully understands the neurological processes that control these muscles. Nonetheless, some basic information is helpful.

Of major interest are two ring-like muscles that surround the anal opening: the anal sphincters (see Figure 2). One is known as the *external sphincter*, the other is the *internal sphincter*. These muscles overlap somewhat. Later you will discover that these muscles are quite capable of function-

54

Figure 2
SCHEMATIC DIAGRAM OF PELVIC MUSCLES

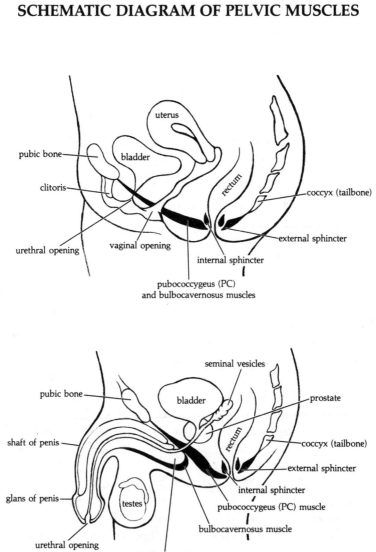

ing independently of each other because the neurological mechanisms that control them are different. For now, it is enough to know where these muscles are and that usually they work together (if one is tense, they are both tense).

Other separate, yet interrelated pelvic muscles are of importance to us (look again at Figure 2). These muscles are close to the anal sphincters and in direct or indirect contact with them. In general, these muscles can be referred to as the *perineal muscles*. They support the tissues around the anus and in the area between the anus and the genitals. This area is called the *perineum* after which the muscles are named.

Two specific perineal muscles deserve special comment. The first is called the *bulbocavernosus* muscle which, in men, envelops the bulb of the penis close to the anus, and in women, surrounds the outer portion of the vagina. Another important pelvic muscle is called the *pubococcygeus* muscle (PC for short). It is part of a large, flat, supportive muscle system known as the pelvic diaphragm. The PC muscle is so named because it is anchored at the front to the pubic bone and at the rear to the coccyx (tailbone).

The late gynecologist, Arnold Kegel, is well known for his studies of the PC muscle in women. Noting the role of the PC in controlling urine flow, he devised some simple exercises (now called ''Kegels'') to strengthen the PC in women who were bothered by stress incontinence (loss of urine when laughing, coughing, running, etc.). Many of his patients reported some welcome side effects of doing Kegels: increased sexual sensitivity and responsiveness. Kegel then became interested in the sexual functions of the PC muscle. He found that the tone of the PC was related to a woman's sensitivity to vaginal stimulation.

In both men and women, the PC muscle contracts randomly during arousal and rhythmically during orgasm. Its condition is probably a factor in the intensity of pelvic erotic sensations. In addition, men and women can voluntarily contract the PC and other pelvic muscles in order to enhance the pleasure of orgasm or, in some cases, influence the timing of orgasm.

My clients have found Kegel exercises to be of value in

improving anal sensitivity. When the PC muscle is contracted, many other pelvic muscles, including the anal sphincters and the bulbocavernosus, tend to contract simultaneously. In fact, it is doubtful that the improvements in sensitivity noted by Kegel were solely attributable to the PC muscle, but rather were a result of better tone throughout the perineal area.

Doing Kegels builds sensitivity in a variety of different ways. First, simply doing the exercises requires a certain amount of paying attention. This, all by itself, can enhance awareness of pelvic sensations. Second, exercising any muscle increases vascularity (blood flow) into the area being exercised. Each of us has felt the tingling warmth resulting from vigorous exercise or deep massage. Third, exercising improves the tone of soft muscle tissue. Soft muscles are very inefficient in transmitting sensations to the nerve endings embedded within them. Restoring tone, by repeatedly contracting and relaxing muscle fibers, firms the muscle tissues, which are then better able to transmit sensations to the nerve endings.

Well-exercised muscles are sometimes incorrectly assumed to be bulky, hard and inflexible. The image of the muscle-bound bodybuilder contributes to this belief. Actually, the restoration of tone to muscles usually results in a *lowering* of baseline (normal) muscle tension and an increase in elasticity. Healthy muscles are able to do their job in a firm, yet relaxed state. Conversely, soft muscles require a great deal of tension to *make* them do what they are supposed to do.

Most of the men and women I have worked with have reported improved anal and pelvic awareness and sensitivity after a few weeks of doing Kegel exercises. Most also felt that their anuses became more relaxed. Both of these changes probably result from a combination of paying attention, increased blood flow and improved tone.

Kegel himself did not pay any specific attention to breathing patterns in relation to his exercises. Yet breathing plays an important role in body awarenesss and relaxation, which is why breathing lies at the heart of such disciplines as yoga and the martial arts. When we are threatened, afraid, or in pain, our breathing becomes shallow, using only the upper portion of our lungs. The lower portion becomes immobile. To get enough oxygen, we take faster, erratic breaths instead of long, deep, slow ones. This restricted breathing is one mechanism that we use to limit our feelings and sensations. We can and do use the same mechanism to suppress or limit pleasurable feelings. *Shallow breathing is one way we learn to obey parental and societal prohibitions against having too much pleasure.*

To begin to reverse this process, to become as aware as possible of pelvic and anal sensations, it is necessary to breathe deeply, which depends on your diaphragm. The diaphragm is a large, flat muscle that lies below the lungs. In full breathing, the diaphragm swings downward, creating a bellows effect, allowing oxygen to fill the lungs. When you exhale, your diaphragm pushes upward against your lungs, expelling gaseous wastes. Full inhalation and full exhalation allow you to use your entire lung capacity. If you are using your diaphragm, your stomach and intestines will push outward somewhat as you inhale. *You cannot breath fully and hold your stomach in at the same time.* Breathe deeply before, during and after doing Kegel exercises and as often as you can remember all day long. Your entire body will feel more open, relaxed and alive.

The association between breathing and the anal muscles has been known, if not completely understood, for a long time. Anal contractions are apparently related to tensing of the diaphragm because it is very difficult to exhale whenever the anal sphincters are under much tension. Therefore, *when combining breathing with Kegels, you will want to contract your pelvic muscles during (or after) inhalation and relax as you exhale.* This is what your body tends to do naturally.

EXPERIENCE

In order to do Kegel exercises, it is first necessary to locate the muscles to be exercised. The best way to do this is to sit comfortably, feet flat on the floor and imagine that you are urinating. Then contract the muscles you would use to stop the flow of urine. If you cannot do this by imagining, then actually stop and start the flow the next time you urinate.

The PC muscle is the one that does this. It also contracts involuntarily during orgasm.

Once you get a feel for this, voluntarily contract and relax the PC a few times while noticing where in your pelvic area you feel the contractions. Place your hand on your perineum (between your genitals and anus). You will be able to feel the contractions there. Notice that your anus contracts, too.

Now that you have located the muscles, there are two different exercises to do with them. First, inhale deeply and contract the muscles. Hold the muscles and your breath for a few seconds and then relax as you exhale completely. When you contract, do it as tightly as you comfortably can. When you relax, visualize the tension "draining out" completely with your breath. Repeat the exercises throughout the day, every day, as often as you like. About 90 contractions per day are recommended.

The second exercise involves inhaling deeply and contracting the muscles as rapidly as you can, about ten contractions at a time. Exhale completely as you relax. Do about 20 to 50 rapid contraction sets per day.

A third exercise is helpful, although it is not a Kegel exercise. It is done by inhaling deeply and gently pushing out and pulling in the pelvic muscles as if you were sucking in and then expelling water through your anus. Then exhale and relax completely. This exercise can increase blood flow and, for some women, may increase natural lubrication of the vagina. The increased blood flow is important for men, too. About 25 of these movements are recommended throughout the day. Your muscles may feel tired at first. This is to be expected. If doing the exercise causes any pain, you will want to go to a doctor and find out what is causing it.

You can do these exercises whenever you are lying, sitting or standing still (watching TV, driving, doing dishes, etc.). Nobody has to know you are doing them, although at first you may want to do them in private. Results will be better if you do the exercises every day. It is easier to develop a routine if you associate the exercises with other daily activities (e.g., getting up, eating meals, driving to work, preparing for bed). Such regularity is important for the first few months. Thereafter, exercises can be done less often, though they will continue to be of value for the rest of your life.

RESPONSE

Some people find it difficult to locate and exercise these muscles. The rapid contractions seem to be the hardest for most people. The more difficult it is for you to control these muscles, the more you are in need of the exercises. As you do them, you will find it increasingly easy and quite pleasurable. After all, you are making your muscles do the things they do spontaneously when you are enjoying sex. Best of all, the more you do the exercises, the more you will start noticing sensations in your pelvis and anus, sensations you might hardly have noticed before.

Kegel exercises can be helpful even if they are done rather routinely. But their impact can be much greater if you use the exercises in a more creative way. This can make them *your* exercises because you will be doing them in ways that are unique to you.

I suggest combining the Kegel exercises with lots of free movement in a variety of settings. The positive effects of this movement will be limited, however, if you hold your pelvis rigid while moving the rest of your body. In fact, habitual, chronic, pelvic "holding on" is one major reason why so many people need Kegel exercises. Holding the pelvis requires muscular tension which restricts movement. Restricted movement allows muscles to deteriorate. Deteriorating muscles, in turn, require more tension to get them to work, which further restricts movement. It's a vicious cycle leading inevitably to decreased pelvic sensation.

Another factor is at work, especially for men. As boys, we learn in subtle ways that "being a little man" requires careful avoidance of swinging hips. Most of us overreact, learning to restrict pelvic movement so as not to be seen as "sissy." Consequently, pelvic rigidity has become characteristic of men in our culture. Girls are usually taught not to move their pelvises too much for fear of appearing too "sexy." So many women hold on as well, though for different reasons.

Try doing Kegels while moving your pelvis in a "hula

hoop'' motion, or thrusting forward and back and side to side. Also do Kegels while dancing, walking or running, breathing deeply and allowing your pelvis to move as freely as you can. There is no danger of becoming a ''sissy'' or ''too sexy'' except perhaps in the eyes of certain frightened and rigid people. You are far more likely to discover an open gracefulness and expansiveness in which you are in harmony with your body rather than working against it.

6

MIND AND BODY

Understanding How the Anus and Emotions Interact

Now that you have located your anal-pelvic muscles, learned something about their structure and begun a program of exercise to build tone, elasticity and sensitivity, you are, no doubt, already noticing more sensation in this area of your body. As you continue exercising—and looking and touching, too—you will be aware of even more sensation.

You may have already seen that anal and pelvic *un*awareness can get progressively worse. This cycle can be broken and started in the other direction. In this chapter, you will be asked to observe carefully how your anus responds and contributes to various emotional states. People often ask if anal tension and discomfort is a physical problem or "all in my head." Now you can discover the answer, which is always the same: *Both*. Body and mind—anus and emotions—are in a constant state of interrelationship.

STRESS AND ANAL TENSION

In order to understand the interplay between anal muscles and your emotions, it is important to have an accurate picture of how you, as a total organism, prepare to meet any threat to your integrity and survival. Let us start with a dramatic example: Suppose you are confronted by some external, very real danger, such as a violent person or dangerous animal. Instantly, without any conscious planning whatsoever (there is no time for that!) your entire being prepares to meet the threat. Blood rushes to the internal organs, particularly heart and lungs, which begin working at a feverish pace. Blood rushes *away* from the surface of your skin. This is why you tend to feel cold and clammy when you are threatened. Tactile sensitivity drops, reducing the possibility of being distracted by pain, should a confrontation occur. Muscles tighten to provide a rigid armor against attack. Breathing, restricted by the tense muscles, becomes shallow and rapid. Adrenaline flows. Your entire body is guarded and closed, ready to fend off or escape from the danger. These reactions are part of a total *stress response* involving mind and body in absolute unity.

In such an extreme situation, the natural tendency of your body is to defecate, getting rid of all excess weight to aid in escape or battle. Animals and human infants exhibit this spontaneous defecation reaction in response to severe threat. However, as a result of toilet training, we learn that this response is inappropriate. Therefore, when adults are under stress, their "natural" response is to *tighten* their anuses in an effort to counteract the urge to defecate. That is why most adults learn to associate a tense anus with fear.

Most of us do not confront situations like this often, but our lives are full of less serious threats, all of which produce stress responses to a greater or lesser degree. In civilized society, many of our stress responses are reactions to *internal threats*. These are specific fears (e.g., "I am going to lose my job, or get laughed at or rejected") or general anxieties (e.g., "I am not the person I *should be*. I am bad. I am not perfect"). Such internal threats—usually triggered or exaggerated by external events—can produce exactly the same stress responses as an attack by a wild animal. Most of these are fears and anxieties about what might or might not happen in the future. We are constantly preparing for battles that never actually take place or which, in many cases, are already taking place as an internal "cold war" among conflicting parts of ourselves.

To dismiss these internal threats as "all in the head" is to misunderstand the fact that *your body takes all threats seriously, whether internal or external, imagined or real, and responds accordingly.* Seeing the problem as "in the head" ignores another important process. Just as fear causes your body to tense up, the opposite is equally true. When your body is tense, it makes you *feel* fearful. Thus, the anxiety and fears of living are "in your body" just as much as "in your head." If you stop feeling afraid, your body will relax (unless it has forgotten how). Conversely, *if your body relaxes, you will feel less afraid.*

Most of us are under some degree of stress much of the time. We are worried about something, insecure about the future, afraid of losses and rejections. Our bodies also retain leftover tension from painful, frightening, anger-producing events that happened long ago. In fact, there is probably some residue of stress left in our bodies every time we are not allowed to discharge negative emotion. To some degree we must cope with new tensions in the course of even the dullest, most uneventful day. This is the way it is to be human.

When we are severely threatened we get tense all over. Yet all of us have favorite "spots" in our bodies where the little fears, hurts and worries of life are most readily expressed in the form of muscular tension. It is possible to be relatively relaxed except for these individual "tension zones." It is these places where tension from old fears and hurts lingers and festers. Usually we are not too aware of these little pockets of tension unless we get especially anxious about something. Then we notice a pain in the back or shoulder or head or eyes or jaw or anus.

The anus is a very common tension center. Many people are surprised to discover—once they start paying attention—that their anuses are tense virtually all of the time. Particular tension centers tend to run in families. This does not mean that they are hereditary, although this may be a factor in some cases. But mostly it seems that parents communicate their tension centers to their children through subtle verbal communication and "body language." If mom or dad gets anxious and tenses certain body parts, the kids are likely to do the same.

Our experiential goal is to discover ways in which your anus responds to your feelings and vice versa. There are two general possibilities. First, maybe your anus is fairly relaxed most of the time except when you are threatened by particular internal or external worries or dangers. In other words, your anus is *not* one of your tension centers. The second possibility is that your anus *is* one of your tension zones, responding with tension to even minor anxieties and insecurities of today *and* storing up those from yesterday. If this is the case, your anus is probably chronically tense.

Of the clients who have worked with me, over half found that their anuses were chronic centers of tension. The others may have been chronically tense elsewhere, but not in their anuses. These men and women found themselves becoming anally tense only when they felt stressful all over their bodies or, more specifically, when they felt anally threatened (e.g., when someone tried to have anal intercourse with them).

It appears that chronic anal tension leaves the anus particularly susceptible not only to discomfort but to actual medical problems. Among my clients, virtually all those with anal medical problems (except sexually transmitted diseases) are in the group that discovers their anuses are chronic tension centers. Specifically, among my research clients, *all* cases of hemorrhoids were among the chronically tense, as were all concerns about constipation. Likewise, all fissures (small tears or scrapes in the anus or rectum) were found in this group. This is why I have come to refer to these medical problems as "tension-related." (There is a less clear-cut relationship between chronic anal tension and sexually transmitted diseases like anal warts or anal gonorrhea. For more information about these and other medical problems, see Appendix A.)

Your primary tool for discovery will be *observation*. When you notice tension, I will suggest that you simply *become as aware of that tension as you can*. It is useless to *try* to relax. If you can just let yourself become completely aware of tension, you will notice some of that tension fading without struggle or effort. You can see for yourself how this works in your own body.

EXPERIENCE

Sit or recline quietly and comfortably. Close your eyes. Let your attention drift down toward your anus. Can you feel it? Is it tense? Relaxed? In-between? If you cannot feel it at all, do a few Kegel exercises (see last chapter) until your conscious mind begins registering some anal sensations.

Now notice your breathing. Are you holding your breath? Is it shallow or deep and slow? Let your breathing become deep, so that your stomach and chest expand as you inhale. Exhale completely. Notice your anus again. It will probably feel more relaxed than before.

Inhale deeply, hold your breath for a few seconds, and make your anus as tense as you possibly can. Now let it relax as you exhale. Do this a few times and notice your anus. Develop a clear image of your anal muscles and picture them as you exhale. As the muscles relax, picture blood flowing into the area, bringing warmth.*

For at least one week, take a few moments many times each day to notice your anus. You may want to do this in conjunction with your Kegel exercises. But be sure to notice your anus *before* you exercise as well as during and after.

When you find yourself in an anxious or irritating situation (e.g., waiting in line, having an argument, feeling depressed), notice your anus. Take a few moments to breathe deeply. Observe your anal muscles as completely as you can. Notice what happens as you breathe. Do not struggle to change anything. It will help you to make the most of your observations if you carry a notebook with you. Each time you notice your anus, note the day and time and whether your anus is tense, relaxed, in-between or numb.

At first you may not know for sure whether your anus is tense or relaxed. But as you focus on it regularly at different times and in different situations, you will become more able to identify subtle variations in tension.

---

* The technique of visualization is a powerful tool for health maintenance, healing and improving self-concept. Samuel's book, *Seeing with the Mind's Eye*(1975) provides a good overview of the history and current techniques of visualization. However, it is not always effective. One's ability to form an exceptionally vivid mental image is crucial. This ability can be refined with practice, but the degree to which it can be refined may be determined by one's basic personality.

RESPONSE

This exercise sounds so undramatic, maybe even silly, that many people neglect it. *It may be the single most important exercise you will do.* If you expect to enjoy your anus during sensual or sexual activities and forget about it the rest of the time, you probably will not get very far—especially if your anus is a chronic tension center.

If you do take time to observe your anus when you are in a variety of different moods and situations, you can learn a tremendous amount. First, you will learn that your anus *does* get tense, probably *very* tense when you are upset, angry or afraid. It is important to realize that this will happen no matter how familiar you become with your anus, or how relaxed your anus normally is. To expect your anus *not* to get tense under stressful circumstances is to expect your body to give up part of its basic mechanism for meeting danger.

What if you do not feel particularly upset or afraid and your anus is *still* tense? One possibility is that you are really having strong feelings, but you are "playing it cool." Your body does not lie; it cannot rationalize. Maybe your anus is expressing something of which you need to be aware. This is what Jane discovered: "My boyfriend and I were having one of our 'discussions' the other night. He doesn't like to fight. Neither do I. So we *discuss.* For some reason, I noticed my anus was tight, real tight. So tight it was hurting. And I realized I was damn mad! I wanted to strangle him! He was making me so mad, but we were *discussing!* Well, I decided I was going to let him have it. Hell with discussing. We were both really scared, but we came through all right, and my anus felt much more relaxed afterwards."

People like Jane, who hate to get angry, often have an angry body. Your anus can tell you things about your feelings—a sort of early warning system—when you are trying to avoid those feelings.

Maybe you are not withholding any feelings and you are *still* tense. Then there is a good chance that your anus is one of your chronic tension centers. Perhaps you have saved up old hurts or anger from the past and stored them in your anal area. Or perhaps you have learned to hold your anus tight to keep yourself from feeling too much pleasure. You do not have to uncover all the reasons in order to start changing. The key is to observe your anal tension. You cannot force your anus to relax. But as you give it more attention, it will gradually become more relaxed. As it does, *you* will feel more relaxed and open.

This does not happen all at once, although it is quite possible to feel the good feelings associated with relaxed muscles after just a few moments of paying attention and deep breathing. This will motivate you to go on. For a while, perhaps for a long while, your anus will tend to return to its familiar tense state. Do not forget that to the extent your anus has been a chronic tension center, you have developed a habit pattern that will require a lot of attention and perhaps considerable time to change. And remember that struggles or coercion of any kind will only make the tension worse.

If you are a person who struggles with things, who sees a problem and wants immediately to tackle it, you may find this a frustrating exercise. In fact, your tendency to struggle and push yourself may be a central reason why your anus is always tense. For strugglers, everything has the flavor of battle and their anuses are always prepared for a confrontation. Maybe you do not see yourself as a struggler. Perhaps you are a "perfectionist." It sounds a little better, but the dynamics are the same. If you demand a perfectly relaxed anus tomorrow morning, then you will never have one. If your anus feels *just a little* more relaxed now than it did a few minutes ago, you are doing great. Even if your anus does not feel more relaxed, but you are a little more aware that it is not relaxed, you are still doing fine.

Those whose anuses are relatively relaxed except, of course, in specific stressful situations, are lucky. You do not have to go through a lot of this. In just a moment, we will return to concerns that are more relevant to you. In the meantime, perhaps you can benefit from considering what, exactly, your relaxed anus feels like. Feeling *nothing* in your anus does *not* mean you are relaxed. If you are relaxed, your anus will feel pleasantly alive. Maybe you need to check again.

Depending on the extent to which your anus has become a repository for excess tension, two factors may make it especially difficult to do anything about it. The first is the strong prohibition against anal awareness and pleasure and the particular fears associated with that prohibition (e.g., "I'll be perverted or sinful if I play with my anus," "Mommy won't love me"). For some men, the association of anal exploration with homosexuality often produces other irrational fears (more on this later).

Another factor that can motivate you to avoid awareness of anal tension is more practical: If your anus has been very tense for a long time, the first thing you may notice when you discover that tension is pain. You may have a tortured anus. When people start noticing their anuses, they are often amazed at how much they hurt. If this happens to you, it is *important to pay attention to your anal pain*. When you touch your anus, stroke it gently. Take warm baths. Breathe deeply. Soon your pain will subside. If it does not, or if you suspect a medical problem, find a good physician and have a checkup.

If you discover pain, you may feel angry at your anus. Do not deny that anger; it is a natural response to pain. If you can express that anger—at least to yourself—you will be better able to move beyond it. This exchange from one of my group sessions illustrates this:

Dan: I realize I always *hated* my anus. I felt it was dirty, smelly. When I called someone an "asshole," that was really the worst put-down. To be an asshole is the lowest of the low in my book. Yesterday I was feeling all the pain in my anus and hating the damn thing even more.
Leader: What did you do?
Dan: What could I do? I don't know how long it went on, but a friend walked by my desk and said, "What's wrong with you?"
Leader: You and your anus were having a closer relationship at that moment than you probably ever had.
Dan: How do you mean?
Leader: You were *feeling* your anus, reacting to it instead of ignoring it.
Dan: I sure was feeling it!
Leader: What about now?

Dan: Well, when I got home from work, I took a long bath and looked at it. I didn't like what I saw too much. But I started to feel sorry for my ass. It was hurting me because I had hurt it. It was all raw and red. I felt like apologizing to my anus. Crazy, huh?
Group Member: You made up after a big fight.
(Group laughs.)
Leader: Things will never be the same between you again.
Dan: I hope not!

Dan's discovery came after several weeks of avoiding (and resenting, it turned out) his anus. He was not able to feel genuine compassion for himself and his hurting anus until he actually felt the pain. If you try to get your anus to relax without *feeling* it, nothing will change.

Frequently, increased awareness of the anal muscles and their response to stress serves as a catalyst for a more general evaluation of the effects of stress on one's body. Many people begin thinking about what they can do to relax. I recommend that any stress reduction program include: (1) at least one-half hour of vigorous physical exercise such as jogging, brisk walking, swimming, bicycling or dancing at least every other day, (weightlifting is good but does not produce the sustained heart-lung function required for optimum stress reduction); (2) at least one, preferably two, fifteen-minute periods every day devoted to one of the popular relaxation techniques (some form of meditation, self-hypnosis or a progressive relaxation sequence is especially recommended).* Stress reduction promotes overall health, including anal health.

After you learn to pay attention to your anus throughout the day, to explore the ways it reflects your emotions, and to release some of the tension you may have been storing there, you can then turn your attention to more specific con-

---

* A wealth of books on relaxation have appeared in recent years. Almost any technique can work if it is suited to you and *you actually practise the technique regularly.* It is useful to select a few techniques not seen appealing or interesting and then "field test" them in your daily life. *The Relaxation Response*(1975) presents the central elements needed for effective meditation. *The Relaxation and Stress Reduction Workbook*(1980) offers concise directions for virtually all popular stress reduction techniques.

cerns of anal sensuality. What happens to your anus in a sexual situation? To help you answer this question, I will ask that you recall experiences from the past. In the context of your present awareness, the past can be reexperienced from a fresh perspective. If you cannot remember, or if you have had no relevant past experience, you can use your imagination to give you similar information.

EXPERIENCE

Find a private, quiet place to sit comfortably with your clothes off. Have your journal nearby so that you can refer to it or write in it when you want to.

Close your eyes and breathe deeply and slowly as you become conscious of your anus. How does it feel right now? Remain aware of any feelings you might be having until your muscles relax. You might want to place your finger over your anus and stroke it gently.

Let your mind wander, thinking over recent sexual experiences, remembering the behaviors and feelings of those experiences in as much detail as you can. See if you can remember one particular experience where a sexual partner made some kind of tactile contact with your anus.

As you remember, see if you can place yourself in that experience. Try to recall that experience from the standpoint of how your anus feels about being touched by a sexual partner. Are you afraid, apprehensive, open, excited? Return your attention to the present and see how your anus is feeling right now. Has it tensed up a little, or is it still relaxed? If you notice tension, pay attention to your anus until it is relaxed again.

Let your mind focus on one sexual experience where your partner put a finger inside your anus. If you have had no such experience, imagine what it would be like. As you recall or imagine your partner's finger entering your anus, see what you feel. Focus on this as long as you want. When you are ready, return to the present and notice your anus. If you notice tension, pay attention until your anus relaxes.

Now remember a time a partner wanted to have, or actually had, anal intercourse with you. If this has never happened, imagine what it would be like. Remember or imagine every detail. What was said (if anything), what your partner did, what you did. If you have had more than one such experience, relive these too—both painful experiences and pleasant ones. Remember them as your anus "remembers" them.

Return to your anus in the present and see how it feels. Write your reactions in your journal while they are still fresh.

RESPONSE

The key to this exercise is to reexperience past events while remaining aware of your anus now. You will discover that your *body remembers*. That is to say, memories, both pleasant and painful, are retained in your body as well as in your mind. This is why *suppressing memories of painful anal experiences will not relieve tension*. Only new, more positive experiences can do that.

With this in mind, it is important to ask yourself what factors contributed to your uncomfortable anal experiences. These are the things for you to avoid, or somehow change in the future. Here are some common responses. Do any have a bearing on your experiences?

I didn't know what was going on. My partner just tried it without telling me what he/she was doing.

I didn't know anything about anal sex and felt that it was dangerous, dirty or perverted.

My partner was insensitive and rough.

I was afraid to say "no."

I put my partner's pleasure ahead of my own comfort.

I felt vulnerable, like I was being violated or used.

I was angry but afraid to let it show.

I felt I *should* be able to do it and was afraid to say that I was afraid.

As you consider the effects of these and other factors on your anal muscles, you will realize that during every negative experience you were essentially out of communication with your anus. To be in communication with your anus is to listen *and respond to* the neuromuscular messages it gives you. Often awareness is the missing link in unpleasant experiences with anal sex, i.e., maybe you did not know your anus was tense. Awareness alone, however, is not enough. It is common for people to be aware that their anuses are tense but to decide (or let their partner decide) to go ahead anyway. In that case, the missing link is *action*, i.e., taking concrete steps to protect yourself from anal discomfort.

I always ask people how they would have liked these painful anal experiences to have been different. Usually the response is something like this: "I wish I could have relaxed and enjoyed it!" This is understandable enough, but let's look at it more closely. Here is an admittedly loose, but probably accurate translation: "I wish my anus had felt different than it actually did so that I wouldn't have had to think about it." If you understand this, you can see that fantasizing "ideal" solutions (e.g., relax and enjoy it) is, in reality, part of the problem—an unwillingness to acknowledge and act on the fact that when you're afraid, your anus will be tense. And while some people are willing to suppress their fears in the interest of something "greater" (e.g., their partner's pleasure, their image as a sexual sophisticate, etc.), their anuses are probably *not* going to participate in the suppression. *To the extent that you create ideals, expecting your anus to go along with them, conflict is generated within you. Tension is the result.* Your anus, left to protect itself, will struggle valiantly. It may lose, but not without a fight.

This is an appropriate point to challenge one of the most widely held and destructive myths about the insertion of a finger or penis into the anus: that a certain amount of pain, particularly at first, is an inevitable part of anal sex, and that if a person is willing to endure a little pain, it will soon vanish, making the experience more pleasurable. When you approach anal sex in this way, this is what happens: Your anus is tense (from fear or habit) but you decide to go ahead anyway. Your anal muscles resist with all the force they can muster to repel the uncomfortable invasion. Eventually, however, the muscles collapse. They can fight no more. Then, if no physical damage has been done (there sometimes *is* damage), the pain goes away. The result is usually not pleasure but neutral toleration. Once you start this drama, it usually has to be repeated again and again. Your anus will never really feel comfortable. You and your anus will remain enemies until communication (awareness *and* protective action) is restored. *The unmistakable difference between real anal pleasure and neutral toleration is reported universally by men and women, once they give up the use of force.*

If this makes sense to you, this is a good time to reaffirm the agreement that you will *never* deliberately submit your anus to any pain. This affirmation is the foundation for all anal pleasure.

Obviously, you can also learn a great deal from positive anal experiences you've had or imagined. What made the experience a good one? Here are some typical responses:

> I was in a good mood and feeling relaxed.
>
> My partner was sensitive and paid a lot of attention to my anus.
>
> I trusted that my partner would never deliberately hurt me.
>
> Our encounter was slow and sensual.
>
> We would have had a good time with or without anal sex.

Your list may contain other items. But if you look closely at your positive anal experiences, you will no doubt find that you were *playing with* your anus instead of *working against* it. Some people take so many drugs that their sense of pain—and pleasure—is severely diminished. Then they may call the experience "good" even though they hardly remember it.

It is not unusual for enjoyable anal experiences to happen unexpectedly. When this is the case, people come to feel that good anal experiences depend mostly on their partner(s), "luck," or other factors beyond their control. If, however, you look closely at what made an experience good for you, you will discover that each experience was affected by *your* behavior, whether active or passive. This is also true of the negative experiences.

Later you will be focusing, in more detail, on how to bring this awareness into present and future experiences of anal sensuality or sexuality with partners. You will learn how to enhance pleasurable experiences and how to avoid ever having unpleasant ones. For now, it is enough to reevaluate your past experiences, seeing that your anus was never a passive receptacle for sex, but rather an active participant in an emotional event. You can arrive at the same understanding by imagining a variety of sexual experiences and noticing how your anus reacts.

7

INSIDE THE ANUS

Learning Voluntary Muscle Control

As you have seen, awareness of what you are actually experiencing—and not some ideal notion of perfection—is the essence of all bodily enjoyment. As you remain sensitive to what your anus is telling you, you can begin to develop voluntary control over your anal muscles. This is not an authoritarian type of control ("Do what I tell you!"), but rather *a natural sense of oneness between what you intend and how your anus responds.*

In order to learn voluntary anal control, you need information about your anal muscles and how they work. Then gradually, as you feel comfortable, you will learn to use your finger as a sensitive probe to explore inside your anus.

ANATOMY AND PHYSIOLOGY OF THE ANAL CANAL

The anal canal is a tube-shaped entryway, less than an inch long, which leads into your rectum. The outer two-thirds of the anal canal is made of the same soft, sensitive tissue that is visible on the surface. The inner third of the anal canal is lined with mucous membrane. This part of the canal is less sensitive to touch than the outer two-thirds, but is very sensitive to pressure. In fact, muscles in the rectum tend to contract in response to pressure. This always happens during bowel movements. This is why insertion of fingers or objects into the anal canal for pleasure should never involve force, but rather should be accomplished through *relaxation*.

The folds of anal tissue give the anal canal a striking capacity for expansion, depending on the level of muscular tension. For example, during rectal surgery, under anesthesia, a person's anal muscles can be easily dilated so that the surgeon's entire hand can pass through the anal canal. This same expansiveness is called upon in "fisting" or "fist fucking," which is a popular sexual activity among a few people. These extremes are not experienced by most people, but they illustrate that anal tissue can easily and safely expand for fingers, penises, etc.

Below the surface of the anal canal, veins and arteries pass blood through cavernous (filled with spaces) columns of tissue called *anal cushions*. There are three of these cushions running the short length of the anal canal. The cushions are anchored by connective tissue and muscle fibers to the internal sphincter muscle. Within the anal cushions, blood passes from arteries to veins without any capillaries (the tiniest of blood vessels that usually connect arteries and veins). This means that blood flows with extreme ease through the anal cushions, which swell to accommodate it (similar to the penis or the clitoris).

During a healthy bowel movement or during the insertion of something into the anal canal, blood leaves the cushions as the anal sphincters relax. However, if the sphincters are *not* relaxed, the anal cushions remain congested with blood. This is what happens when a person strains to force a bowel movement or uses force to insert something into the anal canal. The result is an uncomfortable stinging sensation or actual pain. If such straining and forcing is done regularly, a variety of medical problems such as hemorrhoids (protrusions from the anal cushions) or fissures (tears or cracks in the anal lining) can result. To prevent or eliminate this discomfort and the possibility of damage, it is necessary to know how the two anal sphincter muscles work.

The anal canal maintains its tubular shape because of two ring-like sphincter muscles (see Figure 3). The sphincters are very close together, overlapping somewhat. The two sphincters are quite capable of functioning independently, and often do so. The *external sphincter,* which is closest to the anal opening, is under the control of the central nervous system, the same system that activates muscles in hands, arms, etc. With a little concentration, a person can make the external sphincter tense or relax at will, in the same way that fingers can be moved at will.

The *internal sphincter* is quite different. It is neurologically controlled by the autonomic nervous system, the same system that makes adjustments in blood pressure, respiration rate and other "involuntary" body functions. Because the internal sphincter normally functions reflexively, most people cannot tense and relax it at will. When fecal material passes from the colon into the rectum, the pressure of fullness triggers the *rectal reflex.* This involves the automatic relaxation of the internal sphincter and a partial draining of blood from the anal cushions. Then the voluntary relaxation of the external sphincter allows for a quick and easy bowel movement.

Three factors can and often do disrupt this course of events. First, many people have been taught to ignore the urge for defecation caused by the rectal reflex. Instead, they hold back, not wanting to be bothered going to the toilet. Perhaps they were taught long ago that bowel movements ought to occur only at certain predetermined times (a notion fostered by over-strict toilet training practices). When it is chronically ignored or overridden, the rectal reflex fades, the internal sphincter stops relaxing. Once this has occurred, almost every bowel movement *requires* pushing and straining. Any person who wants a healthy and relaxed anus must learn to pay attention to the rectal reflex. Gradually, the natural urges it produces will again become strong.

Another factor that can inhibit the rectal reflex is the common habit of avoiding the passage of flatus (intestinal gases)

Figure 3

INTERNAL AND EXTERNAL ANAL
SPHINCTER MUSCLES

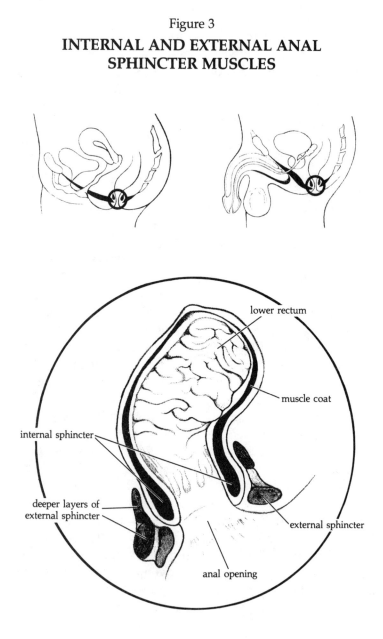

through the anal opening. Gases are formed during food digestion. Chronic attempts to hold in these gases inevitably result in unnecessary and potentially destructive muscle tension (Levitt, 1975). Certainly one will want to exercise some control over the timing of flatus release. However, it is a mistake to adopt a policy of never "farting."

The third, and perhaps the most important factor that disrupts relaxation of the internal sphincter during bowel movements is the absence of adequate bulk in the fecal material. Feces should be *soft*, yet well-formed and bulky. This requires adequate fiber in the diet. Small, hard feces do not provide the fullness necessary to trigger the rectal reflex. Once again, the person must resort to straining whenever bowel movements are attempted. *If your stools are not large, well-formed and slightly moist, your goal of anal awareness, pleasure and health will be very difficult to reach unless you add significant quantities of fiber to your diet every day.* With adequate fiber, your rectal reflex can be more easily triggered. This will help you immensely in learning how to relax your internal sphincter muscle. The best sources of fiber are legumes (beans and peas), nuts and fresh fruits and vegetables (Lappe, 1975). In addition, two tablespoons of unprocessed bran (available in most grocery stores) can be taken in liquid *before* each meal.

The ease with which you do have bowel movements and the pleasure you receive from anal stimuli will be greatly enhanced if you can learn how voluntarily to relax the internal sphincter muscle. How can a person learn voluntary control over an "involuntary" body process? That such control is possible at all has just recently been "discovered" in the West. In the East, practitioners of disciplines such as yoga have known these things for centuries. In the West, the turning point was the development of *biofeedback*, which involves the use of mechanical or electronic devices to provide a person with visual or auditory information about what the body is doing. Put simply, it has been found that if a person can get clear, immediate feedback (in the form of a changing tone, flashing light, etc.) about some "involuntary" body function (e.g., blood pressure, brain waves, skin temperature), before too long he/she will be able

80

to affect that function just by paying attention to it. The development of biofeedback has opened up a whole new area of research, with any number of potential applications (Brown, 1974).

The key to voluntary control of the sphincter muscles, particularly the internal one, is a steady, accurate supply of information about what the muscle is doing. Happily, no electronic instruments are needed to provide this information. Your body is already equipped with a supersensitive "biofeedback device" that you can begin to use at any moment: *your finger.* By inserting a finger into your anal canal, locating the two sphincters, and paying attention to the information your finger will provide, you can learn to relax the muscles at will—as long as you feel safe.

Before you begin to explore inside your anus, you should know that your anal canal and rectum do not normally contain any solid masses of fecal material. Your rectum and anal canal are passageways for feces which, during a bowel movement, are moved by muscular waves (peristalsis) out of the colon, into the rectum and out through the anal canal. Feces are not normally *stored* in the rectum for long periods of time. However, those who have learned to ignore the rectal reflex or whose feces are not well-formed may encounter some feces in the lower rectum, a situation that can be remedied by changes in diet and "toilet habits."

Bathing is usually adequate for cleaning this area, especially when you learn to feel comfortable putting your finger in your anus as part of bathing or showering. If, however, you are concerned about cleanliness, you might want to give yourself an anal douche.

ANAL DOUCHING (ENEMAS)

An enema involves the introduction of liquid into the anal canal and lower rectum, holding that liquid inside for a few minutes, and then releasing it. Most people use enemas for the purpose of initiating bowel movements. Some children are forced to submit to enemas as treatment or even punishment for constipation. The regular use of enemas for initiating bowel movements is not a good idea because it can foster dependency, i.e., the inability to have a bowel movement naturally (Consumer Reports, 1980). And enemas containing harsh chemicals can irritate mucous membranes. Serious conditions such as hemorrhaging and infections have been associated with the frequent use of chemical enemas (Darlington, 1973).

The use of plain water enemas solely for the purpose of cleaning the anus and lower rectum is harmless. Many people find that the feeling of cleanliness that results makes them feel more relaxed because they are no longer concerned about encountering feces during anal play. The term *anal douching* is becoming more popular since it avoids the connotation of enemas as treatment for constipation.

There are four means of anal douching. First, you can buy a disposable enema at the drugstore. It comes in a plastic bottle with a lubricated nozzle for insertion into the anus. Just empty out the unwanted chemical solution and fill the container with warm water. It can be used over and over again. Or you can buy a "hot water bottle" and hose designed for vaginal douching. Third, you can buy a plastic turkey baster with a rubber bulb. Finally, some products specifically designed for anal douching are now available. One of these even connects to a shower head. This can be convenient for regular use, but it must be used with *very* low water pressure.*

Some people enjoy the process of anal douching as well as the cleanliness that results. Others don't like it, perhaps being reminded of childhood enemas. If anal douching makes you uncomfortable, don't do it.

LUBRICATION

The inner part of the anal canal produces mucus to keep the tissues moist and protected. But anal mucus is not the same as the excellent lubrication secreted by the vagina nor is it as plentiful. For this reason, extra lubrication should

* A few people are experimenting with beer, wine or hard liquor enemas. Since alcohol can be absorbed throught the rectal tissues, it is possible to become intoxicated this way, but it can be very irritating to your anus and rectum. Hard liquor can burn delicate tissues. Those who feel compelled to try this would be wise to dilute their favorite beverage with plenty of water.

always be applied when you insert your finger (or anything else) into the anus.

Talking to anal enthusiasts about lubricants is like talking to wine connoisseurs about wine—everybody has a different opinion about which one is best. This is something you will want to decide for yourself. A few guiding principles, however, are helpful. First, use a lubricant with as few chemical additives as possible. Your anus and rectum are not used to a steady assault of harsh chemicals as is the rest of your body. Scents, colors and emollients are all chemicals that can irritate anal tissues. Second, lotions and creams do not lubricate well because they are absorbed too quickly. Water soluble lubricating jellies (available in drug stores) are good because they clean up easily with water. For this reason they are the most convenient for anal exploring with your finger. Later on, if you decide to try more prolonged anal stimulation, greasy or oily lubricants are probably better because they last longer. Vegetable shortening, safflower or peanut oil and virtually any of the newer commercial preparations designed for anal lubrication are all fine. It is a matter of personal preference. Water soluble lubricants and lightweight oils should probably be the only ones used in the vagina (if extra lubrication is desired or needed) because the vagina is a cul-de-sac from which heavy lubricants like petroleum jelly are difficult to wash out. The rectum is an efficient self-cleaning system. Any leftover lubricant will be cleaned out during your next bowel movement.

EXPERIENCE

Begin with the bathing and anal looking and touching that you began in Chapter 4. Gently apply a small amount of lubricant to your anal opening and finger. Use the finger that seems most comfortable. Make sure your fingernail is trimmed and smooth.

Inhale deeply, contract your anal muscles and gently press your finger against your anus. As you exhale, let your anal muscles relax and your finger will move into your anal canal. Use no more than a gentle pressure. Go in only as far as feels completely comfortable. Just a quarter of an inch at first is fine. If you feel discomfort or pain, it means you are pushing too hard and should use less pressure.

When your finger is as far into your anus as you want it to go, stop there and let your anal muscles get used to the presence of your finger. Your anus will begin to relax as it discovers this is not an invasion, but a friendly expedition. Be sure to breathe deeply and slowly. Feel the relaxation, but *do not* push your finger in any further. Do this as long as it is comfortable and then pull your finger away slowly and take a break.

Each time you repeat this exercise, you will find that your finger will comfortably go in a little more. At each step, spend a few minutes moving your finger slowly in a circular motion. Stop *before* you feel uncomfortable or bored. Soon, you will be able to put your finger all the way inside your anal canal. You will be entering the lower rectum, which will feel soft and open.

Experiment with moving your finger in and out, back and forth and around in a circle. Never use force. Do only what your anus will accept without protest. If you realize you have gone too far or too fast, back off a little. But do not pull out completely, and avoid ever pulling out rapidly. Jerky movements are more likely to make your anus tense.

When you can move your finger around freely, slowly pull your finger out so that only the tip of your finger is in your anal canal (about one half to three quarters of an inch). Gently press against the walls of your anal canal. You will be able to distinguish your external and internal sphincter muscles as two separate rings with a small space between them (less than a quarter of an inch). The external one will probably feel more relaxed than the internal one. Notice how you can tense and relax the external sphincter while the internal one seems to have a mind of its own.

Notice that your internal sphincter frequently changes spontaneously, tensing up a little, relaxing a little. Just pay attention. When your internal sphincter relaxes, say to yourself, "Relax, relax." When it starts to tense up again, repeat to yourself, "Tense, tense." Just describe what is happening. Do not try to control it.

Spend a few minutes each day if possible doing the same

things. Gradually (do not rush!) you will find that thinking "Relax, relax" can affect your internal sphincter. But whenever your sphincter ignores relaxed thoughts and tenses anyway, do not fight it; just repeat, "Tense, tense."

As your sense of influence over your anal muscles increases, you will quite easily be able to insert two fingers at a time. To do this, follow the same gradual progression already described.

A variation of the exercise can be tried whenever you feel the urge for a bowel movement. (Remember: If you have learned to ignore these urges, you may have to pay close attention.) As soon as possible, go to the bathroom. As you sit on the toilet, breathe deeply and imagine your anal muscles relaxing. Allow the muscles of your colon and rectum to expel the feces. Do not strain in any way. If nothing happens, don't push. Leave the bathroom and return the next time you feel the urge.

RESPONSE

Exploring inside your anus can be a turning point in your desire for anal pleasure. Especially if you have abused your anus in the past (allowing uncomfortable sexual experiences, straining during bowel movements, etc.) it may take your anus a while to trust the presence of your finger. Patience is crucial. If you push yourself, your anus will reflect your impatience by getting tense.

Once inside, even a little, you will experience some new sensations. Some will be pleasurable. Others may feel rather strange. When you encounter a new sensation, your automatic impulse may be to assume that it is uncomfortable and to pull your finger out until the sensation goes away. This, of course, is exactly the thing to do if you really do feel discomfort. But take a moment to ask yourself: *"Is this new feeling uncomfortable, or just different?"* If you decide it is just different, and not particularly uncomfortable, then you can leave your finger inside and see what the new sensation is like.

Exploring your anal canal is also likely to trigger some memories and emotions. Pay attention to these, rather than trying to change or suppress them. Write your responses in your journal after each session; then you will be able to look back at changes in your feelings as you progress. This can be helpful if you encounter a rough spot later on in your exploration.

Pay attention to your resistance, e.g., forgetting to do the exercises or never finding time. Observe your behavior until you discover the fears behind your avoidance. By doing this, Beth made an interesting discovery: "I've been having trouble getting near my anus until the other day when I was just sitting there and it struck me. I was feeling the same way about my anus that I used to feel about my vagina during my period, that it was sort of like a wound, that it was sick or diseased or God knows what. It just wasn't right to put my finger inside a wound. I guess all these years I've been waiting for my anus to heal! After this, my finger went in pretty easily. I can't say I'm enjoying it exactly, but—it's embarrassing—I was delighted to find no blood."

Pete's experience was different: "I've always hated fingers in my ass. Every time some guy would put his finger in there I was bracing myself to get fucked any minute. My asshole reacts the same way to my own finger. It's getting ready to be raped, I guess. That's what it always felt like before—*rape!* I guess, in a sense, I've been raped many times. But I went along with it. No wonder my ass is so tight."

As you experienced in the last chapter, your anus has a memory (it shares yours). However, most people find that the anus does not hold a grudge. Instead, it will respond quickly to a new situation if you just give it a chance. Once your anal muscles start to respond to your own caring touch, progress is usually rapid. You can then begin to "train" your internal sphincter, not with intimidation, but with patience. Under coercion and pressure of any kind, your anus will automatically assume its instinctive protective posture.

Learning a more natural approach to bowel movements can also increase your capacity for anal pleasure and dramatically reduce the negative effects of straining. To the extent that you usually push your way through a bowel movement, undoing this habit will require special attention. Recent research into the processes of habit change indicates the value of making adjustments in the *behavioral routines* that accompany unwanted habits. For example, people who read in the bathroom have probably learned to associate reading with prolonged straining, even though awareness of straining may have disappeared. Removing all reading material from the bathroom will help such a person concentrate on sensations of relaxation in the anus and rectum. A well-functioning rectal reflex, in combination with a diet rich in fiber and reduced anal sphincter tension should result in bowel movements being completed in about a minute. The need for more time strongly suggests that the relaxation responses are still being inhibited (Goliger, 1967).

Modifying the ways in which you have bowel movements can be more complex than you expect. Social demands placed on many children can be a source of great embarrassment, fear and anger. This is especially true when parents believe that anal muscular control can only be fostered by threats of ridicule and coercion. (Actually, there is no reason why anal control shouldn't occur as naturally as walking and talking.) Depending on your experiences as a child, you may find that the reduction of anal *over*control, and a return to a more natural elimination pattern, brings with it a rush of unexpected feelings. Many people find themselves spontaneously crying when they first experience a natural, unforced bowel movement. Then there is often anger: "Goddamn her," said Meg, referring to her mother, "It's so *easy!* Why did she have to make it such a scary ordeal?"

Others, as they learn to release the tension of chronic overcontrol, have "flashbacks" of fear as they remember parental warnings of accidents if control is not maintained. If this is true for you, it may take a while to relinquish completely the conviction that chronic anal tension is the price that one must pay for controlling feces. It may require repeated reminding that the tension serves no useful purpose. The natural tone of your anal muscles is all that is needed for adequate control.

Although it often sounds silly to people at first, almost all my clients report that a quiet sense of joy accompanies relaxed bowel movements—those in which the body's finely-tuned system of elimination is allowed to function properly. This, of course, is not silly at all. Similar experiences of joy usually accompany optimal functioning of any body system. Put simply, *bodily health is inherently pleasurable and it normally produces a positive emotional state.*

8

ANAL EROTICISM

Including the Anus in
Self-Pleasuring and Masturbation

All experiences of anal exploration have the *potential* of being highly sensual or erotic. The degree to which you have been getting more familar with your anus is probably the degree to which you have found your anus to be a source of pleasure. Thus far, however, I have not emphasized the erotic potential of your anus because anal eroticism is so negatively charged for many people.

If you look at the development of your own sexuality over the years, you are likely to realize that many things that are now highly erotic to you were, at first, explored in a more matter-of-fact, less passionate way. For instance, children casually play with their genitals, discovering that this feels good, long before they experiment with more focused masturbatory activity. It is important to explore your anus without having to be sexually excited in order to do it. Some people include their anuses in sexual activities in the rush of erotic passion, but may resist looking at or touching their anuses when they are not aroused. In these instances, anal eroticism *per se* does little to increase anal awareness.

You have been doing a lot of anal exploring in a variety of different ways and have gathered a great deal of information about your anus and how it responds. Fears you might have had have now subsided or perhaps disappeared completely. This is a good time to consider (or reconsider) the erotic capacities of your anus.

As you move into the area of anal sexuality, it is important to pay attention to your sexual responses in general, because the entire body—not only particular parts—is inevitably involved in sexual arousal.

SEXUAL RESPONSE AND THE ANUS

Sexual responsiveness is a highly personal thing. What turns you on, how you feel about it, the subtle combination of factors that make for a good sexual experience is unique to you. Yet you also share some elements of your sexual response with virtually all human beings. This commonality is especially evident on the physiological level, because the body is our most basic human heritage.

Masters and Johnson are well known for their studies of physical sexual response. In the laboratory, Masters and Johnson observed about 600 men and women (ages 18 to 89) doing things they like to do sexually. After observing about 2,500 cycles of sexual response, they found that some generalizations could be made about the sexual response cycles of men and women. The information can be of value to you in exploring your own sexuality as long as you place the information in the context of your uniqueness, being careful not to assume that the generalities are standards for normalcy.

Masters and Johnson divide sexual response into four phases: excitement, plateau, orgasm and resolution. Generally, each phase flows into the next. Yet certain physiologic events can be seen as landmarks for each phase. Your body responds to sexual stimulation in essentially the same way regardless of the kind of stimulation or its source (as long as what is happening is interpreted as erotic *by you*). Thus, whether you give yourself stimulation or get it from a loved one or a stranger, there is no physiological difference in the sexual response.

It is important to remember that these are descriptions of physiological response to sexual stimuli. There is a great diversity in the way arousal and orgasm are perceived by the person experiencing them. A few people have become so turned off to sexual situations that they feel no pleasure or they feel nothing although their bodies are undergoing these physiological changes.

Figure 4 graphically represents three common response patterns for men and women. Line A is the most frequent pattern. In men, pattern A is so frequent that Masters and Johnson describe only this pattern for males. However, some men experience, at least on occasion, pattern B, in which excitement builds to plateau, perhaps fluctuating, but does not lead to orgasm (this pattern is called inhibited or absent ejaculation). Since no orgasm occurs, the body's return to an unaroused state is usually slower. In pattern C, excitement builds in rapid steps directly to orgasm, followed by a rapid return to an unaroused state. Plateau does not occur as a discrete phase. (In men this pattern is sometimes called premature or rapid ejaculation.)

For women, patterns B and C occur more frequently than they do for men. Pattern B, which is very common, is called

Figure 4
SEXUAL RESPONSE CYCLES

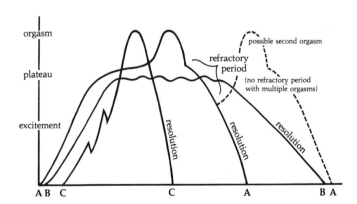

a non-orgasmic or pre-orgasmic pattern. However, some women describe the extended and fluctuating excitement of plateau as "mini-orgasms." The most significant difference between the men's and women's patterns is that it is possible for some women to have two or more orgasms without detectable loss of excitement, if effective stimulation continues long enough. The vast majority of men, by contrast, require a partial loss of excitement after an orgasm before it is possible to have another. The period after orgasm during which no additional orgasms are possible is called the refractory period. It varies from minutes to hours. Some women also require such a period.

In each graph, the movement of the line from left to right represents the passage of time, which may range from minutes to hours. The movement of the line up and down represents the increase or decrease in sexual arousal with particular reference to two fundamental processes: vasocongestion and myotonia. *Vasocongestion* means an increase in blood flow to the tissues of certain organs and muscles in such quantity that more blood is flowing into the area than out. Engorgement is the result. Vasocongestion is primarily the result of dilation (opening up) of tiny blood vessels. Sexual response involves widespread vasocongestion, not just in the genital region.

Myotonia means an increase in muscular tension or tone above the usual baseline firmness of the muscles. Sexual response involves widespread myotonia both voluntary and involuntary—such as the contractions of orgasm. These mechanisms will be discussed as they function during each of the four phases of the sexual response cycle.*

In each section I will include what is known about the involvement of the anus. I will also include information about several anatomical *sources of pleasure* related to the anal-rectal systems of both men and women. Masters and Johnson made relatively superficial observations of the anus, which was not of primary concern to them. No other similar research has been done to fill the gap. Therefore, I will include personal observations, as well as information gathered

* For more detailed information read Brecher and Brecher, *An Analysis of Human Sexual Response* (1966) or Masters and Johnson's more technical *Human Sexual Response* (1966).

from extensive subjective reports. Remember that such reports are quite unreliable since people are notoriously and appropriately unobjective when sexually aroused.

Phase I: Excitement

Sexual excitement is the body's natural response to erotic stimulation. Stimulation may be received via any of the five senses or be solely dependent upon thoughts or images (fantasy). Whatever the form of stimulation, it must be *interpreted* by the individual as erotic in order for it to trigger sexual response.* The mind may assign sexual significance to virtually any sensation or image. Conversely, stimulation that might seem erotic to one person may be interpreted as downright dull to someone else. In general, humans seem to receive most erotic stimulation through the senses of touch and vision, but there is great variation. Some people respond strongly to sounds, smells or tastes. Stimulation that is erotically experienced is called *effective sexual stimulation.*

Effective sexual stimulation affects the entire body. As excitement builds, respiration, heart rate and blood pressure increase. Vasocongestion may affect the skin anywhere on the body, resulting in perspiration, feelings of increased warmth, and flushing. Myotonia, though usually slower than vasocongestion, is also widespread, affecting arms, legs, face, as well as the pelvic region. Myotonia is responsible for erection of the nipples, experienced by virtually all women and about 30 percent of men. During sexual excitement there is usually a perceived increase in sensitivity to pleasurable touch and sometimes also a blunting of sensitivity to pain. In short, a wider range of things feel good when a person is aroused.

With men, the most noticeable sign of excitement is erection, which may occur within a few seconds of any effective stimulation or more gradually, depending on each in-

---

* It is often assumed that people are conscious of the erotic significance various stimuli have for them. This is not always the case. We can learn to deny erotic feelings, even when our bodies are responding. A study by Heiman (1975) suggests that women do this more than men. It is reasonable to assume that the anal taboo could motivate many people to be unaware of the erotic impact of anal stimulation.

dividual's response pattern as well as his age, level of arousal and sense of comfort and safety. Erection happens without conscious control when the arteries that feed blood into the penis *relax*, allowing the columns of absorbent tissue to fill with blood. The capacity for erection is inborn and operates from birth. It requires no skill, learning, power or virility (contrary to some still-popular myths). Attempts to *make* an erection happen usually assure failure. Strong anxiety or fear inhibits erection. An overemphasis on the meaning or importance of erection or insecurity about one's sexual desirability and "adequacy"—all worries about sexual performance—increase fear and inhibit erections.

In the early stages of excitement, erection is somewhat unstable and will respond to minute changes in excitement as well as to distractions. As excitement is prolonged, the erection becomes more stable. In addition, the scrotum thickens and contracts, becoming less "baggy," though this response is variable. Inside the scrotum, the testicles, suspended in part by the vas deferens (the tubes that carry sperm from the testes) begin to elevate.

With women, the first genital response to sexual excitement is the lubrication of the vagina through the vaginal walls, probably as a result of vasocongestion. Vaginal lubrication, sometimes seen as analogous to male ejaculation, actually corresponds to erection both with regard to physiology and timing. As vasocongestion continues, the vaginal walls thicken and grow darker. The inner two-thirds of the vagina expand and lengthen. The outer and especially the inner lips darken and swell.

Also during excitement, the clitoris becomes engorged with blood and grows somewhat larger. But the clitoral prepuce (hood) does not usually permit it to stand out like the penis. The uterus responds to excitement by growing larger and beginning to elevate from its normal position.

In both men and women, the anus is involved in the excitement phase. The anal tissues, rich with blood vessels and blood-absorbing spaces, become congested, resulting in a noticeable deepening in color in some people. Usually moist, the inner anal canal may secrete more, sometimes dramatically more, mucus. Perspiration around the anal canal also contributes to increased moisture. These fluids should not be confused with lubrication of the vagina. A few people become so moist that no extra lubrication is required even for anal intercourse. It is not known if the amount of anal moisture is related to how sexually excited the person is.

Myotonia also affects the anus and is most noticeable as random contractions of the anal sphincters in response to direct stimulation or in sympathy with other pelvic muscles. Just as men and women may contract pelvic muscles voluntarily to enhance pleasure, voluntary contractions of the anal sphincters can heighten pleasure as well. Many people enjoy the sensations of the anus contracting *around* something such as a finger, dildo or penis.

Anal contractions during excitement should not be confused with chronic anal tension or anal tension related to fear of anal insertion. These patterns of anal tension actually inhibit the spontaneous contractions of the anus during sexual response. I have observed, and it is almost universally reported to me, that the *range* of anal muscular activity (contractions and relaxations) increases during sexual excitement for those whose anuses have become more generally relaxed. This observation needs further investigation because, as we have seen, anal relaxation goes along with anal awareness. It could be that people who report more muscular activity have simply become more self-aware. It also seems reasonable that anal awareness might motivate a person deliberately to relax and contract the anus to enhance pleasure.

Sensitivity to anal touching appears to increase (for those who like it) during sexual excitement. This is no doubt related to attention as well as vasocongestion and myotonia. Within the anal muscles and nearby perineal muscles are a great many (proprioceptive) nerve endings that can be stimulated not only by contractions but also by external massage.

For a man, two additional sources of pleasure may become involved when a finger (his own or his partner's) is inserted into his anus. First, because the bulb of the penis is so close to the anus, movement in the direction of the bulb (toward the penis) can feel similar to masturbating from the inside. Finger, penis, vibrator or dildo can also provide stimulation or massage of the prostate gland. The prostate can be stimulated by inserting a finger about three inches into the anus and lower rectum and moving the finger in the direction of the navel. (Generally, the prostate cannot easily be felt as a separate organ during the excitement phase because it is soft like other organs in the vicinity.) Some men experience prostate stimulation as extremely pleasurable. Others find it irritating. Poking the prostate, rather than stroking it, however, is almost universally unpleasant. The importance of prostate massage in anal pleasure is over-emphasized by some men. Women seem to have no less a potential for anal enjoyment even though they have no prostate gland.

For some men, focused anal stimulation, especially internal stimulation, results in a partial or total loss of erection. Some are concerned about this, others are not. Sometimes this loss of erection is clearly a reflection of discomfort or fear. Other times, however, no such fear is evident. In fact, the man may be thoroughly enjoying himself. The mechanisms involved in this loss of erection are not understood, though it may simply mean that erotic attention has shifted from the penis to the anus. It is not known if, or how often, a similar phenomenon occurs among women.

Phase II: Plateau

The plateau phase is a stabilized high level of excitement that usually leads into orgasm within seconds or minutes. Sometimes, plateau is absent as a discrete phase.

During this phase, vasocongestion and myotonia are at a high level all over the body, although different body zones may be affected in different people. Hyperventilation (rapid breathing) is marked. Some people hold their breath with alternate deep breathing. The person is clearly very aroused, unless his/her reactions are being kept under careful control.

With men, the penis may become even more erect. The glans (head) of the penis becomes enlarged and takes on a purple hue. The testicles become more enlarged (50% to

100%) and become fully elevated against the body cavity. The scrotum may be drawn up tightly too or, by this time, may have relaxed and become more "baggy." The tiny Cowper's glands secrete a small amount of clear fluid that may appear at the opening of the penis (meatus) in some men; sometimes there is enough secretion to dribble. The fluid is unrelated to semen, through it may contain stray sperm. Its function appears to be to prepare the penile urethra for the passage of sperm.

In women, the outer third of the vagina congests with blood and forms the "orgasmic platform." Later, orgasmic contractions will be obvious here. The inner portion of the vagina expands still further. The uterus becomes fully elevated, contributing to the enlargement or "tenting effect" of the inner vagina.

The clitoris retracts under the clitoral hood during plateau, particularly if it is being stimulated directly. Full congestion of the inner lips results in a deepening of color and signals an approaching orgasm. The Bartholin glands, like the male's Cowper's glands, secrete scantily during plateau, contributing little to vaginal lubrication, which slows down or ceases completely during the plateau phase.

The anus continues its irregular contractions during the plateau phase. If direct anal stimulation has been a part of the excitement phase, many men and women report that the anus feels particularly receptive and open just prior to orgasm. Pelvic thrusting movements, during intercourse or at other times, appear to increase these anal sensations for some people, while others like to be still, quietly focusing attention on the anal area.

Among men, erection loss as a result of anal stimulation seems to be less common during the plateau phase, though it still does occur. Again, this is not fully understood except when fear is a factor.

During the later part of the plateau phase, many men find their prostate gland to be particularly sensitive to stimulation through the wall of the lower rectum. In preparation for orgasm, the prostate expands in size and becomes firm and lumpy rather than soft. At this point it is possible for a man using his finger to feel the shape and movement of his prostate.

Phase III: Orgasm

Orgasm is a discharge of sexual tension through spasmodic, involuntary, muscle contractions. It is a reflex and is not subject to direct voluntary control. The occurrence of orgasm can, however, be influenced by voluntary adjustments in stimulation, muscular tension and thoughts. And orgasms can be inhibited by trying too hard. In this way, orgasm is very similar to crying. One *allows* it to happen, usually with a subjective sense of surrendering or letting go.

The entire body is involved in orgasm. Arms and legs may become rigid and extended. Hands may grasp. Facial muscles become contorted. The person seems to be gasping for breath and may moan or scream, perhaps even laugh or cry.

In men, orgasm begins with contractions of the ''secondary'' internal sex organs: vas deferens, seminal vesicles and prostate gland. These organs pour some of their contents into the dilated (open) ejaculatory duct. This movement of fluid (emission or first stage orgasm) is experienced subjectively as ''I'm about to come.'' Indeed, once these fluids are in the ejaculatory duct, ejaculation is inevitable. Any attempts to stop the ejaculation must be made prior to this ''point of no return.'' In second stage orgasm, contractions spread to the more powerful perineal muscles. Muscular contractions against the bulb of the penis, as well as contractions of the urethra, propel the semen out of the penis. An exception to this course of events occurs with ''retrograde ejaculation'' in which semen is propelled backwards into the bladder. This happens during certain illnesses or occasionally with the use of some tranquilizers. It is not harmful and usually transitory, but may be quite disconcerting to the man. Seminal fluid contains a very small volume of sperm (produced by the testicles), and also small amounts of secretion from the seminal vesicles and sometimes the Cowper's gland. Almost all of the semen, however, is produced by the prostate.

In women, the most noticeable focus of orgasmic contractions is the outer third of the vagina. The intensity and frequency of these contractions are tied to the subjective experience of orgasm. The inner portion of the vagina does not contract, but continues its "tenting effect." Rhythmic contractions do take place in the uterus. In some women, there are also some contractions of the urethral sphincter. This is why some women lose a little urine during orgasm, especially if the bladder is full at the time. The clitoris remains hidden under its hood during orgasm.

All phases of the sexual response cycle happen physiologically in exactly the same way regardless of the source or type of stimulation. This is no less true for orgasm. Distinctions that have often been proposed between different kinds of orgasms are subjective and not reflected in physiology.

Following orgasm, almost all men require a refractory period during which no further orgasms are possible. This involves a rapid partial loss of pelvic vasocongestion. Many women experience no refractory period. If effective stimulation continues after orgasm, excitement can mount immediately to another orgasm. Multiple orgasms are thus possible for women.

The anus shares the contractions of orgasm, though these subside more quickly than other pelvic contractions such as those of the outer vagina or penis. My observations and reports I have received suggest that with increased anal awareness, anal orgasmic contractions are more pronounced and long-lasting. Anal contractions are most noticeable when the anus is contracting *against* something (finger, penis, etc.). This is also true with vaginal contractions. These contractions, which begin involuntarily, can be continued on a voluntary basis, thus increasing pleasure.

Phase IV: Resolution

Resolution is the body's return to an unaroused state following orgasm. Blood drains from congested tissue, respiration and heart rate return gradually to normal. Generally, myotonia has been discharged during orgasm. Of course, an orgasm does not always occur in which case the resolution phase is more prolonged.

Most people feel profoundly peaceful and relaxed during the resolution phase. If the person was tired before sex, he/she may feel like sleeping. Others may feel elated, playful and energized. For some, resolution is a time for feeling guilt about what they have just done, or fear of possible consequences. For these people, the pleasure of the resolution phase is clouded by a desire to forget or even escape the situation.

When resolution is comfortable, the anus is likely to be relaxed. In fact, people commonly report that their anuses feel more open following orgasm than at any other time. For this reason, resolution is sometimes a preferred phase for anal exploration. Some people even find anal intercourse to be easier and more enjoyable after they have experienced orgasm. For those bothered by anal pain, orgasm often relieves anal tension—and thus the pain—better than any pill. This is indicative of the profound relaxation that can follow orgasm.

EXPERIENCE

When you are in the mood, find a comfortable, private place for self-pleasuring and masturbation. You might begin this in the bathtub and then move to another room. Choose lighting, positioning and perhaps music that suit your preferences. Gather any paraphernalia you might want to include in your self-pleasuring. Remember to have some lubricant close by. Massage oil, vibrator, erotic pictures, etc., can also help to make this encounter with yourself special.

Begin by touching yourself, paying attention to your entire body, not just your genitals. At various points along the way, stimulate your anal area, including the sensitive perineum (the area between your genitals and anus) and buttocks as well as the anal opening itself. You might want to stimulate other favorite body areas at the same time using your other hand. Using a small amount of lubricant, slowly insert a finger in your anus, experimenting with different movements, rhythms and positions. A reminder to women: It is not a good idea to insert the same finger in your vagina that you insert in your anus without washing first. It is preferable to designate one finger for anal stimulation and use the others for vaginal stimulation, if both are desired.

If anal play becomes a turn off or gets boring, stop for a while and enjoy other things. Come back to your anus again when you feel more aroused. As you get aroused, see how your anus feels during different levels of sexual excitement.

Allow your fantasies to come and go as they please. Try not to suppress them. If you want to, explore fantasies of anal sensuality or intercourse. Do not push your fantasies. If one fantasy is not going anywhere for you, abandon it and try something more enjoyable. Enjoying the physical sensations without fantasy is, of course, fine too.

Stop when you feel finished—according to your feelings. Being sensual and sexual with yourself need not lead to orgasm. Pleasuring activities can stop and start anytime and anywhere. When you do feel like having an orgasm, or if it just happens, pay attention to ways in which anal stimulation and sensations contribute to your enjoyment.

Explore your anus after orgasm as well. If you notice good feelings in the anal area, allow yourself to continue the experience even if you had one or more orgasms. Because some people tense up right after orgasm, you may want to withdraw your finger gently and slowly.

RESPONSE

Most people find that including their anuses in auto-erotic activity seems natural and welcome, when it follows earlier, non-erotic forms of anal exploration. Quite a few people do it spontaneously from the very beginning. Others are surprised and delighted at how erotic the anus can be, like Frank: "I've been doing all this stuff with my ass lately but I never knew it could *feel* so good. Touching it turned me on!" Or Angela: "It was great. Fantastic. I never enjoyed masturbating so much." Such responses are typical.

However, things can get in the way of anal eroticism. Some people do not masturbate, or if they do, it is very quick and genitally focused. Most people I work with masturbate and enjoy it at least sometimes, the men more frequently than the women. Others either do not enjoy masturbation, see it as a substitute for "the real thing," associate it with loneliness, or feel guilty about it. A few women have never masturbated at all and do not know how they would feel about it. If any of these feelings remind you of your own, you have two options. You can consider a new attitude toward masturbation or you can skip this section and move on. Think carefully about the first option before choosing the second.

Masturbation is one of the best ways to learn about and expand erotic response. Undistracted by others, you can concentrate completely on what gives you pleasure. Masturbation can be a way of making love to yourself.*

Occasionally, those who enjoy masturbation still find it difficult to touch their anuses. This usually represents more guilty feelings. Such feelings should be acknowledged and experienced. This is the only way to move beyond them. Suppression of feelings is the surest way not to change.

Men—straight, gay or bisexual—may find that anal eroticism brings up their "homophobia," irrational fear of homosexuality. Typically, the ultimate gay male sex act has been seen as anal intercourse. Exploring anal eroticism may make a straight man fear he will become gay or a gay man experience or reexperience his discomfort about being gay. Women rarely have such homophobic reactions to anal eroticism. But many men and women fear that if they enjoy anal eroticism with themselves, they will *have to* receive anal intercourse from others. Obviously, such a thought can cast an anxious shadow over even the best masturbation experience. It is important to be very clear with yourself that what you do alone can be completely unrelated to what you choose to do with others.

Some practical concerns about anal eroticism also deserve attention. Rodney expressed some of these with humor: "I like to play with my anus, but it can be such a hassle. The other night I was in the mood to get it on with myself, but I had to find the lubricant. My roommate was home, so I had to get

---

* Those who would like to see and read about the masturbation patterns of twelve men (different sexual orientations, ages, races, body types) might be interested in my book, *Men Loving Themselves: Images of Male Self-Sexuality*. The book contains 135 black and white photographs. A written section entitled, "The Psychology of Male Self-Sexuality," will be useful to those who are exploring new ways of thinking about and enhancing masturbation. See ordering information in the back of this book.

dressed. Then when I was getting into it, I wanted the mirror which I couldn't find. Finally, I just gave up and beat off!'' These practical things can get in the way, making anal eroticism seem like an ordeal. Rodney did not mention another common concern, the whole routine of cleaning up afterwards, wiping off the lubricant, washing, etc. This can be greatly simplified by a little planning. Keep lubricant and a mirror handy. Use a water soluble lubricant because it is easier to clean up. Masturbate before you plan to take a bath, or do it in the tub. With a little experimentation, it can all progress smoothly. Be careful that you do not use these practical concerns to cover up or avoid uncomfortable feelings about your anus.

As I mentioned earlier, men sometimes lose their erections when they stimulate their anuses. If this happens to you, see if you can allow it to happen without concern. Your erection will return, and besides, you do not always need an erection to have a good time sexually. Frequently, such erection loss is simply a reflection of a little uneasiness that will soon go away when you get more accustomed to anal stimulation. If, however, anal stimulation actually turns you off (a loss of erection does not necessarily mean you are turned off), then you need to take it a little more slowly, perhaps exploring your anus again in a non-erotic way. At first you may want to wait until you are really excited before touching your anus, especially before putting your finger inside. The important thing is to have fun and not take it too seriously.

One sign of taking self-sexuality too seriously is the feeling that it must result in orgasm. In fact, some people get so focused on ''coming'' that they do not enjoy the process. Masturbation is a form of self-pleasuring. It does not have to *lead* anywhere. You do not have to continue unless you really want to. And it certainly is better if you do not rush. Try taking breaks from self-stimulation, getting up and moving around and maybe coming back to it later. This can be a good way of becoming less orgasm-oriented and more pleasure-oriented.

Erotic fantasies can be a source of either joy or concern. This is especially true of fantasies involving anal intercourse. ''Why is it,'' James asks, ''that I like fantasizing about getting [anally] fucked, but I can't actually do it?'' Ruth echoes the same concern: "When I think about it [anal intercourse], it's always a turn-on. I've even fantasized that Mel [her lover] was really inside my anus during vaginal intercourse, especially when he enters from the rear; but every time we try anal sex it's no fun at all." One reason for James' and Ruth's feelings might be that they do not want to receive anal intercourse in actuality but like it very much as a fantasy. After all, there is no direct relationship between fantasy and behavior. People frequently fantasize things they would not actually want to do. Another possibility is that James and Ruth would like to receive anal intercourse but find the actual experience frightening. Either way, it's best if you can enjoy your fantasies for themselves right now. Later, I will suggest comfortable ways of exploring what you would like to do with a partner.

Other men and women discover that *neither* fantasy nor actual anal stimulation is very erotic. Some experience a significant *decrease* in excitement. If you are one of these people, the more at ease you become with anal fantasies or actual anal stimulation, the more your fears will subside. By deliberately introducing fantasies of anal stimulation at moments of high excitement, you can gradually eroticize the anal area.*

Some people are particularly concerned about "S & M" (sadomasochistic) or "top-bottom" fantasies. They occur in many forms—from being penetrated, taken over or swept away by a powerful man, to being forced into anal sex, perhaps even tied up or raped. Obviously, these fantasies are reflections of the power dimensions of human sexuality, i.e., wanting to surrender to or control another. Some people find that they better understand the power dynamics in their relationships as a result of S & M fantasies or roleplaying. Allow yourself to have these fantasies, recognizing that you need not act on them unless you want to. Writing them in your journal can help you clarify and accept your fantasies.

---

* The mechanism that makes this possible is called *stimulus pairing*. When two stimuli (in this case, anal fantasies and feelings of arousal) repeatedly occur together, they become associated with one another. By using this technique, you can condition yourself to respond erotically to previously non-erotic stimuli.

DRUGS AND ANAL EROTICISM

People have always looked for substances that can alter their sexual experiences in some desired way. Sought-after effects include an increase in sexual interest, relaxation or suppression of inhibitions, and sensory intensification during sexual activities whether alone or with a partner. Today, non-medical, recreational drug use preparatory to or during sex is commonplace. It is, therefore, not surprising that many who enjoy anal sex have experimented with chemicals specifically to enhance their enjoyment of the anus and rectum. And among those who want to enjoy anal eroticism but find it difficult to do so, chemical help is frequently sought.

Anal relaxation or erotic enhancement claims are often made for four types of popular drugs: (1) alcohol and other depressants, (2) marijuana, (3) cocaine and other stimulants and (4) volatile nitrites. All except alcohol are illegal (the legal status of volatile nitrites is not clear) and all have a variety of negative side-effects, some of them potentially serious, when the drugs are over-used. But because they are commonly employed with anal stimulation, it is important to describe them briefly with regard to their effects on anal relaxation and eroticism.

Alcohol and Other Depressants. Because alcohol depresses the central nervous system, and because it is legal and readily available, it is by far the most popular drug for lowering anxieties and inhibitions prior to sexual activities. Other drugs have very similar effects. Short-acting barbituates—secobarbital and phenobarbitol (marketed as Seconal and Nembutal, respectively)—are almost identical to alcohol in their effects. A person who develops tolerance for alcohol will simultaneously develop tolerance for barbiturates. Also subjectively similar to alcohol are the anti-anxiety drugs, sometimes called minor tranquilizers, such as benzodiazepine compounds (marketed as Librium and Valium) and meprobamate (marketed as Miltown and Equanil). These drugs are probably more popular for sex than barbiturates because they calm anxieties and inhibitions with less sleepiness. The minor tranquilizers also have some muscle-relaxing qualities which, in some instances, may reduce anal tension slightly. Currently, the most popular depressant among sexual sophisticates, other than alcohol, is methaqualone (formerly marketed as Quaalude, Sopor and Parest *). Methaqualone is a hypnotic-sedative which, enthusiasts claim, reduces inhibitions dramatically, while providing a feeling of vitality and energy. It seems to be particularly popular in casual sex settings. Many people say it helps them relax anally, and it is true that methaqualone has an anti-spasmodic effect throughout the intestinal tract, no doubt including the anus and rectum.

The inhibition-reducing and anti-anxiety effects of all central nervous system depressants occur, for most people, at relatively low doses, e.g., one or two glasses of wine or one-half of a large (300 mg) Quaalude tablet. At higher doses, these drugs have a sedative effect and sensitivity is reduced. Obviously, these effects are not in the interest of enjoyable sex, whether or not the anus is involved. Combining alcohol and other depressants is unwise because each intensifies the effects of the other, often unpredictably. Users of any depressants should also be aware that tolerance for these drugs develops fairly rapidly so that larger doses are needed to get the same effect. This characteristic gives users of these drugs a relatively high potential for development of dependency. Heavy use of any depressant with anal stimulation deprives the user of the awareness needed to guard against anal damage, especially when vigorous internal stimulation is practiced.

Marijuana. Although marijuana is still illegal and not nearly as available as alcohol, the smoking of marijuana to enhance sexual experiences is almost as common among some groups as alcohol ingestion. For many, marijuana appears to have relaxing and inhibition-reducing qualities similar to those of alcohol and other depressants, without the sedative effect. But the effects of marijuana are quite variable. For example, some people regularly use marijuana specifically as an aid to sleep while others are energized. Marijuana enthusiasts virtually always mention its

* As of June, 1984, methaqualone is no longer manufactured or sold in the U.S.. Street drugs touted as quaaludes are either illegally imported (usually from Colombia) or are not methaqualone, but diazapam (generic Valium).

sensation-intensifying properties as one of the main reasons they use it with sex. Many people do find that smoking a "joint" contributes to anal relaxation and appreciation of anal sensations or erotic fantasies. However, others report that marijuana makes them anxious, jumpy, even "paranoid" (intensely worried that others are thinking negatively of them)—feelings not conducive to anal enjoyment.

One of the advantages of marijuana as a recreational drug is the fact that higher doses rarely produce any increase in negative side effects, as is the case with alcohol and most other drugs. Another positive attribute of marijuana, from the standpoint of anal health, is the fact that it appears never to deprive the user of the sensitivity needed for anal self-protection.

Cocaine and Other Stimulants. A white powder derived from coca leaves, cocaine is usually inhaled to produce a short-lasting, euphoric-stimulant effect. Its increasing popularity as a recreational drug is remarkable given its pro-hibitive cost. Aphrodisiac claims made for cocaine are overstated. Its stimulant qualities can, in some instances, intensify sexual interest, fantasy and sensations, including anal sensations. On the other hand, because cocaine not on-ly stimulates the central nervous system, but also the sym-pathetic nervous system (Kornetsky, 1976)—the part of the autonomic nervous system that activates the body's reac-tions to stress (see chapter 6)—the anal muscles may actually *contract* involuntarily as a result of cocaine use. This reac-tion occurs particularly when a person is feeling anxious to begin with.

The fuzzy line between stimulation and stress also tends to make other stimulants (such as amphetamines and amphetamine-like chemicals) counterproductive for anal relaxation, even though they may intensify the subjective feeling of anal eroticism. For some people, though, cocaine and other stimulants help divert their attention from wor-ries about sexual performance. Consequently, the tension producing tendencies of these drugs may be offset by in-tensified excitement. This sort of trade-off probably accounts for the popularity of MDA, a drug that is both a stimulant and a psychedelic. MDA is sometimes called "speed for "trips" last up to eight hours.

Volatile Nitrites. Popular among gay men, and increasingly so among straight sophisticates, are the volatile nitrites (Sigell, et al., 1978). Used medically for the relief of chest pain, pharmaceutically-produced amyl-nitrite (the prototype of this group of drugs) comes in thin glass capsules covered with a fabric webbing. To use, a capsule is crushed, allowing the fumes to escape and be inhaled. The sound of the capsule breaking has resulted in the nickname "poppers" for all volatile nitrite liquids, whether or not they are packaged in glass capsules.

Poppers produced for non-medical purposes are usually either isobutyl or amyl-nitrite. In either case, inhaling the fumes causes blood vessels to dilate (get bigger). This causes a rapid *drop* in blood pressure, followed by an increase in heart rate as the body attempts to stabilize blood pressure.* Within a few seconds of inhalation, the person experiences a "rush," which is said to enhance the intensity of sensation and feeling of abandon during dancing or sex. The entire experience lasts only a couple of minutes. Some people claim that the inhaling of poppers helps the anal muscles to relax and therefore makes it easier to receive a finger, object or penis into the anus and rectum. It has been known since the late 20's that volatile nitrites do have a mild antispasmodic effect on the gastrointestinal tract (Holmes & Dresser, 1928). Poppers can also enhance relaxation by providing a feeling of flushed sensation all over the body, which may increase desire for anal stimulation or divert one's attention from worrying about it. Many people feel anything but sexual abandon when they inhale poppers. Instead they feel scared and even panicky as their bodies react to the disequilibrium caused by the drug.

Because volatile nitrites are the shortest-acting of all popular recreational drugs, many users inhale them over and over again in the course of a sexual encounter. Used this way, poppers not only become decreasingly effective but may also produce headaches and a feeling of depres-

---

* In addition, a wide variety of other physiological effects resulting from volatile nitrite inhalation have been noted (Haley, 1980).

sion. Therefore many experienced users seek to maximize the desired effects by limiting popper use to one or a few "high points" during sex—such as just before orgasm.

Variability of Effects. It is not accurate to say that any drug "causes" most of the effects ascribed to it. Responses to all drugs vary widely from person to person. And one person's responses can vary strikingly from situation to situation. With experience, most people learn to predict their own responses fairly well, taking into account the many important factors that affect them (e.g., emotional state, setting, expectations, reactions of others, dosage and interactions with other chemicals).

While all drugs trigger varied responses, some are more variable than others. For example, large quantities of alcohol invariably produce the symptoms universally recognized as "drunk." But how much alchohol it takes to produce drunkenness and whether a drunk person staggers joyfully, tearfully or looking for a fight depends on factors other than the alcohol itself. The effects of other drugs, most notably marijuana, vary so widely from person to person that no particular response can be expected consistently. In fact, one investigator has called marijuana an "active placebo," reflecting how much expectations and learning determine the nature of marijuana highs—or lack of them (Weil, 1972).

Nowhere is the variability of response to drugs more obvious than it is with anal eroticism. A drug that appears to obliterate the last vestiges of anal tension and inhibition for one person may make another person tense, frustrated or totally uninterested. Any drug may conceivably help reduce anxiety about anal eroticism, increase it, or have no effect either way. Those who claim that a particular drug *makes* a person more open to anal eroticism are simply misinformed.

What to Do. Especially if you have trouble associating erotic feelings with the anal area, or find it difficult to relax sufficiently to enjoy them, it can be tempting to search for a drug—as one client put it—"to open doors that I don't even know how to find." And it cannot be denied that the use of a drug can, on occasion, trigger a breakthrough in the erotic enjoyment of the anus. Nonetheless, recreational drug use should be kept to a minimum, or avoided altogether, during the early stages of anal erotic exploration. Certainly, if a glass of wine or a ''joint'' will help you relax and focus on pleasurable sensations, then there is no reason, other than a moral or legal concern, for not using it.

Healthy recreational drug use requires that the drug primarily be used to *enhance* experiences. This is possible only when the person can also enjoy that experience without using the drug. If a person believes that a certain drug is *required* for the full enjoyment of anal eroticism (or anything else), then he/she has become dependent on the drug. Dependency of this type, reinforced over time, is highly likely to be detrimental to one's enjoyment of sex as well as one's health.

If you find yourself using more than moderate amounts of a drug (variable from person to person) or using a drug more than occasionally when you explore anal eroticism, then you are probably looking for a chemical solution to inhibitions that can be more safely and effectively reduced through gentle, persistent self-exploration.

Later, once you become fully at ease with anal eroticism, you will be in a much better position to decide which recreational drugs, if any, you would feel comfortable using, in what quantity, how often, and under what cirumstances. Take the time to gather much more information than I have presented here about any drug you might consider using or are already using. Even though research on the effects and risks of most drugs is far from conclusive, it is still possible to weigh potential risks against likely benefits and structure one's drug use to keep the risks (whether legal, physiological or psychological) to a minimum. Especially since the AIDS crisis began, self-affirming men and women have been carefully evaluating — and often reducing or eliminating — their use of recreational drugs. Heavy drug use suppresses the immune system, possibly making a person more susceptible to the AIDS virus (see Appendix A).

Drug use that is primarily motivated by a desire to reduce anal pain is virtually always unwise. Anal pain that accompanies the insertion of an object into the rectum signals the need for relaxation or indicates a medical problem. It is not helpful, and may eventually contribute to anal medical problems, to try to deaden anal pain chemically. The application of over-the-counter local anesthetics, cocaine or any other sensation-reducing agent to the anal tissues, therefore, is very unwise, even dangerous.

9

DISCOVERING
THE RECTUM

Exploring Rectal Shape
and Sensations

Thus far, you have explored the anal opening, short anal canal and lower rectum. As you have seen, these areas can easily be reached with your fingers. We now turn our attention to the inner rectum, which you cannot reach with fingers. For some people, greater awareness of the rectum can offer additional possibilities for pleasure. The rectum is stimulated by feces going out during a bowel movement or by soft objects (such as a dildo or vibrator) going *in*, or by a penis during anal intercourse. In any case, exploration of your rectum requires the sensitive use of an object longer than your finger.

ANATOMY AND PHYSIOLOGY
OF THE RECTUM

The rectum is a tube-like structure made of loose folds of soft, smooth tissue. Its total length is about eight or nine inches. Normally, the rectum is more open and spacious than the anus. Like the anus, it has a striking capacity to expand. The entire length of the rectum is supported by muscles which, during a bowel movement, contract and relax in wave-like motions (peristalsis) moving feces through the rectum and out the anal opening. The tension level of these muscles varies from person to person reflecting, among other things, emotional states and habitual muscular patterns. Chronic, non-rhythmic contraction or tension of the rectal muscles can contribute to constipation and other medical problems of the lower digestive system. Rectal muscles are not nearly as powerful as the anal sphincter muscles (with the exception of one related muscle that I will discuss shortly). Nonetheless, if they are very tense, they can inhibit the entry of an object or penis into the rectum.

While the rectum is tube-like, *it is not a straight tube*. It takes two curves along its length (see Figure 5). Knowledge of these curves is essential for the rectal explorer. The lower rectum is tilted slightly toward the navel. After approximately three inches, it curves in the opposite direction, toward the backbone. This curve is the result of a strong supportive muscle known as the *pubo-rectal sling* (shown in the separate detail of Figure 5). After a few inches, the rectum curves back slightly toward the front once again.

It is the first curve and the pubo-rectal sling that are most likely to give a person trouble in allowing an object or penis to enter the rectum. Figure 6 shows that an object entering the rectum at an improper angle runs into the rectal wall at the first curve. If the object is inserted with force, it can cause pain. If a lot of force is used (e.g., when a man insensitively rams his penis into the rectum), a tear (fissure) in the rectal wall can result. Figure 6 also shows that a slight adjustment in the angle of entry easily prevents this. Difficulty in moving beyond the first curve can be exacerbated if the pubo-rectal sling muscle is tense, making the curve more pronounced and less flexible. The pubo-rectal sling, like all anal and rectal muscles, becomes tense in response to fear, stress, chronic straining or improper diet.

It is estimated that the pubo-rectal sling is responsible for about 80% of continence, i.e., prevention of unwanted passage of feces, liquid or gas (Karkowski, et al., 1973). Therefore, even people with damaged anal sphincters can still retain a high degree of continence.

When a person feels pressure associated with the need to defecate, the pubo-rectal sling is tensed to hold back feces and gas until an appropriate time (hopefully not very long!).

115

Figure 5
ANATOMY OF THE RECTUM

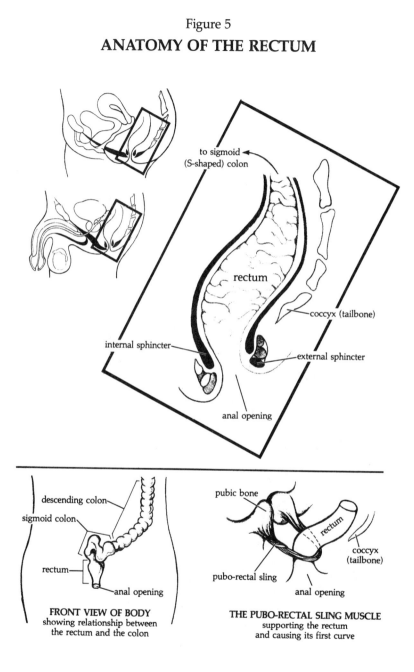

FRONT VIEW OF BODY
showing relationship between
the rectum and the colon

THE PUBO-RECTAL SLING MUSCLE
supporting the rectum
and causing its first curve

Figure 6

EFFECTS OF ANGLE OF ENTRY ON RECTAL INSERTION

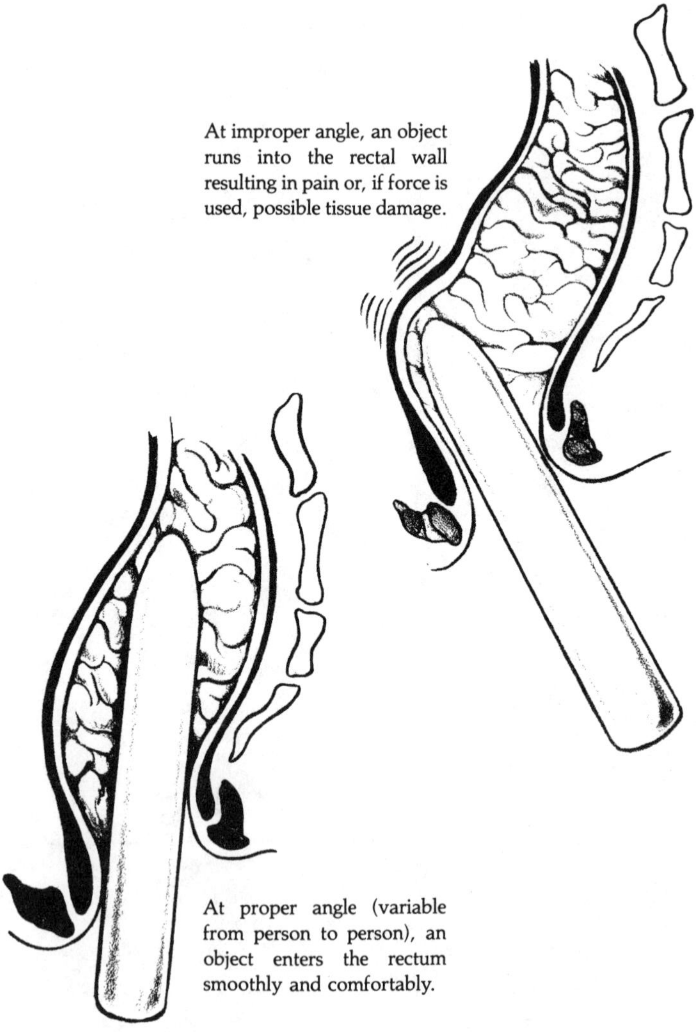

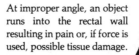

At improper angle, an object runs into the rectal wall resulting in pain or, if force is used, possible tissue damage.

At proper angle (variable from person to person), an object enters the rectum smoothly and comfortably.

Any stimulation of the pubo-rectal sling or pressure at the upper end of the rectum (where it joins the colon) can trigger this response.

This is useful in understanding two phenomena commonly experienced when objects are inserted in the rectum: (1) the feeling of an imminent bowel movement, even when this is not going to happen, and (2) the tensing of the pubo-rectal sling making the insertion more difficult. Clearly, these two experiences are related. Pressure from rectal insertion is perceived as an urge to defecate which, in turn, results in tensing of the pubo-rectal sling.

Comfortable rectal insertion requires a relearning of this response. This is relatively easy to do for most people because the sling can readily be brought under voluntary control. A person simply needs to learn that the urge to defecate associated with rectal insertion is an illusion. This awareness allows relaxation of the sling.

The second curve in the rectum is less pronounced and usually more flexible. Consequently, it rarely is a source of difficulty or discomfort during rectal insertion. When it causes discomfort, slight adjustments in the angle of entry will remedy the problem. Generally, any body position that places the legs at right angles to the body (e.g., sitting, squatting, lying on your back or side with knees pulled toward the chest, or on your knees in a ''doggie'' position) will straighten the rectum a little. No position, however, completely eliminates the rectal curves.

Within this general description, rectal shape and size vary from person to person. Inserting objects into the rectum may be easier for one person in a particular position or angle of entry, while another position or angle is better for someone else. Differences are no doubt a combination of physiological variations and personal preference. Anyone who states that one position or angle is ''the best'' for rectal entry is generalizing from personal experience. There is no substitute for individual exploration and experimentation.

In contrast to the anus, the rectum contains relatively few nerve endings, making it less sensitive than the anus. The rectum has this in common with the vagina, the entryway being far more sensitive than the inner portion. In general, rectal nerve endings pick up and transmit mostly sensations of pressure. Some people find these pleasurable immediately while others find it necessary to get used to them. The intense pleasure that some people feel from deep thrusting during either vaginal or anal intercourse is mostly a response to factors such as total body contact and psychological satisfaction, and is far less dependent on internal nerve stimulation. A few people, however, appear to have a remarkable sensitivity in their rectums. To some extent this sensitivity appears to be a learned capacity developed through paying attention. There may also be hereditary differences in nerve ending distribution. And keep in mind that verbal reports of how something feels are of limited value in comparing one person's experience to another's.

When a penis or penis-sized object is inserted into the rectum, only the anal canal and rectum are involved. Penises or objects longer than 9 or 10 inches may pass beyond the rectum into the sigmoid ("S-shaped") colon (shown in Figure 5). Sometimes this occurs without difficulty, because the muscles of the lower colon tend to relax at the same time as the anal and rectal muscles. There may, however, be some initial muscular resistance at the entrance to the colon. In addition, the likelihood of encountering feces in the lower colon is greater than in the rectum. It is a natural function of the colon to collect feces until there is sufficient quantity to enter the rectum in preparation for a bowel movement. Those concerned about feces will want to consider how much time has passed since the last bowel movement whenever entry into the colon is desired.

"FISTING"

The colon is of particular interest to those experimenting with a more dramatic form of manual-anal stimulation popularly called "fist-fucking" or "fisting." This activity involves gradually relaxing the anal muscles until several fingers and eventually the whole hand (and sometimes forearm) can enter the rectum and colon. The awareness, gentleness, and trust recommended for all anal exploration are doubly important for safe experimentation with fisting. Those who wish to explore fisting (giving or receiving) will find the exercises and information in this book useful. However, most readers, while perhaps curious about fisting, are probably not themselves planning to do it.

Although increasing numbers of people (especially, but not exclusively, gay men) are experimenting with fisting, relatively few people appear to be able to relax sufficiently to accommodate something as large as an entire hand. Those who do enjoy fisting sometimes become devoted enthusiasts.* Receivers of fisting report deeply satisfying sensations of fullness and pressure and often describe it as the ultimate experience of receptivity. Those who do the fisting are not usually as enthusiastic as the receivers. Some, nonetheless, are intrigued and excited by the sensation of exploring deep inside their partner's body.

Accommodating a hand and forearm in the rectum and colon requires tremendous self-awareness, relaxation and trust. Some describe the experience as a form of meditation (i.e., relaxed, focused concentration). A "fisting session" takes time (maybe several hours), gentleness and patience.

Unfortunately, many (perhaps most) experimenters with fisting have not developed the self-awareness necessary for doing it safely. Instead they rely on large quantities of drugs and often use force, sometimes tolerating considerable pain. These problems are intensified when fisting is employed as part of S & M roleplaying. When this happens, the rough movements that may enhance the S & M fantasy can increase the risk of physical damage. Whenever attempted with large doses of drugs or force, fisting, like other forms of rectal stimulation, can be quite dangerous.

Very little research has been done on either the positive or negative effects of fisting. One investigator (Lowry, 1981) coined the term "brachioproctic eroticism" for fisting and collected questionnaires from 102 males involved in fisting. The average respondent had been active for nearly four years, with 40% participating at least once a week. Thirty seven percent were insertors most often, while 18% were usually receivers. Forty five percent experienced both roles equally. Twenty four percent had even received two hands simultaneously.

Three of the men reported bowel perforations from fisting,

* At least two organizations have been formed to provide information and support to "fisters" and "fistees" and facilitate their meeting one another.

requiring hospitalization. Lowry speculates, extending from his findings, that there may be one serious injury per 2,000 fisting episodes. Eighty five percent described their fisting experiences in extremely positive terms. A few of the men mentioned that fisting seemed to improve their anal health by promoting deep relaxation.

Of course, the arrival of AIDS on the scene has brought new cause for concern. AIDS researchers warn that fisting is likely to cause abrasions, sometimes too small to notice, in rectal tissue, providing an entry point into the blood stream for the AIDS virus (which appears to be highly concentrated in the semen of an infected partner). Many fisting enthusiasts are curtailing their activities until a vaccine becomes available. At the very least, fisting recipients should take great care not to expose their rectal tissue to semen or blood. To this end, some recipients now insist that their partner wear surgical gloves.

EXPERIENCE

Begin by bathing, relaxing and touching your body in a self-loving, sensual way. Explore your anus with your fingers. Feel your muscles relax. When you are completely comfortable, apply a lubricant to your anal opening and inside your anus.

Also lubricate a smooth object. I recommend a soft dildo, a flexible vibrator or a tapered, wax dinner candle. If you use a candle, use the base, not the tip. Make sure that it is smooth with no rough or sharp edges (a knife can be used to smooth the base of the candle). Some people prefer a more natural object such as a carrot, cucumber or zucchini. These are fine as long as you wash them thoroughly (you do not want any pesticides in your rectum) and make certain that they are smooth all over. Whatever the object, it should be about the diameter of two of your fingers (or smaller). Figure 7 shows a variety of objects commonly used for rectal insertion.

Select a position in which you can easily reach your anal area without strain. Inhale deeply, pushing your anal muscles slightly outward. Gently press the end of the object against your anus. As you exhale, allowing your anus to relax, the object will easily slide inside your anal open-

Figure 7

OBJECTS USED FOR RECTAL STIMULATION

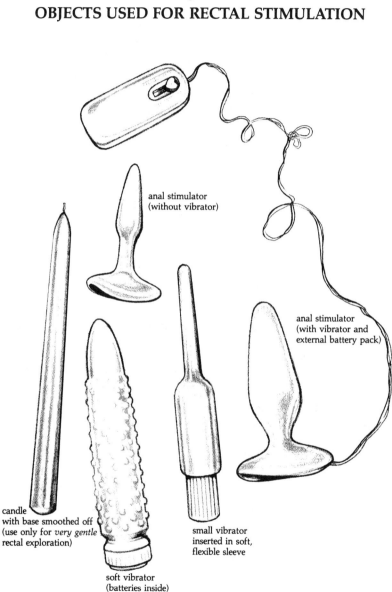

anal stimulator
(without vibrator)

anal stimulator
(with vibrator and
external battery pack)

candle
with base smoothed off
(use only for *very gentle*
rectal exploration)

small vibrator
inserted in soft,
flexible sleeve

soft vibrator
(batteries inside)

ing. Do not push. If it does not go in easily, go back to using your finger until you are more relaxed.

Once past your anal sphincters, the object will slide easily into your rectum. After a few inches, the object may stop as if it has run into something. This is your first rectal curve and the pubo-rectal sling muscle. If the object stops here, *slowly* pull it back out *just a little*, move it to a slightly different angle, and slowly push in again. By experimenting with different angles and positions, you will find one or more combinations in which the object will slide past your first rectal curve without resistance. Notice exactly which angle and positions work best for you.

You are likely to experience new sensations once the object is inside your rectum. When this happens, ask yourself (as you have done before) if the sensations are actually uncomfortable or *just different*. If uncomfortable, back off to a point that feels good and remain there.

A common sensation, mentioned earlier, is the urge to have a bowel movement. If this bothers you and prevents you from relaxing, try inserting the object when you are in a safe environment such as on a plastic sheet or in the bathtub. Tell yourself that is all right even if you *do* have a bowel movement. Then allow yourself to relax completely. Visualize the relaxation of your pubo-rectal sling and other rectal muscles as you breathe deeply and slowly. You will discover that even though you feel like you are going to have a bowel movement, it will not actually happen. You have always associated rectal sensations with such an urge, and now you are learning to reinterpret these sensations in a new way. As you learn this, the sensations will feel more pleasurable and the object will move much more easily.

Do not push the object so far into your rectum that you lose your grip on it. Contrary to some myths, your rectum will *not* pull the object out of your hand, although there may be a slight feeling of suction. Occasionally an object does end up inside a person's rectum out of reach. This *only* hap-

---

* If you should happen to "lose" an object inside your rectum, *do not* panic. If you relax, the object will usually come out by itself. Feeling panicky increases tension and there is no reason to rush. With just a little care, this will *never* happen to you, so do not worry about it.

pens when the object has been *pushed* into the rectum, not because the rectum "swallowed it up."*

Explore your rectum when you are not aroused as well as when you are. Rectal stimulation can be an enjoyable part of masturbation. If you discover that you like to thrust an object vigorously in and out of your rectum, it is a good idea to use an object with a larger base (like some dildos) so that even in a moment of passion, you will not be able to push it all the way into your rectum. While a wax candle is fine (and inexpensive) for slow, gentle self-exploration, it is not recommended for erotic play because it is too hard and brittle.

If you find a tender or sore spot in your rectum, go to a supportive doctor (see Chapter 15) and make sure that everything is all right.

When you include your rectum in erotic self-pleasuring, allow yourself to have any fantasies that might come into your mind. Afterwards, write them and your feelings in your journal.

At some point, explore your rectum before, during and after orgasm. Note the different sensations. After you have finished, pay attention to how your anus and rectum feel throughout the day.

RESPONSE

Learning to enjoy the insertion of an object into your rectum is primarily dependent on three factors. First, the muscular awareness, control and relaxation that you developed earlier with your anal muscles must be expanded to include your rectal muscles. This has happened already to a great extent because your rectal muscles tend to function in harmony with your anal muscles. For most people, a little patience, paying attention, deep breathing and visualization of the rectal muscles relaxing is all that is needed. If this does not work, you are probably trying to go too fast and you should go back to using your finger for a while. While the vast majority of people find that inserting their finger is the best way to begin, a few people discover that inserting objects is easier and more pleasurable for them. If this is true for you, naturally you will want to do whatever is easiest.

The second, and perhaps more important factor is becoming intimately acquainted with the shape of your rectum and accommodating your movements to that shape. Uncomfortable or painful anal-rectal experiences are, as you have discovered, the result of muscular tension. And, in circular fashion, anal tension is often a response to pain that results from strong pressure against the rectal wall, usually in the area of the first curve. Internal rectal medical problems related to anal intercourse are often the result of ignorance about rectal shape. These problems can be eliminated by learning about your own rectum and exploring the angle and positions in which objects can travel the length of your rectum unobstructed. While your rectum does not like to be jabbed or pushed, *it is not nearly as delicate as you might think.* If guided gently, objects can be moved around freely in several directions as you experiment.

The third factor involves becoming accustomed to new sensations. This can best be accomplished through frequent experiences in which you give yourself plenty of time to feel and get used to the new sensations. Some people, of course, react strongly to any new sensation, making an association between *new* and *dangerous.* Others react to new body sensations with curiosity rather than fear. If you find yourself afraid, ask yourself what you are afraid of. Take steps to protect yourself from whatever you fear. See if you can adopt a positive, non-pressured curiosity.

It is important to apply the same positive curiosity to any sensations that occur after rectal stimulation. Sometimes these include a slight burning sensation in the anal-rectal tissues. This is probably due to increased blood congestion in the area. The feeling can be "tingly" and pleasant, or it can be irritating. If it is irritating, you probably did too much too fast, or else you were a bit tense and went ahead anyway. It is also possible that you are simply becoming more aware of sensations that have always been there, probably the result of chronic rectal tension. If irritation persists, it is a good idea to consult a physician just to be certain that you do not have a medical problem. Another common sensation is mild bladder irritation that may be particularly noticeable when urinating. This seems to be reported much more often by women than by men. Usually, with both men and women, this is the result of indirect stimulation of the bladder. Generally, it can be greatly reduced by being more gentle as you become accustomed to rectal stimulation.

10

ATTITUDES TOWARD RECTAL STIMULATION

Confronting Psycho-Social Blocks

Not everyone is immediately delighted with the ability to insert objects in the rectum. Although many people have not been aware of it before, insertion of objects into the rectum is not simply a sensual experience for them. It has a more a complex meaning as well. For example, Mavis felt this way about it: "Now that I'm enjoying this [rectal stimulation], it makes me feel like a more relaxed and sexually versatile woman." Drew said, "I feel more receptive and less uptight—like I don't have to be in control all the time."

These and other ideas about rectal stimulation are negative and frightening for some people. The person's ability to enjoy pleasurable sensations can become partially or totally blocked. Certain ideas about rectal stimulation are so frightening that the insertion of an object remains an impossibility. No matter how relaxed the anal muscles are, the moment an object begins to enter the rectum, the muscles go into spasm.

In these cases, the only effective approach is to face the troublesome attitudes and ideas directly. Facing them does not guarantee that they will immediately (or ever) completely go away. Usually, however, bringing deeply ingrained attitudes into consciousness greatly reduces their emotional charge and, in turn, their negative impact.

Because the majority of my clients want to be able to enjoy anal intercourse eventually, most are delighted to discover that they can enjoy insertion of objects approximating the size of a penis. Once making this discovery, some are quick to arrange for a partner to have anal intercourse with them. Although this works well for a few, most find that moving too quickly to anal intercourse rekindles old anxieties and tensions. This, understandably, is experienced as a "setback." Do not worry about anal intercourse now, even if you want it. Instead, enjoy rectal stimulation by yourself until you are totally at home with it.

FECES

The most consistently negative attitudes that block the enjoyment of rectal stimulation are those associated with feces. You may already have confronted this when you first touched your anal area. But rectal stimulation, reaching into inner regions of your body is more likely to trigger powerful feelings about feces. Some people associate rectal stimulation with a threatening descent into the mysterious "underworld" of intestines or "guts," punctuated with taboo images of darkness, dread and defilement. Peter expressed something like this when he said, "I just don't feel I should mess around in there. I get the weird feeling of being where I'm not supposed to be. I can't take it lightly like some of the rest of you."

Clearly, such intense feelings, to the extent that you have them, are remnants of your personal anal taboo and will not make rectal exploration any easier. As with other strong feelings, vehement denial of their existence is a good indication that your have suppressed them. Out of consciousness, they are likely to haunt you in the form of tension and displeasure.

Freud observed that infants show no disgust with their own feces, examining them and even taking pride in them as "gifts." Early in life, however, most of us change our attitudes quite dramatically. We learn to see feces as dirty, repulsive and foul-smelling. Freud felt that adults, while expressing a conscious dislike of feces, often retain an un-conscious attachment to them. Most adults I have talked with will admit to more than incidental interest in their own feces, e.g., gazing at them before flushing the toilet. For most people, that is about as far as they would want to go. One thing is sure, the intense feeling of revulsion that is commonly focused on feces goes far beyond a concern about hygiene. It reflects a fundamental ambivalence toward the body's natural functions.

One way in which our culture expresses its traditional mistrust of the body is through relentless efforts to cover up or eliminate all natural body odors and secretions. With cultural values tending toward one extreme (compulsive cleanliness) it is not surprising that a few people express the opposite extreme, making odors or feces the center of their erotic interest. One extreme is not any "worse" than the other. In a sense, they complement each other. People at either extreme could benefit from a more balanced, less "driven" attitude. I encourage people to look at their feces and become more relaxed about them. I suggest the same approach to perspiration, semen, vaginal secretions, mucus in the mouth or nose, and urine. It is not necessary to *like* feces in order to enjoy your anus and rectum. Few people are ever really going to like feces, but it is possible to learn not to hate them.

There is no way to avoid the fact that the anus and rectum are passageways for feces. However, negative feelings about feces can be partially avoided by remembering that feces are not normally stored in the rectum except when the body is preparing for a bowel movement. The consistency of the feces determines how much is left inside after a bowel movement. Soft feces leave traces whereas better-formed feces come out more cleanly. The feces that result from a healthy diet are almost universally reported to be less repugnant. On days when you notice that your feces are especially soft, avoid inserting anything into the rectum or take extra precautions such as douching or washing inside the anus with your finger.

These precautions assure that feces will not be *directly* encountered in anal and rectal stimulation. Yet the underlying negative attitudes are not easily or quickly changed.

Looking more closely at your attitudes toward feces and perhaps initiating discussions with friends can help you gradually become more accepting of the least likeable aspect of your body.

HOMOPHOBIA

Those who do not wish to receive anal intercourse (or are not sure) are more likely to have other feelings instead of, or in addition to, delight with their new-found ability to enjoy rectal stimulation. They may be concerned that it will be difficult to say "no" to somebody who wants to have anal intercourse with them because they know they have the physiological capacity to do it—if they want to. Obviously, straight or bisexual women and gay or bisexual men are most likely to have to deal with situations like this. Yet any person can be confronted with concerns related to self-image.

One of the most powerful of these concerns among men is a deep, irrational fear of homosexuality called homophobia. "Putting things in my ass," says Ralph, "makes me wonder if, underneath, I might be gay. I like gays okay, but I've never thought of myself this way before." Ralph's concern is exacerbated by the popular idea that anal stimulation is the exclusive interest of gay men as well as by psychoanalytic notions that the desire for rectal stimulation signals "latent homosexuality." According to Kinsey, 37% of the total male population has had at least some homosexual experience to the point of orgasm between adolescence and old age. Another 13% react erotically to other males without having overt sexual contact. It is silly automatically to label all such men "latent homosexuals."

Most of the straight men I have worked with freely acknowledge occasional interest in other men and several have had some incidental sexual experience with other men. These men are not in a "homosexual panic" and can talk quite openly about their feelings. Such concerns as Ralph's do not fit the profile of the "latent homosexual." They are the natural worries of men in a homophobic society.*

* In our society, men fear being labeled gay by others for good reason. An excellent study by Rodney Karr (1978) showed that men who were

Understanding this, and getting a little reassurance from others, helps these straight men to enjoy their anuses and rectums without worrying that it necessarily indicates anything at all about their sexual orientation. Sexual orientation is a matter of erotic and affectional partner preference. It has nothing to do with the enjoyment of rectal stimulation.

A few men in my research group were, in fact, in the early stages of "coming out." Their reactions to rectal exploration were usually much stronger. Often they were unable to enjoy it or even talk about it. A few dropped out of therapy. Reassuring such a person that the desire for anal pleasure bears no relationship to sexual orientation is useless because he knows that he *does* want to explore his gay interests. For these men, anal tension is a natural reaction against real desires they are having trouble accepting. Consequently, enjoyment of anal/rectal pleasure may have to be delayed until they feel more accepting of their sexual orientation. Unfortunately, for most people this takes time. Supportive psychotherapy can be helpful, but most gay men seem to choose to go through the early stages of coming out alone.*

Homophobia is not just a problem of straight or not-yet-gay men. Virtually all men in our society learn negative attitudes toward homosexuality early in life. Those who turn out to be gay internalize the same anti-gay messages, sometimes to a greater degree than straight men. Even openly gay men who appear to have accepted their sexual preference are likely to feel some deep residual doubts about their erotic and affectional interests, and certain experiences can bring these feelings into consciousness. Rectal stimulation, even with no partner present, is one such experience.

lead to believe a man was gay tended to view him far more negatively (weaker, less manly, less intelligent, dirtier, etc.) than when the same man was assumed to be straight. Usually, this devaluation occurred unconsciously. Not only that, but the man who labeled the other man gay was seen more positively for having done so. It seems that in our society, men receive positive reinforcement for labeling others as gay, thereby isolating presumed gays from "the male club."

* For men involved in the coming out process (even those who are well under way), there is no better book than Don Clark's *Loving Someone Gay* (1977).

This is what happened to Lee, a successful and apparently self-confident gay man: "I had just managed for the first time ever to get a large vibrator into my rectum. I was about to get excited when everything stopped. I thought, 'You know, if I were a *real man*—I meant straight—I wouldn't be sticking things in my ass!' And it was as if my muscles pushed that vibrator right out and clamped shut! I haven't been able to do it again since."

Many gay men are surprised at the intensity of their actions, especially those who have fooled themselves into believing that they are free of all *internalized homophobia*. The development of "gay pride" balances internalized homophobia, but, unfortunately, pride is sometimes used by gay men to keep from confronting their doubts about being gay. For such men, facing the remaining guilt and self-hatred is uncomfortable but almost always results in a reduction of tension, often including anal tension. One gay man, after a long walk in the woods during which he experienced the intensity of his self-hate, found himself sobbing. Afterwards he "squatted down and took a 'cosmic shit.' I never felt so open and free in my life. I'd been holding in all the shit my father had told me about queers."

MASCULINE/FEMININE

The more that homophobia is studied (among men of all sexual orientations), the clearer it becomes that it is *not* closely correlated with traditional sexual morality, as might be expected. Rather, it appears that fear of homosexuality is primarily the consequence of narrowly defined sex-role behaviors and rigid gender identity (one's sense of masculinity and femininity) (MacDonald, et al., 1973). While it is true that homosexuality has no direct relationship to masculinity and femininity, most people, including gays, are convinced that it does. Therefore, men's fear of homosexuality is liable to bring up another, more basic fear: the fear of being viewed by self and others as unmanly and feminine. A great many men try to suppress, at all cost, the soft, receptive aspects of themselves. They fear their masculinity will be compromised and, therefore, their value as people reduced. For example, men who are labelled homosexual tend to adopt increasingly exaggerated masculine behavior as a compensation, even if they are *not* gay (Farina, 1972). Among men, then, homophobia could just as well be called "femiphobia"—an irrational fear and devaluation of femininity. Such attitudes pervade our culture; even mental health professionals are likely to view stereotypically masculine behavior as "more healthy" than behavior considered feminine (Broverman, et al., 1970).

In this environment, it is little wonder that receptivity to anal stimulation, with its physiologic similarity to vaginal receptivity, provides fertile ground for femiphobia. Although there is nothing inherently feminine about enjoying rectal stimulation, men who *believe* such a connection exists are unlikely to give up this conviction. The solution for these men has to include a relaxation of their sex-role stereotypes. Gradually, they must come to realize that the acceptance of their femininity (if that's what receiving anal stimulation represents to them) does not constitute a loss of masculinity. On the contrary, *the ability to relax, to receive, to voluntarily abandon control is a psychological and interpersonal asset, not a loss.* *

Straight men are most likely to consider this—if they haven't already—when they discover that women are often attracted to and enjoy the company of men who can be receptive. The women's movement is, without question, the most important social force encouraging, sometimes demanding that men give up their traditional roles and explore a wider range of behavior. The still-embryonic men's liberation movement has been one forum for men to begin to discuss these issues with each other.

For gay men, the most crucial factors that allow them to accept their femininity are a reduction of internalized homophobia and an increase in self-acceptance. Otherwise, receptivity will probably continue to be associated with feel-

---

* The psychological theories of Carl Jung are particularly relevant in this regard. Jung recognized through his analysis of dreams and other symbolic material (such as art and myths), that a conscious integration of one's masculinity and femininity is a crucial aspect of psychological wholeness for both men and women (Jung, 1951). The person who reduces internal conflict between masculinity and femininity is called *androgynous* and this more balanced approach called *androgyny* (see Singer, 1976).

ings of unworthiness. It is virtually impossible for a gay man to reduce his homophobia without experiencing considerable anger or rage at those whose attitudes have supported his hatred of himself.

Many of my male clients, whatever their sexual orientation, have found that experimentation with rectal stimulation can be a symbolic way of becoming more at ease with receptive feelings. Sometimes this occurs without any conscious intention, as it did for Burt, a man with a super-masculine image. He began anal exploration only because his wife refused to learn how to relax anally unless he did, too. At each point he resisted, fearing that he would be "contaminated" by femininity. However, at each step he found that he actually enjoyed the sensations of anal stimulation. He especially resisted internal anal simulation because of its association with intercourse, which he definitely did not want. This is what he discovered: "I was trying to get my wife's vibrator in my rectum—which I once thought I would never even try. And boy was I trying, pushing like I do with almost everything. I'm not a violent guy, but I guess I use force a lot. Naturally it didn't work. The harder I tried, the tighter I got. Finally I just let go. Liz [his wife] says I became receptive. Anyhow, it worked. I now have some idea of what receptivity, passivity—whatever you want to call it*—feels like. It's not bad."

Others deliberately set out to develop a receptive feeling before even attempting rectal stimulation. Many men discover very quickly that their subjective feeling determines both the ease with which they can receive objects into the rectum and the extent of their enjoyment of rectal stimulation. Initially, however, the inherently good feeling of being receptive is often overshadowed by their femiphobia.

---

* The terminology *is* troublesome and is itself part of the problem. The concept of passivity is negatively charged for most men (and some women) because it connotes lack of involvement and loss of will. Receptivity is better, but is difficult to distinguish from passivity—until it is experienced. The term, *passive will*, proposed by Brown (1974) and other biofeedback researchers, is a good alternative. By combining words normally seen as opposites, it communicates the androgynous quality of receptivity. It is intentional, voluntary surrender of control with total involvement.

VIRGINS AND WHORES

None of the women I've worked with has experienced homophobic responses to anal stimulation. This does *not* mean that women are free of negative attitudes about both homosexuality and femininity. It is unlikely, however, that rectal stimulation will trigger these feelings for women. Instead, it is far more common for women to recall long-forgotten commitments to the ideals of chastity as well as fears of becoming "whores," "sluts" or "loose women." They tend to associate anal stimulation with promiscuity. They fear that if they allow themselves to enjoy it they can no longer retain their self-images as "good women." Jan discovered that "deep down inside I guess I feel that anal sex is 'kinky.' It's for prostitutes and weirdos."

This attitude is shared by many sexual sophisticates and is certainly not limited to women. Sexual sophistication is sometimes a thin veneer used to cover up the effects of anti-sexual training. In general, it seems that the more attached a person is to playing the role of sexual libertarian, the more he/she is likely to be harboring remnants of sexual prudery. Among some people, it is a curse worse than death to be labelled a prude. Yet, it is hard to imagine how anyone could grow up in this culture without any vestiges of anti-sexual feeling. It is much better to become aware of these feelings than to hide them behind a mask of sexual nonchalance.

Rectal exploration provides a great opportunity for a person to come face-to-face with his/her real sexual values—including those not currently in vogue. When a person becomes conscious of them, sexual values can be modified, or, in some cases, intentionally retained. In the course of therapy, I ask people about their sexual ethics. Many are put off by the very idea, associating all ethical judgments with the moralisms they have rejected. It is not unusual for men and women to assert that they make no judgments about sexual behavior ("Whatever turns you on"). Too often, the result is a silent inner battle, waged on the edges of consciousness, between opposing emotional extremes—the virgins against the sluts. I sometimes ask clients to act out their "prudish selves" and later their "liberated selves." It is fascinating (and fun) to start a dialogue between the two selves. Sexual partners can learn a great deal about themselves and each other by acting out these roles if they are willing to take the risk of acting a little silly and perhaps discovering that the inner prude is still very much alive.

11

OPENING A DIALOGUE

Enhancing Verbal Communication

To the extent that you have been paying more attention to your anus and rectum, you can now begin making choices as to whether and in what ways you wish to include this area of your body in the sensual/sexual experiences you have with others. These decisions do not have to be made all at once. Consider your private anal explorations. Before you began, you could not know for sure what they were going to be like. What you thought, felt and did unfolded progressively in the light of new information and experiences. The same will happen as you begin looking more closely at the shared aspects of anal pleasure.

Receiving anal stimulation from another is very similar to giving it to yourself. Either experience is best in the context of a positive, non-threatening relationship. So far you have learned a lot about ''relating'' to your anus. You may *not* be so sure how to be equally comfortable involving others.

The basis of all relationships is communication. Your anus does not use words, so in building that relationship you relied on nonverbal communication through your senses of sight and especially touch. You have been learning the neuro-muscular language your anus speaks. With other people, it is advisable to begin with words, because words are usually perceived as a less threatening form of communication. For most people, touching *seems* more intimate even though non-communicative touching can and often does leave people feeling isolated and empty rather than full and satisfied.

Even people who touch each other regularly often do not talk intimately. They use words, but the words are guarded, defensive or meaningless. The really important things remain unsaid. In the area of sexuality, many people do not speak with each other at all. Others, feeling more sexual freedom, like to talk about sex frequently. Then there are those who hide behind words, using them as a shield instead of a means of contact. Even frequent sex-talk can be restrained by unspoken barriers. Two of these barriers deserve special attention because they are so common and because they inevitably block communication.

The first barrier is the unspoken rule that while it is all right to discuss one's latest sexual desires and adventures in great detail (perhaps exaggerating a bit), it is *not* all right to discuss sexual fears, doubts, dislikes and questions. We do not want to appear silly, prudish, weak or old-fashioned. So we pretend that everything is just fine, even if it is not. We might like things to be quite different, but we keep it to ourselves. The result is a gnawing feeling (if not an absolute conviction) that we are the only ones who get anxious about sex, have questions and still have some growing to do.

Talking about sex as a seduction technique, a means to an end, also tends to inhibit communication. Such "sex talk" is almost always shallow and phony. It leaves each person wondering what the other is *really* thinking and what is going to happen next. It rarely brings people closer together. Instead, this sort of "communication" fosters mistrust—even though it may be very exciting. (When sex talk is used as a form of sexual play and not as a manipulative technique, it can enhance erotic encounters).

In addition to these two barriers, sexual communication is often limited by what some people insist is "spontaneity." They do not feel comfortable speaking up whenever they have something to say. They have to wait until the subject "just happens" to come up. Of course, there is nothing spontaneous about this. The person in fact fears the consequences of speaking up. For this reason, many people rarely talk during sensual or sexual encounters. They fear that words will "break the flow." There may, in fact, be very little flow to break. It is a good guess that people who rarely or never talk during sensual/sexual play are behaving according to an unspoken sexual script. On the other hand, a few people are at the other extreme, talking incessantly and rarely *feeling* anything. Full exploration of shared anal pleasure requires that barriers to verbal communication be recognized and overcome by developing new skills.

EXPERIENCE

Think of some people you know or would like to know better. You do not have to be close friends. However, select a person you trust and with whom you have good rapport. It makes no difference which sex the person is or if you have had sex together before or even if you are sexually interested in him/her.

Talk to one or more of these people. Say that you are exploring your sexuality and that one of the things you want to do is talk more about sex. Ask if he/she would be interested in spending an evening with you during which the *primary* agenda is to have an in-depth dialogue abut sensuality and sexuality. Give the person complete freedom to say "yes" or "no."

If this person is an actual or potential sexual partner, *make an explicit agreement that you will not have sex together that night even if you want to.* Be very clear that this is not a sexual "come on." When you get together, discuss all aspects of your sensual/sexual self—past, present and future. You probably will want to start with the least threatening material (usually the past) and move into more intimate areas as you become more comfortable with each other. To help you get started, you might discuss the first time you had feelings which, in retrospect, seem to have been sexual.

When you have gained each other's trust, discuss any sexual fears or questions that concern you. Explain what you have been doing with regard to anal exploration. Find out your partner's feelings and attitudes toward anal pleasure.

Here are some other things you might discuss:

    what turns you on and turns you off
    sexual relationships
    peak sexual experiences
    uncomfortable sexual experiences
    masturbation
    sexual fantasy
    things you would like to do in the future
    sexual values

Remember, neither one of you needs to reveal anything unless you want to. But if you do not feel comfortable talking about something, *avoid making up a phony story*, as this will eventually have a negative effect on your communication. Simply say you do not feel comfortable talking about it right now. That is all you have to do and it is completely honest.

Pay attention to how you interact with each other, not just the content of your words. Include your moment-to-moment feelings in the conversation. If your friend says something that bothers you, say so. If something makes you feel good, say that, too. Before you say goodbye, discuss your experience.

RESPONSE

Some people readily see the value in this experience and do it, even though they are nervous about it. With rare exceptions, they have thoroughly positive encounters. Others are more reluctant, questioning how this could possibly be relevant to anal exploration. Some feel that requesting such a conversation is artificial and embarrassing. Ironically, those who talk frequently about sex are often the most resistant, insisting that they have done it all before. A closer look usually reveals that they have *not* done it before, at least not this way. Their previous sexual communication has been blocked by one or more of the barriers described earlier. Overall, willingness to explore verbal communication skills is an accurate predictor of the level of comfort with which people are later able to share anal pleasure.

The differences between this kind of discussion and most other sexual discussions are what make it potentially valuable. Several important communication skills can be enhanced by doing it this way—as contrived as it might appear. First, you will learn that you do not have to wait for sexual discussions to occur "spontaneously." Rather, *sexual communication is available when you need it or want it.* Second, *you will learn how to initiate and honor explicit interpersonal agreements whenever they can help make things more comfortable between you and your partner.* This will be true even if the person with whom you talk is not an actual sexual partner.

Both of these skills will be extremely useful to you in your interpersonal and anal exploration process. In fact, all sexual exploration can be greatly enhanced by these two skills. For example, in sex therapy, clients agree to eliminate anxiety-provoking behaviors (such as intercourse) for a certain period of time. By doing so, they can redirect into more pleasurable activities the energy they might otherwise have spent worrying. The practical use of this technique for those who wish to explore anal intercourse will be discussed in Chapter 13.

THE FUNCTIONS OF
SELF-DISCLOSURE

In addition to developing these two communication skills, the act of sexual self-disclosure is a powerful tool for growth in and of itself. As you disclose who you are to another, you not only reveal something of your present level of self-awareness, you also expand your own awareness and self-acceptance.

The late psychologist Sidney Jourard noted that sexual material tends to be particularly difficult for people to discuss (Jourard, 1971b). This corresponds with my experience. Most people have difficulty revealing sexual information about themselves, especially if they feel that the information might make them look bad or stupid. Almost everyone finds it particularly uncomfortable to express feelings about anal sensuality. But self-disclosure about these things is universally reported to be very liberating.

Talking about yourself is, at its best, not a passive reporting of what you already know. Change-producing self-disclosure is an *active mutual journey* that both points to *and* fosters growth. In therapy, people regularly surprise themselves with what they disclose. "I never knew all these things about myself" is a frequent reaction. If your self-disclosure does not uncover something new, if it does not bring you *closer to yourself*, then you are probably holding back, discussing only what is safe. The full value of verbal communication becomes obvious only if you risk disclosure of those aspects of yourself that are not yet fully known.

As you discuss your experiences, feelings, values, needs and fears, it will be clear that your sexuality is *special and unique*. By discussing your sexuality as a whole rather than in disjointed fragments, you will see more a realistic picture of how your sexuality is unique and why that is important to you.

This is only half of the picture. Something else happens simultaneously: *you discover that your sexual uniqueness takes shape against a background of a profound human commonality in which you are intricately involved.* Both uniqueness *and* commonality are important. For this reason, I suggest that you have several conversations with men and women of varying ages, sexual orientations and lifestyles. If you avoid those you feel are "too different," you will miss the opportunity of fully learning about, accepting and celebrating both your uniqueness and commonality.

After each conversation, write about the experience in your journal. Think about how you responded to each person and vice versa. To what extent did you "edit" your disclosures and why? Did you have a pre-determined picture of what your friend was expecting? The way a person typically *talks* about sex is often indicative of the way he/she *behaves* sexually. For example, those who have their receptive "antennas" always attuned to what others are thinking (or might think) are likely to be guarded and cautious both verbally *and* physically. This might be something you will want to work on within yourself. The first step is to become more aware of the fears that prevent you from being open.

On the other hand, it is unfair and inaccurate to assume that all communication blocks are within you. Look more closely. Did your partner say or do anything that encouraged your insecurity and caution? An entire conversation can be rendered superficial because of some little thing one person says at the beginning, e.g., a judgmental remark about somebody else, an offhanded comment that gives an impression of narrow-mindedness, or a particular way that person has of expressing personal opinions that makes them sound like the "gospel truth." If you look back and discover that something about your interpersonal dynamics made you uncomfortable, arrange another evening with the *same* person in which you talk about how you felt. This might include telling the person that certain of his/her behaviors make it difficult for you to talk freely. Obviously, being so frank can be threatening, but your partner can benefit as much (or more) from your feedback as you will benefit from being able to give it.

Joan made an interesting discovery about her communication with her friend, Dick: "I really like this guy, but it's so hard for me to talk with him. I think I'd like to go to bed with him—I *know* I would. But I have no idea how he feels about me. The first time we talked it was just awful! I was so phony. I think he was too. I felt he was being seductive, and I guess I was too. Anyway, I was watching every word. I felt bad about it all week. So I called him up, and we got together again last night. I told him how I felt scared and he turned me on and I didn't know what he was thinking. We got it all out in the open. It was really hard for me. I was shaking like a leaf. We ended up having a beautiful evening. He admitted his attraction, too, but we decided not to make love right away. I really feel close to him. Saturday we're going out to dinner, but we're not going to have sex until we're really ready."

Joan was able to overcome her blocked communication with Dick because she was willing to reveal her feelings *in spite of* the fact that she was anxious. Perhaps the single biggest block to honest sexual dialogue is the idea that you can talk only about what is comfortable. This limitation eliminates the things most in need of discussion. It is uncomfortable to be anxious, but it feels even worse to be anxious *and* to feel you have to hide it. Most people can cope with their anxieties. But anxiety complicated by attempts to suppress it can be totally debilitating.

These communication skills will be of greatest value if you can find ways to integrate them into your daily life, whether you are talking about sex or something else. My clients tell me that they now use the same assertive approach to raise the subject of conflict in a relationship or a frustrating situation at work. One man used this approach to help break through unspoken conflicts with his family. He wrote his parents that during an upcoming visit he wanted to schedule an evening of intimate conversation. He explained that he valued his relationship with them and wanted it to be better. When it actually happened, they were all very nervous and defensive at first. By the end of the evening, they were even talking about sex, a development he never expected would be possible. He was surprised to discover that his parents were sexual beings too and that he had misread their silence about sex as meaning they were opposed to it. In reality they were only uncomfortable talking about it—just as he was.

A final note: As I have said, these dialogues usually work out very well. Yet there may be some people with whom you simply *cannot* feel open, no matter how much you work on it. It is part a self-affirming attitude to acknowledge and accept this situation (including any disappointment, frustration and anger) *and then to ask somebody else.*

12

MUTUAL EXPLORATION

Non-Demand Anal
Stimulation with a Partner

You can now learn to combine verbal communication with tactile communication. Some people find this a natural next step while others experience it as a risky "leap." Unfortunately, many people neglect verbal communication the moment they begin touching. This chapter will focus on both aspects of communication, one enhancing the other.

I will suggest a variety of experiences that can help you develop or refine additional skills for improving the sensual/sexual pleasure you share with others. These include the ability to make and receive explicit requests, the ability to say "no" without fanfare or apology, the ability to experiment playfully without pressure or demand and the ability to ask for and receive feedback. Obviously, these skills are useful not only for anal exploration and pleasure but for all forms of shared pleasure.

In this chapter, anal intercourse will *not* be suggested. This means that all of it can be used by any couple. The experiences suggested here can also be used to humanize group sex experiences. However, it is a good idea if each participant first feels comfortable doing them in the less complex setting of a one-to-one relationship.

CHOOSING A PARTNER

Your first concern will be the selection of a partner. If you are in a monogamous relationship all you need to do is encourage the positive involvement of your partner. Usually this is simply a matter of making a clear request. Then, any resistance can be discussed and you can reach agreements that will help to make the experience comfortable for both of you. It is possible that your partner will refuse to participate in any experimentation and will share pleasure only in old, familiar ways. When this happens, you can decide it's not important enough to pursue in this relationship, become more assertive in insisting that negotiations continue (perhaps with the help of a professional counselor) or terminate the relationship. The last option is quite drastic and rarely happens. When it does, this specific conflict is obviously representative of a deeper, more serious one.

Those without a monogamous partnership have some choices to make. If they are involved in a non-monogamous but primary relationship, most people choose their primary partner for anal exploration. However, this is not always the case. Some find it easier to try new things in a relationship with fewer established patterns. But choosing a non-primary partner can be a serious threat to the primary relationship. This is the case not because of sexual involvement *per se* (many couples have little or no difficulty with additional sexual involvements) but rather because the ''secondary'' relationship may end up becoming more open and comfortable than the primary relationship. Serious conflicts can arise unless you are able to incorporate the new communication processes in your primary relationship as well.

For those considering going outside of a primary relationship, or for those who are not involved in such a partnership, focusing on one major question can be helpful in choosing a partner: *In what kind of sensual/sexual relationship will you feel most comfortable experimenting and exploring?* For instance, do you want to be romantically involved (''in love'')? For some people this is a ''must.'' Such people feel that they are really sexually free only when swept along by romantic intensity. For others, the intensity of romantic feelings is an inhibiting factor because the stakes are so high. There is a lot to lose if things do not work out. In addition, relationships with high romantic intensity are also likely to be those with the least direct communication; the partners rely instead on powerful fantasies as a primary source of information about each other. This is particularly true in the first phase of romantic relationships.

For people who feel inhibited in romantic relationships, a sexual friend is the preferred choice because the rapport and trust exists without the high intensity and dependency. A few people prefer a totally new partner who has not known them in the past. These people find it easier to move beyond old behavioral roles and expectations in the context of a fresh involvement.

None of these choices is inherently better than the others. The important thing is to become aware of which is best for you.

Any person you choose may be reluctant to work with you. Overcoming the resistance of a reluctant partner requires persistence, tact and often patience. Your partner will be more willing to experiment if you make it clear that *both* of you have something to gain from the experience. Your partner's reluctance is likely to soften if you express willingness to discuss or experiment with something he or she wants (as a trade off). For example, Laura convinced her lover to try non-intercourse-oriented sensual touching by suggesting that this might help her feel more at ease giving him oral stimulation (something he had wanted for a long time). Another couple agreed that they would try sensual experimentation one night in exchange for going out dancing the next.

Some gentle probing may be required to discover specific fears that make your partner uneasy, especially because your partner may not be aware of any specifics. Unless he/she gives your requests serious thought, the initial reaction may only be vague anxiety. But often there *are* very specific concerns that, once acknowledged, are easy to take care of. For instance, worries about the cleanliness of the anal area can be countered by agreeing to shower or bathe together before doing anything else. Similarly, your partner's feelings of awkwardness with the unfamiliar may result in fears that he/she won't be able to ''do it right.'' Mutual reassurance that you're both exploring new territory and that there's no "right" or "wrong" way to do it can help a lot.

If your partner has not done any anal exploration private-ly, he/she may fear that you will want to explore his/her anus as well. This fear is especially common among men in heterosexual relationships. Depending on how you feel, you can offer assurances that one-way anal touching is accept-able to you. This may be difficult for couples who feel that every sexual or sensual activity must always be mutual. But wanting your anus (or any other place) touched doesn't mean you *have* to reciprocate. You may feel very comfort-able by now about touching your own anus and ready to try being touched by a partner. But you may not be ready to touch your partner in the same way. Especially if your partner is already an anal enthusiast, you need to make your limits clear.

EXPERIENCE

Make two explicit agreements with your chosen partner: (1) that you will spend some time together when the only goal is exchanging pleasurable touch all over your bodies including your anus (and, if desired, your partner's anus as well) and (2) that you will *not attempt* intercourse during that encounter.

Begin by taking a bath or shower together. Find a com-fortable place (not necessarily the bedroom) in which to *take turns* pleasuring each other's body. When you are being touched, do not *do* anything. Just lie or sit back and enjoy it. See if you can focus all your attention on the stimulation you are receiving. Likewise, when you are doing the touching, see if you can focus all of your attention on what that feels like *for you*. When you touch, make no attempt to read your partner's mind ("Does he/she like what I am do-ing?" "Should I be doing something else?" etc.). Instead, *assume* that what you are doing feels just fine unless you hear otherwise. Remember, you are not trying to get turn-ed on or to turn on your partner—just find out what feels good to each of you.

It will be possible to do this only if you know *from experience* that your partner really will take care of him/herself by tell-ing you if something feels unpleasant. Verbal agreements to this effect are important, but they are not enough. *Test* your agreement by *deliberately* finding a way to touch your partner that does not feel good (it tickles, irritates, etc.). In this way you can be sure that your partner will indeed give you feedback about unpleasant touching and will not just ''grin and bear it.'' (Don't conduct this ''test'' secretly; tell your partner what you intend to do.)

Touch your partner all over. There is no rush. Explore every detail. A massage oil reduces friction and can be very sensual. Expensive massage oils are unnecessary. Safflower or peanut oil works just fine. If desired, you can add a few drops of scented oil. Massage oil can also be warmed up by placing the container in hot water.

If you have not had this kind of experience before, you will probably want to have at least one session that does not include anal stimulation by either of you. After as many non-anal sessions as you need, you can agree to include anal touching the next time.

If you have agreed that anal exploration will be mutual, find a comfortable position in which to explore your partner's anus visually and through touch. Your partner might want to use a mirror and watch what you are doing. Ask for permission to put your finger inside his/her anus slowly and gently. If you get permission, apply a little lubricant to your finger and his/her anus. Ask your partner to breathe deeply as you gently press your finger against the anal opening. Make an agreement that each will ask the other to stop *before* anything you are doing becomes annoying or uncomfortable.

When you are ready, switch places so that you are the one being explored and pleasured. It does not matter in what order you do this. You might want to change positions several times.

Making requests. Later on (or perhaps another time) pleasure each other in the same way, one at a time. Only this time agree that nothing will happen unless the person being touched *requests* it. He/she begins by making a simple request (e.g., ''I'd like you to massage my feet''). Do what is requested until you get a new request (e.g., ''Would you do it a little harder or softer or slower,'' or ''Now I'd like you to move up to my calves''). Spend plenty of time doing this until you both feel completely comfortable making and receiving detailed, explicit requests. This is an effective way to find out about each other's preferences, even though you may feel self-conscious at first.

Saying no. If it is difficult for many people to ask for things directly, it is even more difficult to say "no" After you both become skillful requesters, spend some time deliberately saying "no" to many of your partner's requests, whether you really want to or not. Do this until "no" becomes just another word, producing no special emotional reaction. Discover that when your partner says "no," you can ask for the same thing again later on. You might get a "yes."

Taking breaks. Take frequent breaks during your activities. Once you start pleasuring, feel free to stop and come back to it later. Maybe you will just want to sit or lie quietly together. Or you might want to get up and go do something else. Even when you are both very excited it can be nice to take a break. Learn that when you or your partner requests a break, the session is not over. Discovering this can help to replace a rigid, "scripted" approach to sex with a more natural, spontaneous rhythm. When you do things this way, sexual arousal will almost certainly fluctuate. A man's erection may come and go. A woman's lubrication may start and stop. Reassure each other that this is natural and does not reflect a lack of interest. If your erotic interest *does* wane, you can still enjoy yourselves. It is good to be able to give and to receive pleasure when you are *not* aroused.

Coping with anxiety. If at any point you feel anxious, uneasy or are wondering about something, these steps can help you relax again: (1) *Tell your partner* how you feel (e.g., "I'm afraid you're getting bored," "I'm afraid this is going to hurt," "I'm wondering if you mind having your finger in my anus"); (2) *Stop what you are doing;* and (3) *Do something new* that you can enjoy with complete comfort *or* get the reassurance you need to continue what you are already doing. Lying quietly together, taking deep breaths in unison can be a good way to relax.

As you experiment with each new skill, apply it to anal exploration and pleasure *when you are ready.* State your feelings *while you are having them.* Help each other to locate your anal sphincter muscles and talk about how they feel. Ask for feedback about which kind of anal stimulation feels the best.

If you want to, explore each other's rectum with a dildo or vibrator. No matter how exciting this gets, keep up the verbal feedback and remember your agreement not to attempt anal intercourse.

If one or both of you want to have an orgasm (it is not necessary), continue touching afterwards. See if your anus feels different from the way it felt before and during arousal.

RESPONSE

For most of my clients, this kind of communicative sensual/sexual encounter is an important landmark in the development of their capacity to experience anal pleasure with another human being. Those who have never before included their anuses in erotic play are usually able to do so comfortably once they exchange direct permission with their partners. Those who have tried to enjoy their anuses with a partner in the past were generally so concerned that anal pleasure might lead to anal intercourse that they rarely enjoyed it. The explicit agreement not to have intercourse sets the stage for a new kind of anal experience.

Nancy, in therapy with her lover Tom, had this to say: "We've been together for three years now, and this is the first time we've agreed it's okay to touch each other's ass and talk about it without me feeling pushed and without Tom feeling guilty for raising the subject. It was great!" Then Tom added, "Doing all this together, I realized that I've never really *looked* at Nancy's vagina either. We've done a lot of touching and we both like oral sex but—how can I explain—it's completely different to investigate a person's body for no reason except that it's fun. Usually I'm trying to *do* something like get her turned on or make her come. I didn't do much of that stuff this time, but I think we got more turned on than ever, didn't we, Nancy? But we didn't *have* to. I guess that's it." And Nancy agreed.

Reports like this are common, but only part of the picture. Steve's experience was just as positive but in a different way: "It seems that most of you [in the group] had a good time with this. I didn't. When my lover touched my ass I went up the wall. He said, 'What's the matter?' and I said,

'Nothing.' Of course, that was a bunch of crap, and he knew it. He said, 'Look, I thought we were going to be honest.' So I told him I hated it. It was really hard to say that, but he said, 'So what else do you want to do?' That was a week ago and it was only last night that he was able to touch my ass and it felt pretty good. I never knew I was so uptight about it.''

At first, Steve thought that everything had to go like clockwork or else he had ''failed.'' Soon he came to understand what was really important about his experience: It is impossible to fail if you give yourself permission to be completely yourself. You can be anxious, angry or bored. If you communicate these feelings and go on from there, you have been true to yourself and your partner. I have talked with very few people for whom anal stimulation (or any sexual activity for that matter) is *always* pleasurable. If you expect this, then you are setting yourself up for disappointment and failure.

Many people report that what feels good is quite different from what they think is *supposed* to feel good. For instance, people often assume that an in-and-out motion of a vibrator or finger has to be ''the best'' because of its association with intercourse. Actually, quite a number of people report that a gentle circular motion around the anal opening is much more pleasurable. This is understandable because many more nerve endings are near the anal opening than in the rectum. But anal pleasure is more than nerve-endings and motions. It is the total response of an individual to a unique set of circumstances.

The suggestions made here are for a particular kind of encounter that is slow, relaxed and accompanied by dialogue. Not every encounter will or should be like this. However, adding a little structure to an encounter (with, of course, your own creative variations) can provide opportunities not only for fun and learning new skills, but also for making some discoveries about the ways you typically share pleasure.

The basic principle is that by deliberately *over* doing things that may not come naturally to you, you can integrate these skills into your repertoire of comfortable behaviors. For instance, usually you will *not* want to talk so much unless a specific request would enhance your pleasure. Sometimes you will *not* want to go slow. It is unlikely that you will always want to "take turns." But it is good to be able to lie back once in a while without having to do anything. Neither will you want to say "no" so much or take a lot of breaks. Nevertheless, your ability to do these things can add to your comfort and pleasure. Specifically with regard to mutual anal pleasuring, these skills are crucial.

Obviously, not all the potentials inherent in these communicative touching experiences can be realized in one session, or two or even ten. Sensual/sexual communication is both a skill and an art. There is always room for refinement. Yet those who try these experiences almost universally report a greater sense of freedom in sexual situations, reduction of performance anxiety, increased feelings of intimacy and more pleasure.

As always, those who have the most difficulty doing these things, who find them threatening or silly, are usually those who most need to do them. Some feel that it takes all of the "mystery" out of sex. This concern is more likely based on a fear of sexual communication than any real interest in mystery. An authentic sense of sexual mystery— abandoning the need for predictability—is actually enhanced by full communication. People who rarely talk during pleasuring are usually following a "cookbook" approach to sex from which all the genuine mystery has been carefully removed.

People who are strongly influenced by a behavioral pattern called the *Nice Person Syndrome* tend to have a difficult time with these communication skills. The Nice Person Syndrome is an exaggerated role adopted during childhood as a means of getting approval and affection. Nice People are carefully trained to be, at all costs, "good boys" or "good girls." They are steeped, too soon and strongly, in the value of unselfishness, cooperation and the importance of pleasing others. Consequently, they grow up feeling that it is natural to defer to the wishes of others, putting their own desires in second place (or ignoring them altogether). I use the word Nice (capital N) to describe adults who still act like good boys and girls. Such people are often highly intuitive, but they use their sensitivity mostly for the purpose of learning what is expected of them. They have a profound need to be liked and will violate, if necessary, their own integrity for even the possibility of love and affection. They usually *are* accepted and well liked, but they are not satisfied, because they know they have withheld something of their true identity. As a result, Nice People often live in fear that nobody will ever really love them—including their weaknesses and blemishes. They feel they must be perfect. Yet they are constantly and painfully aware that they are not perfect. A good number appear to have bodily symptoms of chronic inner conflict (e.g., anal tension).

Nice People operate on the basis of one central conviction: *The only way to get what I need is to do what other people want.* They are usually very good at getting what they want (without asking for it) but there is always something missing. Spontaneity is difficult since each interpersonal encounter is, in a sense, a performance. Remaining a Nice Person requires constant vigilance, since all "bad" qualities (e.g., anger, selfishness, competitiveness) must either be suppressed or rechanneled in such a way that they at least *appear* nice.

I have deliberately presented a somewhat exaggerated characterization. But in it, you may be able to see aspects of yourself. If you do, I suggest that you look more closely at the negative effects this pattern can have on your relationships and your sex life. The impact of the Nice Person Syndrome is likely to be heightened in the presence of a significant other, such as a sex partner. This helps explain why some men and women can feel very relaxed and safe when they are alone, but tense up again when they are with someone else. In fact, people who have trouble sharing anal pleasure with a partner when they can easily give it to themselves almost always discover that they are playing the Nice Person role.

Nice People have trouble making explicit requests. Instead, they tend to be more manipulative, perhaps dropping a few hints or else *giving* what they, in fact, want to *get*. One man, Bill, expressed his strategy for getting what he wanted from people as "nicing them into submission." Nice People know that if they are just good enough, others will automatically know what they want and give it to them. When this does not happen, they feel hurt. They would feel angry, but that is not nice.

Nice People are usually "rescuers." This is a concept developed by Transactional Analysis (T.A.) (Berne, 1964). It refers to an interpersonal pattern or "game" in which a person is constantly taking care of others. Most of us play this game at one time or another. We rescue somebody each time we withhold or distort our true feelings, not wanting to hurt or anger the other person. We do the same thing when we go along with something that we really do not want to do. What we usually do not realize is that in rescuing others, we treat them as "victims," helpless people who cannot take care of themselves. Rescuing somebody (except in instances when someone genuinely needs help) is a subtle put-down.

Nice People save up little grievances each time they play rescuer because they rarely let themselves say "no" when they want to. As a result, they are often chronically angry. My clients report that they usually have tense anuses when they play rescuer. It's as if their anuses say "no" when their mouths will not. People often protest, "Why should I do this exercise of saying 'no' to my partner's request whether I really want to or not? It seems so *negative!*" In reality, people who cannot say "no" (even when they have permission to do so) are likely to be profoundly negative, even though, on the surface, they appear sweet and cooperative.

In sex, as elsewhere, *it is impossible for a person authentically to say "yes" to anything unless he/she simultaneously feels complete freedom to say "no."* Bioenergetics therapist Alexander Lowen states, "The expression of affection is *not* to be trusted until the repressed negative feelings have been vented. Until this happens, the positive expression is in most cases a defense against the underlying negativity." Lowen often has people pound with fists or feet while shouting "No! No! No! I won't!" until they are able to discharge the physical/emotional effects of years of "cooperativeness" and repressed "no's" (Lowen, 1971). While you may want to try an intense discharge like this, the less dramatic exercise of saying a lot of "no's" during sexual activities can also go a long way toward changing this destructive behavior pattern.

Because Nice People have trouble saying "no," they are likely to associate potentially pleasurable situations with feelings of obligation and duty. Having begun a sexual encounter, they feel they must go through with it to the bitter end. They feel like they always have to be doing something or they will be seen as selfish. This is why taking frequent breaks is so valuable. If you and your partner are both able to start and stop as you please, then you can each be assured that, when you are sharing pleasure, it is because you want to and not because of a sense of obligation.

All of the experiences suggested here can help you become more "creatively selfish." To get the most out of them, you and your partner must agree to take reponsibility for your own pleasure instead of trying to read each other's minds. To do this, you must have or develop trust in your partner's capacity to take care of him/herself and to accept you as you are. You may also need to develop greater ease in accepting differences in personal preference.

Non-manipulative communication is the only way to remain simultaneously in full contact with yourself and your partner. If you abandon contact with your partner, touching can become an exercise in alienation. But what many fail to recognize is that if you abandon contact with your own needs and feelings, then you have very little to share. In either case, your anal muscles are likely to respond with tension. Whereas, if you are in full contact with yourself *and* your partner, you are much more likely to feel safe and receptive.

"RIMMING"
(ORAL-ANAL STIMULATION)

One form of anal stimulation that you and your partner(s) may want to discuss is oral-anal stimulation, technically called analingus but popularly called rimming. Because the lips and tongue and the anal opening are all highly sensitive and potentially erogenous, it is not surprising that many people enjoy bringing the mouth and anus into intimate contact. Rimming involves kissing or licking the anal area. Occasionally the tongue is partially inserted into the anal opening and moved in-and-out or in a circular motion. Some people have a strong, perhaps even exclusive preference for either rimming or being rimmed. Others enjoy both, perhaps taking turns or else experimenting with positions that allow mutual, simultaneous rimming (for many, such positions are too awkward to be enjoyable).

Of all forms of anal stimulation, rimming is the most likely to trigger strong reactions of revulsion and disgust. Most of us learned early in life that when something is dirty, we should definitely avoid putting it in or near our mouths. For this reason, partners would be wise to avoid pressing each other into experimentation with rimming. If someone is not comfortable with it, even the thought of rimming can be a complete "turn off."

Those who decide to explore rimming usually want to try it during or immediately after showering or bathing. This can reduce discomfort with the odors commonly found in the anal area. This also reduces the possibility of encountering feces. There are a few people, however, who find anal odors highly arousing. For these people, washing reduces the excitement.

Frequently, those who are squeamish about rimming feel the same about being rimmed. Others enjoy being rimmed even though they would never consider rimming their partner. Sometimes rimming is a part of S & M roleplaying. In this case, the rimmer is invariably seen as the "bottom" (submissive) and the rimmee is the "top" (dominant). For these people, the notion that rimming is degrading and humiliating is usually an important aspect of their arousal. Those who do not enjoy feeling degraded will not enjoy rimming until they view it as pleasurable rather than degrading.

Unfortunately, for those who enjoy rimming, there are serious health risks involved: contracting or spreading diseases like hepatitis and intestinal infections. And virtually all AIDS researchers consider rimming to be a high risk activity, especially when practiced casually. Those who want to experiment with rimming should read Appendix A, carefully consider the risks, and decide under what circumstances, if any, the risks would be outweighed by the positive aspects of rimming. For example, thorough washing substantially reduces the risk of infection. Limiting the number of partners with whom you practice rimming also reduces the risks. The risk for monogamous partners is extremely low. However, a person can have an intestinal infection, even for a long time, without realizing it. There is a similar possibility of previous, unrecognized infection with the AIDS virus. (Note: In casual sexual settings, especially the kind available to gay men, a partners' penis could easily have just had contact with someone else's anus. In this case, the risks of oral-penile sex are similar to those of rimming. Similarly, engaging in oral-vaginal contact after rimming can sometimes spread intestinal infections to the vagina.)

Thinking about and discussing these issues, and deciding what seems best for you, may make you uneasy. Perhaps you'll be tempted to ignore the entire subject of rimming. However, my clients virtually all discover that discussing rimming (and other sexual activities) helps them to be less anxious in sexual settings, because they know what they want and don't want. This frees them to enjoy whatever they choose to do. See Appendix A for help in developing safe sex guidelines that are suited to you.

13

ANAL INTERCOURSE

Approaching it Safely and Comfortably

This chapter is for men and women who wish to explore anal intercourse. Others might want to read it for the information or to develop a better understanding of those who enjoy anal intercourse. Or you may wish to skip it altogether.

People who want to be able to enjoy anal intercourse usually view it as the culmination of their anal exploration activities. However, many clients report that their intense focus on intercourse decreases during therapy, as they discover that other forms of anal pleasure can be equally satisfying. At the same time, most continue to feel that including intercourse is an ordeal. Consequently, only about one quarter are able to move easily from other forms of anal stimulation to anal intercourse. This is especially true for those who have been hurt by intercourse in the past. With patience, however, most are eventually able to enjoy anal intercourse.

There is little likelihood that anal intercourse will become enjoyable unless anal *self*-pleasuring has *first* become comfortable. Of all my clients, only a few are exceptions to this ''rule.'' These few, mostly men, never do much anal self-exploration at all. Instead, once given permission and information, they can enjoy anal intercourse almost immediately. With these exceptions, those who report persistent difficulties with anal intercourse are usually also unable (or unwilling) to enjoy their anuses alone. For this reason, anal intercourse should not be attempted until most of the experiences suggested thus far have become enjoyable. This is a caution to those of you who skipped or skimmed the first twelve chapters because they seemed too elementary.

Those who pay attention to developing the interpersonal, verbal and tactile communication skills discussed in the last two chapters usually find the transition to anal intercourse far less anxiety-provoking and thus more enjoyable than those who do not try these exercises. Virtually all of the women and most of the men I've worked with feel that a partner with whom they have already shared other experiences is the natural choice for experimentation with anal intercourse. However, a few of the men prefer a partner whom they do not already know. Rather than learning how to create a comfortable atmosphere for experimentation with anal intercourse, these men decide to wait until they are "in the mood" to receive intercourse and then just do it. Once again, for a few people this approach appears to be satisfactory. Unfortunately for this group, the AIDS crisis requires that they apply more forethought and planning.

In general, it can be said that once anal self-pleasuring and mutual pleasuring (not anal intercourse) have become enjoyable, the positive transition to anal intercourse is almost totally dependent on *how* anal intercourse is attempted and the *nature of the relationship* in which this takes place. Some people abandon all they have learned about their anal muscles and expect them immediately to yield to intercourse without giving themselves a chance to relax and trust their partner. A few give up all previous agreements and resort to coercion; then they are frustrated and disappointed when pain is the result. The focus of this chapter is to help you explore anal intercourse while remaining in contact with both your partner and your own needs.

EXPERIENCE

In this section I will describe the approach that has proven to be the easiest and least anxiety-producing for most people. Keep in mind, however, that a different approach might be easier for you. Trust your intuition and experience.

Choose a man with whom you have earlier shared other forms of anal pleasure. Be clear with him (as you no doubt already have been) that you would like to receive anal intercourse but that you *do not* want to feel obligated or pressured. Reassure one another that you can still have a good time together even if you discover that anal intercourse is not going to be comfortable during that encounter.

If you and/or your partner is a non-monogamous gay or bisexual male, you should become familiar with the latest information on AIDS and discuss the health guidelines you will follow (consult the AIDS section of Appendix A, pp. 214-226). If either of you has participated in any high risk activities with other partners in the last few years, use a condom. Doing so may feel awkward at first. But with practice and a little patience, condom use can become a natural and easy aspect of intercourse. Inevitably, using a condom will reduce or change the sensations, but not as much as you might think. New materials and manufacturing techniques make condoms thinner and stronger than they used to be.

On the other hand, you may decide that it's better not to engage in anal intercourse at all right now, enjoying instead, other less risky forms of anal stimulation. For one thing, fear of AIDS has understandably made it more difficult (or impossible) for many people to relax sufficiently for anal intercourse. Even some who used to find it easy are now having trouble. It is important for partners to be patient and understanding with each other whenever they encounter such fears.

If you do decide to proceed, begin by showering or bathing and trying some of the same sensual and erotic pleasures that you have experienced together before. Do not forget your verbal communication skills. When you feel comfortable, ask him to stroke your anal opening gently with his finger(s) or, if you both want it, with his mouth. As you feel your anus relaxing, ask him to lubricate his finger and slide it inside your anus.

Be playful together. If one or both of you is taking all this too seriously, break the tension by talking and laughing about it. If you are anxious over anticipating intercourse, your anus will be tense and you will not be having fun. Talk about your feelings, breathe deeply, making certain that you do not feel rushed. If you find yourself making too big a deal out of this so that you cannot relax, put off any attempt at intercourse until you feel safer.

As part of your play, move together into several positions in which it would be possible to receive anal intercourse (see Figure 8) but ask your partner to *make no attempt to insert his penis.* For now, you are just experimenting with the positions so that you can get a sense of which will be the most comfortable. Notice how your anus responds in each position. Tell your partner which position you feel the most relaxed with and, if you know why, tell him the reasons, too (e.g., a certain position gives you more freedom of movement, makes you feel more in control, less self-conscious or less vulnerable).

Your partner may lose his erection during these explorations. He may be afraid of hurting you or self-conscious about "doing it right." For everything you are doing so far, an erection is *not* necessary. Ask him to talk about his feelings if you sense he is nervous. He may need reassurance, too.

When he does have an erection and you feel comfortable, he can put on a condom (or it can be fun to do this together). When rolling on the condom, pinch about one-half inch of the tip with your thumb and finger to form a reservoir for semen (many condoms are designed with a reservoir tip built in). Select the most comfortable position, apply a lubricant and ask him to place his penis gently against your anus while you breathe deeply. Stay in this position until you feel your anus relax. Then gently bear down with your anal muscles (push outward) and ask him to move the head of his penis gently into your anus as you visualize your anal and rectal muscles letting go. Or if you are sitting over him (which is the easiest initial position for most people) you can lower yourself slowly onto his penis. If you encounter any pain, back off to a more comfortable point and stay there until you get used to it.

When you are ready, think about what you learned about the shape of your rectum and make small adjustments in position and angle to allow the penis to enter your rectum without resistance.

Once his penis is inside, ask him to be completely still until you get used to the sensations. Then tell him which movement (if any) you find the most pleasurable. You probably will want to start with slow movements. At first, his erection may come and go somewhat; this is natural. If at any time the condom slips off, simply reapply it or use a new one. When and if you both desire faster thrusting, your partner may need to hold the rim of the condom in place around the base of his penis. Either of you may stop at any time, according to your agreement. You can enjoy other erotic activities together, perhaps returning to intercourse later. When your partner withdraws his penis, he should hold the rim of the condom so it does not slip off, especially if he has ejaculated. Note: If you are a woman, your partner should remove or change the condom if you desire vaginal intercourse after anal intercourse (perhaps you could do this together).

If this first attempt does not work out exactly as you had hoped, express any feelings of disappointment or frustration. It is important that you don't stop giving each other pleasure just because anal intercourse was not comfortable. Quitting will leave you feeling bad about yourselves and it will intensify your misgivings about anal intercourse. *Acknowledge and appreciate the positive aspects of the experience (e.g., you were able to enjoy being in one or more positions for anal intercourse, you liked it for a little while, the anal touching felt good).*

When anal intercourse becomes comfortable in one position, you will be able to try other positions without difficulty. If, however, you find out that some positions are not good for you, tell your partner. Be assertive about your preferences.

RESPONSE

The success of this approach to anal intercourse depends on your willingness to be direct and specific in asking a partner for what you want. Those who have the most trouble with this usually fear that nobody could possibly be in-

Figure 8

POSITIONS FOR ANAL INTERCOURSE

Figure 8, continued

terested in spending any more than limited time and energy with them. One man, Jerry, expressed his concern this way: "I don't think it's fair to ask my partner to go through all this with me. It seems like I'm asking for an awful lot." Jerry obviously felt that he was not worth any special time and consideration. Yet, he had tried a more rapid approach and found that it just did not give him enough time to relax and feel safe. This left him feeling as if he had very few options. Although Jerry denied it at first, he also felt a great deal of resentment toward his partner for not being more helpful. It took him a few weeks to admit to the anger he was really feeling (and how tense it was making him). He then could see more clearly that he was denying *himself* the attention he wanted, because of his unwillingness to ask for what he needed. Jerry's self-esteem problem was quite persistent and did not go away overnight. But eventually, he *was* able to ask his partner to spend sufficient time with him and, after he talked about his uneasiness, it worked out fine.

Physical sensations. There are very few sensations involved in anal intercourse that you have not felt during the earlier experiences. You have already stimulated your anal opening many times. You have also experienced the sensation of your finger and soft objects inside your rectum. If you had your partner insert a dildo or vibrator in your rectum, you have already experienced the sensations of having somebody else control the movement, pressure and angle of entry (guided, of course, by your words and nonverbal cues). You have explored and interpreted new sensations that may have accompanied rectal stimulation for you. You have also become familiar with the sensations that occur *after* rectal stimulation.

One new sensation is the greater body contact with your partner that is usually a part of anal intercourse. Perhaps you like this feeling. If it makes you feel uneasy, however, you will initially want to select a position that minimizes body contact. For example, many people find that sitting over their partner gives them more control over movement, angle and pressure and reduces their feelings of being "pinned down." Others report that the weight of the partner's body is highly arousing and makes them feel *more* safe and secure. Some prefer to lie on their back (with legs up) so that they can face their partner. These people usually feel this position is more intimate because they can see and touch one another's faces. Some, by contrast, find this position to be awkward and uncomfortable.

Becoming aware of your position preferences and assertively asking for them is extremely important. Many men and women find out that the primary reason for uncomfortable anal intercourse is that they feel obligated to do it in a certain position. For example, as soon as Roseann accepted that she did not *have to* receive anal intercourse on her back (which she found "unaesthetic and humiliating"), she felt greatly relieved and found that she could enjoy anal intercourse without any trouble in a "side-by-side" position. Incidentally, she recognized that she also disliked the "missionary position" for vaginal intercourse. She had gone along with this choice of position for years because she thought it was "natural." After several weeks of assertively refusing to accept this position (happily, with the support of her husband), she found that she could enjoy it once in a while, as long as she did not feel obligated.

Other possible new sensations are those associated with the particular kind of pelvic thrusting used by your partner. Some men like to thrust very vigorously. You may like this. On the other hand, you may find it frightening and irritating. Communicate this to your partner so that you can negotiate a mutually satisfying solution. At first you may want to ask him to lie still and let *you* make the movements.

Talking openly often reveals some surprises. For instance, some people say that their partners automatically start thrusting vigorously and deeply. But when they talk about it, they are often surprised to discover that neither of them derives any special pleasure from such vigorous movement. Instead, their partners feel it is expected of them. Their actions are based on predetermined ideas about anal intercourse rather than their own needs.

Some people also get confused about the "proper" amount of time to engage in anal intercourse. Concern about timing is a very common manifestation of sexual performance anxiety. Not infrequently, for example, men enter sex therapy feeling that they ejaculate "too fast" or "too slow" during vaginal (or anal) intercourse. When asked what makes them feel this way, the answer is often based on expectations the partners have never discussed. One man may, for instance, consider fifteen minutes of stimulation prior to ejaculating to be "premature" while another feels that it is far too slow.

Likewise, those receiving anal intercourse show a tremendous variation in their desires and expectations (often these do not coincide) with regard to timing. Some may enjoy receiving intercourse for only a few minutes (or less) but continue anyway, feeling that they must please their partner. Others want it for as long as possible. Rarely is either partner as rigid about timing as the other thinks. Sometimes partners participate together in activities that each feels are expected but which neither one is enjoying.

Men and women sometimes wonder what they "should" be doing while they are receiving anal intercourse. Should you move? If so, how much? Or should you lie perfectly still, acting as a passive receptacle for your partner's penis? Again, preferences vary widely. Many people prefer to lie still during anal intercourse, concentrating all their attention on the internal sensations. For these people, too much movement is a distraction. Others prefer to thrust their pelvises vigorously and are actually far more active than their partners. These people, of course, prefer positions that allow them complete freedom of movement (usually side-by-side or sitting on top).

Experiment with different ways of receiving anal intercourse, paying attention to what you actually like rather than what you are supposed to like. It will also help if you can transcend your ideas about "passive" and "aggressive" roles, focusing instead on what gives you both pleasure. Keep in mind that you will be genuinely receptive to your partner only to the extent that you are enjoying yourself. *The most pleasurable experiences with anal intercourse occur when neither partner feels compelled to do anything that he/she does not want to do.* These are pleasure-oriented encounters. Performance-oriented encounters, tied up as they are with expectations, are often more hard work than fun.

A good example of this involves the use of voluntary contractions of the anal muscles during anal intercourse. Some people have heard or read about the use of rhythmic anal contractions as a means of providing extra stimulation for their partner's penis (vaginal contractions are reported to have a similar effect). Consequently, men and women sometimes feel that they have to be able to do this right away or else they cannot be "adequate" receivers of anal intercourse. Actually, those who do not worry about these fine points of anal intercourse enjoy themselves more than those who struggle to "do it right." Remember, anal contractions do occur naturally as part of your sexual response cycle. Once you become comfortable receiving anal intercourse, you can then experiment with deliberately contracting your anal muscles (remember the Kegel exercises?) in rhythm with your own or your partner's pelvic thrusts. This *may* enhance your own or his pleasure. But if you feel you have to do it *for him,* you might find your anal muscles tensing involuntarily in response to your efforts to perform.

Some people also become concerned about orgasm in anal intercourse, feeling they have to reach a climax during anal sex. Actually, relatively few people are able to reach orgasm while receiving anal intercourse as the only source of stimulation. More men than women appear to be able to do this, probably due to the proximity of the penile bulb and prostate gland to the anus and rectum. If an orgasm for the receiver is going to be part of anal intercourse, direct simultaneous genital stimulation is usually needed. Not everyone feels a need to reach an orgasm during anal intercourse, although some believe this is expected. Similarly, the partner who is *giving* anal intercourse may feel that he is expected to ejaculate inside his partner's rectum. Some men, however, enjoy entering their partner's rectum very much, but prefer (or are only able) to ejaculate while receiving some other form of stimulation.

Some people expect to be able to feel semen ejaculating inside the rectum and are disappointed when they cannot. Because the relatively few nerve endings in the rectum respond mostly to pressure, and because so many other sensations are likely to be experienced at the same time, it is highly unlikely that ejaculation will be felt. A few people do report incredible rectal sensitivity. However, in the vast majority of cases, the perception of ejaculating semen is probably fantasized in conjunction with other more dramatic signs of orgasm. Of course, if you are using a condom, as I recommend, you definitely will not feel your partner ejaculating.

Insertors in anal intercourse often have their own special concerns. Sometimes these concerns are ignored as attention is focused on the needs and feelings of the would-be receiver of intercourse. Even those men who have actively pushed for anal intercourse may be considerably less than comfortable when the opportunity presents itself. Many insertors feel on the spot, not only pressured to produce and maintain an erection, but also saddled with total responsibility for making the experiment a success. Sometimes the insertor feels so much pressure that he will try to avoid intercourse at the very moment that the receiver is ready to try. Some people will lose interest in sex altogether or aggressively initiate sexual activities other than anal sex.

It is best if the fears of the insertor can be sensitively discussed. But this may be easier said than done. For one thing, if anal intercourse has previously been a subject of contention in the relationship, both partners may feel some lingering resentment about the past. Resentment makes sensitivity difficult, if not impossible.

It's also possible that one or both partners may secretly feel guilty about past difficulties with anal sex. One man, Tim, who kept losing his erection when he attempted intercourse finally realized, "I've nagged Bill about letting me fuck him for so long I just can't believe he really wants it now, even though he says he does. I can see how I made things really miserable for him at times." Not everyone is as honest as Tim. Frequently one partner doggedly clings to a blaming attitude toward the other. More often than not, this is simply a cover-up for guilt. As you can see, in many cases there needs to be plenty of discussion before intercourse is even attempted.

Most difficulties encountered with anal intercourse can be alleviated by proceeding slowly and patiently, focusing on the sensual and practical aspects, overcoming unrealistic expectations and assertively communicating personal needs and preferences to partners.

But what if you are doing all these things and anal intercourse is *still* uncomfortable for you? Ask yourself, once again, if you really do want to be able to receive anal intercourse. People have a remarkable capacity to fool themselves. Particularly those caught in the Nice Person Syndrome find it difficult to differentiate external pressures from their own desires. Perhaps a talk with a close, supportive friend (someone who has no personal investment in your decision) can help clarify your feelings.

If you reaffirm your desire to be able to enjoy anal intercourse, then the next step is to reevaluate the approach you have followed thus far. Have you spent sufficient time exploring on your own? Some people do not take the early anal exploration process seriously because their attention is so focused on the goal of receiving anal intercourse. They simply go through the motions of exploring their anuses in an obligatory way, thinking to themselves, "Okay, I'll do all this if it's absolutely necessary to get what I *really* want." Sometimes unsuccessful attempts at anal intercourse are positive because people are forced to reconsider what they have or have not been doing alone. Then many are able to put aside their feelings of urgency about anal intercourse and reexperience other forms of anal pleasure in a different, less frantic way.

If, however, you *do* feel intimately aware of your anus and rectum and are able to share anal pleasure both with yourself and a partner—but you just cannot seem to relax and enjoy anal intercourse—then it is almost certain that, for you, anal intercourse has negative symbolic significance. For a great many people, intercourse (whether vaginal or anal, given or received) represents an expression of power. It may well be that your enjoyment is being blocked by the dynamics of power at work in your sexual relationships and/or fantasies. Understanding these power dynamics is so important (whether or not you enjoy anal intercourse) that I am devoting an entire chapter to a discussion of power and anal pleasure.

14

POWER AND
ANAL PLEASURE

Understanding Interpersonal
Dynamics

While many people are reluctant to acknowledge it, power dynamics are at work in *every* interpersonal relationship. Whenever two people are together, there are decisions to be made and differences to be negotiated. In most social interactions, differences can be worked out smoothly; neither person is aware of the process. The more intimate people become, the more apparent and persistent are their differences. Those who try to avoid inevitable conflicts (Nice People do this regularly) usually pay a price of distance, smoldering resentment and perhaps a tense, armored body.

The only relationships in which the dynamics of power can be ignored without negative consequences (e.g., resentment and muscular tension) are those in which roles have been established and mutually agreed upon. One person dominates and the other submits; for those two people it's second nature. Although many relationships are structured this way, very few people are fully satisfied with the inflexibility of such relationships. Even those who clearly prefer one role or the other almost always would like to abandon their traditional role once in a while.

It is difficult for many people to think or talk about power in their loving relationships partly because they see the whole subject as anti-romantic, and because they tend to view power only in its negative aspects. They see it as inevitably destructive, manipulative or coercive. Yet power can also be positive. In order for a person to take a creative, self-affirming stand in the world, he/she must feel that his/her decisions and actions will have some effect. Psychologist Rollo May suggests that the experience of powerlessness is the root of violence and despair (May, 1972). People who view power only as negative adopt a role that May calls "pseudo-innocence." This is a reluctance to abandon the innocence of childhood and to confront a world of conflicting wills. The "fall from innocence" requires a recognition of each person's capacity to use power both *creatively and destructively.* People who play innocent often end up being destructive (or destroyed) because they refuse to take responsibility for their actions and the effects of their behavior on other people.

The theories of psychologist Erik Erikson shed some light on the relationship between power and anal tension from a developmental point of view. Erikson contends that the major life issue confronting a child during the period of emerging anal muscular awareness and control ("toilet training") is whether anal self-control will be associated with feelings of autonomy or feelings of shame and doubt. To the extent that the child is allowed to enjoy the new, but rudimentary ability to use the anal muscles for voluntary control and release, he/she will experience pleasure and a sense of physical and psychic autonomy. But when muscular control is *demanded* under threat of punishment or ridicule, both the pleasure of self-exploration and the autonomy of voluntary control are subverted. The anal muscles are thrown into spasm as a protection against future shame (Erikson, 1959).

Unfortunately, there is a tendency to view "toilet training" as an isolated process. Actually, the way a parent approaches toilet training probably reflects the overall, ongoing relationship between parent and child. Does, for example, the parent trust the child's ability to grow and develop without coercion or threats? Does the parent feel comfortable with the child's need for self-assertion even when that need comes out as defiance? If the answer to either or both questions is "no," this will be reflected again and again in an infinite variety of situations, not just toilet training. The result is likely to be an anxious, inhibited child who would do almost anything to avoid the punishment (pain) that has resulted from his/her meager attempts to be autonomous and strong. Or, as sometimes happens, the child's authentic but frustrated need to be autonomous may take the form of fantasies of being all-powerful, perhaps even sadistic. Then, feeling powerful is tied with rage.

Erikson's theory implies an early interplay between the use of the anal muscles and a sense of autonomy or its opposite, powerlessness. If he is right, powerlessness might not only be the root of violence and despair, but also one of the roots of anal tension (and the health problems that result). My own impression is that feelings of powerlessness *are* often reflected in anal tension, especially during sexual encounters. Of course this is not always the case. Many people who acknowledge that they often feel frightened and powerless, are nonetheless extremely relaxed anally. It seems that feelings of fear and powerlessness can be expressed in many body zones, not just the anus. For example, some people have tense, drawn chests, as if armored to fend off attack.

For many (but not all) of my clients, feelings of fear and powerlessness are unmistakably associated with anal tension. For many, sexual relationships are frequently struggles for power, often hidden behind a calm, "nice" exterior. Generally speaking, people are willing to take a closer look at the role of power in their relationships only when they start believing that: (1) power interchanges are unavoidable in human relationships; (2) power can be both creative and destructive; and (3) a positive sense of autonomy and strength is not inconsistent with being sensitive and receptive. On the contrary, *it is impossible for a person to be truly receptive unless he/she feels an authentic sense of power.* Furthermore, it is impossible for a person to abandon him/herself to *play* without this same sense of power. Both receptivity and play require safety. When we feel safe, we can let down our protective barriers, confident that we can protect ourselves, if we have to, against opposition.

Many people do not want to look directly at either their power or powerlessness because they think a concern with power is incompatible with love. They feel that the price they have to pay for intimacy is the suppression of their will. But Rollo May warns, "When love and power are seen as opposites, 'love' tends to be the abject surrender of one partner and the subtle (or not so subtle) domination by the other. . . . . Missing are the firmness of assertion, the structure and the sense of dignity that guard the rights of each of the partners," (May, 1972). Not surprisingly, people who do not want to look at power in their relationships often have the most difficulty learning to enjoy anal sexuality. It seems that the less the dynamics of power are openly acknowledged in relationships the more they are expressed in symbols and rigid roles. In such relationships, anal intercourse (and often vaginal intercourse) can symbolize the power of the "top dog" or "fucker" and the powerlessness of the "underdog" or "fuckee."

Some people resist exploring their attitudes toward power by pointing out that they cannot enjoy anal intercourse in *any* relationship. "How then," they ask, "could the problem lie in my relationships? It's obviously my *individual* problem." The answer, of course, is that we tend to behave in similar ways in all our sexual relationships. Some people carry the same pattern into their nonsexual relationships as well, but destructive patterns are most dramatically expressed in romantic sexual relationships.

POWER AND ROMANTIC FANTASIES

Sexual relationships are, more often than not, charged by romantic fantasies. It may take time for these fantasies to surface, but they are often activated even prior to the first encounter. Therefore, many encounters that appear casual are, in fact, quite serious for one or both partners.

Romantic fantasies take many forms, but their dynamics tend to be similar. On the one hand, they can intensify the potential *meaning* or significance of a sexual encounter (e.g. "This could be *the* man/woman to fulfill my dreams"). In turn, an element of mystery increases the *stakes* of the encounter (e.g., ''Depending on how things go, I will either win or lose this person's affections, which I desperately want''). Especially if both partners are injecting fantasy images into the encounter, the sexual intensity may be feverish.

On the other hand, the romantic fantasy, if taken too seriously, simultaneously activates the most needy aspects of the participants. In many instances, a person's lingering feelings of vulnerability and incompleteness make the fantasy appealing in the first place. The fantasy object is imagined to posess important qualities which the fantasizer desires to internalize or ''import.''* Once this happens, the fantasy is invested with tremendous power. Sooner or later (usually sooner) the fantasizer ends up feeling disappointed, depleted and even more vulnerable.

Many clients, once they become aware of these power dynamics, are amazed to see that they approach many (or even all) sexual encounters vaguely anticipating such a drama. Often, they expect themselves to be the ''losers.'' In this context, receiving anal intercourse understandably represents powerlessness. The only real solution is to become more secure and powerful in sexual relationships.

Men and women who typically adopt the role of ''chaser'' in romantic encounters deliberately have to restrain their tendency to pursue. Doing this allows them to retain more of their power. Self-esteem can also be increased by learning to allow others to approach them. Increased self-esteem always results in reduction of vulnerability. But if chasing is held back as a strategy, without self-esteem as the foundation, it simply won't work. Many people who pretend to be cool and aloof are, in actuality, faking it. This is usually obvious to everyone, especially the Faker him/herself.

---

* The concept that people seek to *import* certain qualities from and *export* other qualities to sexual partners is developed by C.A. Tripp (1975). Sometimes the desire to import qualities from a sexual partner points toward a sense of deficiency in the importer, and a perceived abundance in the exporter. However, the desire to import does *not* necessarily imply a sense of deficiency. Some peple want more in the qualities they already like in themselves, not because they feel lacking, but because these qualities have become eroticized. In these cases, attraction may be high, but vulnerability remains relatively low. Consequently, destructive power dynamics are greatly reduced.

Those who typically play the role of "chasee" in romantic encounters deliberately have to counteract their tendency to withhold involvement in relationships. The chasee tries to compensate for low self-esteem by getting others to pursue. But simultaneously, chasees fear becoming trapped, taken over or dominated by the pursuer and are thus very vulnerable. It is often not recognized that the chasee uses ambivalence as a power strategy. By simultaneously attracting and rejecting the chaser, throwing out a few "crumbs" and then retreating, the chasee avoids the clear statement of intentions that would end the game. Although this may serve to keep the intensity high, in many cases it precludes for both partners the feeling of safety that most people require for enjoyment of intercourse.

The "cure" for the chronic pursuee is the same as for the pursuer—increased self-esteem. As both chasers and chasees feel more secure, they can replace their predictable roles with a more natural give-and-take. This keeps the relationship from becoming boring and renders unnecessary the artificial drama that almost always leads to emotional tragedy. As a result, romantic fantasies can be used more playfully, as a source of sexual excitement and with reduced implications for one's self worth.

SEX ROLES AND POWER

By far the most potent symbols of power in sexual relationships are learned early in life. The qualities considered "masculine" (e.g., strong, aggressive, controlling, independent, firm, competitive) and those considered "feminine"(e.g., fragile, receptive, deferential, dependent, soft, cooperative) are usually assigned according to anatomical sex. The popular conviction, most articulately expressed by some psychoanalysts, is that there is something inherently aggressive about penises and that vaginas (or other orifices) are inherently passive or submissive. Therefore, no one person of either sex is encouraged to exhibit the full range of qualities. The more strict the polarization, the more extreme the qualities tend to become. Ideas of what is masculine move toward dominance and "sadism." Ideas about femininity move toward submission and "masochism."

Traditionally, the most popular images of male-female sexual relationships are unquestionably "sadomasochistic." It is the man's role to dominate and control. The woman's role is to submit and surrender. Gradually, ideas about sex roles have been changing to allow for greater variety and equality between the sexes. Yet traditional sex-role expectations are still very much alive and will be for a long time to come.

What is not usually recognized is that masculinity and femininity are both legitimate and effective power strategies. There are times when assertive action and control is the most effective way to make something happen. For example, success in the world of work usually requires these qualities. At other times, a more receptive, yielding approach is more effective. The ability to yield is regularly required in all intimate relationships and in coping with the challenges of life that are not subject to control. A person who has developed one set of abilities and suppressed the other faces life at a disadvantage.

Our culture values masculine qualities most highly; femininity is associated with social and economic oppression. In the realm of sexual expression, especially vaginal intercourse, many women feel deeply resentful about always being expected to be receptive. To the extent that anal receptivity is also associated with submission and weakness, it will be difficult or impossible for these women to experience it as pleasurable. Many men who wish to receive anal intercourse feel the same way. They want the pleasure of rectal stimulation but they do *not* want to be dominated or controlled.

SPECIAL CONSIDERATIONS IN LESBIAN AND GAY MALE RELATIONSHIPS

In spite of the gradual trend toward detaching sex roles from anatomy, the belief is still pervasive that, with sex, one partner *has* to take a more dominant role. Traditionally, of course, this role has been expected of men and strongly discouraged in women. Boys and girls are carefully social-

180

ized to play their assigned roles, even before they can talk.

It is not surprising that many people simply cannot imagine how two partners of the same sex could be sexual *without* adopting "male" and "female" roles. In addition, the common assumption that *real* sex means the insertion of a penis into an orifice makes it difficult for some to imagine how two women could be sexual together at all.* Modern sex researchers now virtually all agree that most same-sex partners do not adopt consistently stereotyped sex roles in their sexual behavior. Instead, power usually flows back and forth within each encounter and from one encounter to the next. Nonetheless, lesbians and gay men are not immune to sex-role socialization. In the course of developing a satisfying sex life, each gay person is likely to face problems resulting from this training.

In our culture, men are socialized to initiate and choreograph sexual encounters. Women are socialized to wait for men to "make the first move." The woman's role is either to surrender or, in many instances, to resist. It comes as no surprise, then, that lesbian couples sometimes find it difficult to be sexual because each partner is socialized to wait. Both may be reluctant to express sexual desires or push the encounter in a direction that might be exciting. There is too much restraint and not enough assertiveness.**

Once these problems are worked out, however, the result is often an unusually high degree of sexual communication and balance between the partners' needs.*** The mutual sensitivity and ease of emotional expression necessary for this level of communication are important positive aspects of female socialization. Additionally, lesbians do not participate in intercourse (vaginal or anal) and are thus not af-

---

* This is why it is often assumed that lesbians use dildos in their lovemaking, even though lesbians, in fact, use dildos infrequently. And when they do, it is for the purpose of vaginal stimulation, not as a penis substitute. Usually, fingers are quite sufficient for vaginal stimulation because the inner two-thirds of the vaginal canal is relatively insensitive.

** The challenges and joys of sexual relationships among women are sensitively explored in *Lesbian Sex* (Loulan, 1984).

*** In their laboratory observations comparing opposite-sex and same-sex encounters, Masters and Johnson (1979) noted a consistently higher degree of mutual sensitivity in the erotic behavior of same-sex couples,

fected by this particular symbolic power exchange. Although this by no means eliminates power plays from lesbian relationships, it may make it a little easier for two women to find forms of sexual expression that are less determined by tradition.

In some respects gay male sexuality is affected by opposite pressures. Because men are socialized to seek sex actively, it is not surprising that there is so much sexual activity in the gay male subculture. In certain segments of the gay male population, male sex-role socialization has been expressed in an extreme form (curtailed now by the AIDS crisis). The result has been an unmatched availability of potential sexual partners (depending, of course, on one's personality, social skills and the community in which one lives). This ready access to partners has clear advantages, but it also increases the level of pressure to perform. Many gay men feel that their only hope of retaining a sexual partner is to be the "perfect" lover—totally uninhibited and versatile. For these men, receptivity to anal intercourse may be seen not as an opportunity for pleasure but as a requirement.

Men are also socialized to be dominant with sex partners and competitive with each other. This training sometimes makes it difficult for two men to relax together. In spite of deep affection, each may find himself maneuvering for the dominant role. This happens even among men who do not consciously desire to dominate or control. Sex-role images are internalized so early that they are woven into one's fundamental self-concept, independently of his value system. In addition, internalized homophobia may subtly press one or both men to adopt even more extreme stereotypical masculine behavior.

The sexual interaction of two men may be complicated fur-

especially lesbians. They coined the term *gender empathy* to describe and explain this sensitivity. Although physiological and, to a lesser degree, psychological familiarity no doubt contribute to this sensitivity, other factors are involved as well. Particularly important is the greater sense of sexual freedom a person often feels when he/she moves beyond behavioral boundaries traditionally imposed by heterosexual ideals. For example, Masters and Johnson noted that opposite-sex couples tend to move relatively quickly into intercourse, slighting sensual enjoyment of the entire body.

ther by the fact that, physiologically, both are able to give and receive intercourse. If they invest a great deal of symbolic importance in intercourse, anal stimulation may be too emotionally charged to enjoy. This dynamic can manifest in several different forms. First, one partner may be able to receive anal intercourse while the other cannot. If they seek to change this, one or both may resist the change out of fear of altering the power dynamics of the relationship. Second, it may be that neither partner can receive anal intercourse, and that one or both may desire to work in this direction. But their anal exploration may be inhibited by uncertainty about who will end up "on top." Third, both partners may enjoy receiving anal intercourse but with different desires as to frequency. If intercourse is a symbol of power, one or both may insist on "equality" (giving half the time, receiving half the time) as a matter of principle rather than preference. In all three instances, the pleasure of anal stimulation becomes secondary, or sometimes non-existent, until the power struggle is resolved. Male couples who find workable solutions to these complexities discover a flexibility of sexual expression that is not available to those who take their assigned sex role for granted.*

OTHER SYMBOLS OF POWER

Sex roles and romantic fantasies are not unique in their ability to alter or determine the power dynamics in sexual relationships. Virtually any physical characteristic or personality quality can be a symbol through which one person invests power in or withdraws power from another. One female client who normally felt independent and strong would "melt" and "become a helpless little girl" in the presence of tall men with moustaches. Not surprisingly, with such men she was unable to enjoy sex, especially anal sex, because she felt too vulnerable. On the other hand, she had trouble saying "no" to men like this. In spite of the almost infinite variability with which any characteristic can symbolize power, the most common fall within seven categories.

* A fascinating and useful exploration of the development of long-term intimate relationships among gay men can be found in *The Male Couple* (McWhirter & Mattison, 1984).

Appearance. Though beauty is, indeed, in the eyes of the beholder, the mass media have helped to create an unparalleled homogeneity of ideal physical types. Many people, maybe most, consciously or unconsciously place themselves and others on a hierarchy based on appearance. One's place on a hierarchy (as perceived by oneself and others whose opinions are valued) contributes to one's confidence, or lack of it, in the sexual marketplace. Everyone has appearance preferences, some more narrowly defined than others. This selectivity serves to intensify erotic response to favored characteristics. However, when appearance is a major factor in assigning *overall worth* to self and others, the assigner could be called "looksist." The process of ranking people according to appearance is called "looksism."

Looksism terrorizes many people and determines the power dynamics of many sexual relationships. Some people attempt to move up the appearance hierarchy by trying to attract someone whom they see as more desirable than themselves. In doing so, they usually adopt a "one down" position. Their self-esteem depends on winning affection from or possessing the prized object. Appreciating another's appearance, rather than being enjoyable, actually becomes an act of self-deprecation. Protective muscular tension and resentment are likely to result.

Some people find it difficult to become comfortable receiving anal intercourse because they are so accustomed to giving sensual attention to their "more desirable" partners that they rarely receive adequate attention themselves. A few clients enter therapy specifically to learn how to receive intercourse on demand, without any need for preliminary touching. This rarely works.

Age. The differences in appearance, experience, values and perceptions among generations can provide some of the contrast conducive to sexual fascination. However, because of the prevalence of "ageism" (the assigning of overall worth based on age) in our society, youth is a common symbol of power. According to popular belief, a person's sexual desirability increases throughout the 30's and begins to deteriorate in the early to mid 40's. Yet many people become painfully conscious of aging much earlier.

People who are self-conscious about aging sometimes seek out younger partners in whom they then invest great power. A large age discrepancy between two sexual partners frequently (but not always) suggests a parent-child type of relationship. The person in the child role feels dependent on the person who plays parent. At the same time, the "child" resents the loss of autonomy and will often express displeasure with "passive-aggressive," underhanded maneuvers for power (e.g., not following through on commitments, making sarcastic remarks, or withholding affection).

The "parent" both admires and resents the "child." Usually the "parent" hopes that by giving the "child" sufficient love and encouragement he/she will grow up and return some of that love. Occasionally this happens, but more often one or both of them gets tired of the adopted roles and terminates the relationship, usually with considerable psychic pain. A string of similar relationships indicates, with little doubt, that this power dynamic is at work.

Generally, the person who overdoes the parent role needs to learn how to allow his/her own childlike qualities to surface, especially the ability to play. The person who plays child needs to develop just the opposite qualities, such as the ability to make and keep commitments and to be more independent. In a positive relationship with a large age discrepancy—and there are many that work very well—both partners learn to develop needed qualities through mutual appreciation and intimate communication. In most cases, if the relationship continues for many years, the significance of the age gap will be greatly reduced and the partners will become peers. Other people are unable to make this transition and must learn to select partners who are peers to begin with.

It is very difficult to avoid being affected by what our society teaches us to expect as we grow older: less fun, less sex, less attention and less power. Those who learn these lessons well usually get what they expect. But aging doesn't have to be this way at all. In fact, the life process runs counter to these negative expectations. With age can come greater knowledge of and comfort with oneself as well as the capacity for genuine intimacy. For the self-loving man or woman, passing years also bring a clarity of values—the ability to distinguish the truly important from the trivial. For many, however, these positive changes do not compensate for the loss of physical beauty.

Race. Whereas people usually look for characteristics similar to their own when they select non-sexual friends, differences are likely to be of greater sexual interest. For this reason, racial differences are, for some people highly conducive to sexual arousal. Not only is physical appearance obviously different, but movement, language and other behaviors affected by cultural traditions may increase the feeling of fascination. Erotic preference based on race is as legitimate and potentially positive as any other type of sexual preference. And there is nothing inherently racist about being attracted—even exclusively—to people of a particular racial group.

However, racism—the assignment of overall worth based on race—can complicate or ruin sexual relationships between two people of different races. This is because racism assures that certain images will be ''projected'' onto some or all members of a racial group, a tendency that increases with distrust and lack of familiarity. Members of different racial groups usually perform ''mass projection'' on each other. This lends a certain commonality to what an individual of one race will see in or expect of an individual of another race.

For example, black men have told me that sexual partners (especially white partners) often expect them to be supermasculine and always to be ''on top'' in anal intercourse. Many of these black men also feel guilty that they cannot live up to this image, and angry about the implicit racism. Of course, some black men use this image to gain a power advantage over their white partners whom they simultaneously envy and dislike.

Some Asian men (especially gays) complain of opposite pressures. They may see themselves as more ''feminine'' and report that others expect them to be receptive even if, in reality, they have more aggressive inclinations. In this sense, their frustrations are similar to those of women who resent being seen as weak and submissive. Some of these men also feel guilty for wanting to violate the expectations of others. When racial stereotyping is a factor in the sexual power game, persistent assertive action is required to counteract the expected roles.

Economics. One of the most common symbols of power is money. It is also one of the most difficult issues for many people to discuss. When there is a large discrepancy between the income of two partners, it is almost certain that this will create a power imbalance. And when economic differences are combined with other differences, the dynamics are even more complex.

When affluence tilts the power scale toward one partner, some other aspect of the relationship—like sex—usually functions as a counterbalance. For instance, the less wealthy partner may withhold sex or a particular sexual activity or, at the other extreme, may demand more than the wealthier partner is able to give. The more affluent partner may feel used or that he/she is buying the affection of the other partner. In either case, conflict and protective muscular tension may result until all the feelings are aired, and a mutually acceptable solution negotiated. Negotiations of this type are unlikely to succeed unless *specific* agreements are reached about money. These might include: who pays or doesn't pay for which things, how decisions are to be made about amounts to be spent and, perhaps, a mechanism of exchange established for non-monetary contributions to the relationship.

Social Skills. When one partner socializes and initiates relationships more easily than the other, this ability can be a symbol of power. The partner who is more shy or socially inept may feel more dependent on the relationship and therefore fearful when conflicts arise.

Our society values extroverted behavior. The introverted person, rather than being encouraged to develop the assets of his/her personality, is devalued. Introverted people often learn to feel that social ease is a sign of basic worth and are likely to think less of themselves. This feeling may be intensified by the fact that the socially confident person will probably have a wider variety of experiences with different people. The introverted partner may admire and fear this broader experience.

Relationships in which there is a wide introvert-extrovert

discrepancy usually don't work very well. It's difficult for the partners to find sufficient common interests. However, a less pronounced difference is quite workable, especially when the more introverted partner is able to (1) accept his/her personality preferences and (2) realize that social ease is not a sign of worth but simply a set of skills, many of which can be learned like any other skill.*

Sexual Confidence. It is not unusual for one partner in a sexual relationship to appear to be more comfortable with sex or particular sexual activities than the other partner. Sometimes, one partner actually *is* more at ease in sexual situations or more versatile or experimental in sexual preferences. In other relationships, one partner merely plays the confident role or is cast in this role by his/her partner. Whether real or contrived, sexual confidence can be a symbol of power in erotic relationships. This is particularly likely among couples who define sexual confidence as the ability to perform certain sexual tasks (such as anal intercourse) on demand.

When sexual confidence does become a symbol of power, the less confident partner may feel tremendous pressure to perform better sexually or face the loss of the more confident partner. This dynamic is sometimes at work when the less confident partner enters sex therapy alone to get "fixed up." Frequently, neither partner is willing to consider the ways in which they *both* are contributing to their problems. If it should happen that the less confident one discovers ways to feel more comfortable—such as learning to be assertive about what he/she wants—the formerly-confident partner may become fearful and seek to restore the old way of relating.

Conflicts of this type can persist for years, gradually destroying sexual enjoyment for both partners. Eventually, sexual interest will probably disappear altogether unless the partners can agree to support each other's confidence.

---

* A variety of groups are currently available for social skills training. Zimbardo's book on shyness (1977) has been helpful to some people. However, shyness, which involves self-doubt and a variety of fears, is not the same thing as introversion—a basic personality orientation. When free of fear, an introverted lifestyle, with a small number of close, highly valued relationships, can be very satisfying.

Once it has been undermined, sexual confidence will probably flourish again only insofar as they remove performance demands from their sexual repertoire.

Self-Esteem. An enduring feeling of respect as well as compassion for oneself is, by far, the most important and versatile source of psychological and interpersonal power. The development of greater self-esteem in one or both partners will almost always help to defuse destructive power struggles—not by removing power dynamics from the relationship, but by making each person more comfortable with power and, therefore, more willing to discuss power explicitly. Especially if both partners are moving toward greater self-esteem, they will naturally be drawn to some form of negotiation whenever power dynamics are working against intimacy. Initially, the urge to negotiate may be felt simply as a desire to talk honestly.

In addition, because self-loving people have greater internal resources available to them, they are less likely to cling doggedly to the empty power symbols and rituals that spring from insecurity. Instead, the self-loving woman or man is better able to tolerate vulnerability—a prerequisite for the deeper forms of intimacy. This is one of the paradoxes of self-esteem: It simultaneously helps to bring a person to terms with both powerfulness and powerlessness.

POWER AND SEXUAL EXCITEMENT

Thus far I have concentrated on how romantic fantasies, sex-role stereotypes and other symbols of power can disrupt or block sexual enjoyment. Particularly when unacknowledged, these power dynamics can, and frequently do, increase vulnerability, anger and muscular tension. Most people who learn to relax the anal muscles yet are unable to receive intercourse, even though they want to, discover that destructive power dynamics in their relationships are largely responsible for their difficulties.

Clearly, however, power dynamics, even the severe power struggles that many people find so antithetical to sexual enjoyment, are not always negative. On the contrary, many men and women of all sexual orientations find that sexual fantasies or behavior based on extreme power discrepancies, especially sex-role stereotypes, actually intensify sexual excitement. Psychologist C. A. Tripp makes a convincing case, based on modern sex research, that some amount of distance or resistance between partners is necessary if sexual interest is to be sustained over time. He suggests that sexual partners often deliberately introduce subtle or not so subtle conflict into their relationship specifically for the purpose of heightening arousal.* In fact, the intensification of sexual excitement may be one of the central functions of polarized sex-role stereotypes.** To the extent that sex roles are polarized, distance between the sexes is assured, which helps generate sexual excitement. Of course, autonomy or independence of individuals in a relationship can fulfill the same function, without the negative consequences of sex-role stereotyping. Any power differences—including those unrelated to sex roles—can heighten the sense of separateness and increase sexual excitement. Many couples, once in bed, are able to put their conflicts aside, and the sex is sensitive, gentle and highly satisfying. Conflict distances them, sexuality bridges the gap.

Some people enjoy introducing conflict based on amplified power roles *directly* into their sexual encounters, either through fantasy or overt roleplaying. Sometimes the roles are based on exaggerated or reversed sex-role stereotypes. For others, especially some gay men, it is not sex roles, but rather images of all male hierarchies or pecking orders that are given erotic significance. A broad range of erotic fantasies and behaviors are all loosely referred to as erotic *sadomasochism* (S & M). The term *sadomasochism*

---

* Tripp's book, *The Homosexual Matrix* (1975) is not just about homosexuality. It presents a general theory of sexual attraction and interaction, with homosexuality as a case in point. I think it is one of the most thought-provoking books ever written about human sexuality.

** Sex roles have other functions as well. For example, pre-defined roles, when accepted by both partners, simplify decision-making and reduce the need for discussion. In addition, strict sex roles have traditionally fostered economic dependence, which tends to maintain relationships even when they have become dysfunctional. Sex roles are also an important tool in maintaining male economic and political superiority.

originally referred to obtaining sexual gratification from inflicting or submitting to pain. However, in most cases, there is little doubt that when pain is involved in sexual roleplaying, which it usually is not, the pain is secondary; power is of primary importance. Therefore, S & M now refers to all erotic behavior and/or fantasy in which the focus is on dominance and submission.

Sadism and masochism are always combined. Some people consciously enjoy both. Others consistently prefer one fantasy or role, with the opposite suppressed, but usually not very far out of consciousness. S & M roleplaying may include slapping, scratching, biting, pinching and, in more extreme instances, flagellation and beating. Pain and pleasure become intertwined or impossible to differentiate.*
Other S & M fantasies or "scenes" (as S & M roleplaying is popularly called) involve no pain whatsoever. These may include one partner tying up or restraining the other, sometimes in conjunction with verbal humiliation or stylized punishment (called bondage and discipline or B & D). Occasionally urine or feces are used in the encounter to augment the feeling of degradation.

Sometimes S & M is a subtle or invisible aspect of a sexual encounter. For others, the less subtle the better. Some people extemporaneously act out elaborate dramas with each other, perhaps playing master-slave, prisoner-guard, teacher-student, policeman-suspect, parent-child and many others. Not surprisingly, the most popular roles reflect actual power-infused relationships in our society.

Another common source of excitement in S & M is the feeling of naughtiness and guilt that goes along with violating society's ideas of love and romantic expression. Most people are taught that sex is a pure and gentle expression of love. S & M celebrates the seamy, primitive, raunchy side of sex. Virtually all S & M enthusiasts occasionally feel at

---

* In S & M roleplaying, even with intense flagellation, physical damage is quite rare. This is because the body adapts to increasingly intense stimulation. When bruises do result it is usually because the dominant partner provides too much stimulation too soon. Experienced "tops" (who don't *really* want to hurt their partners) learn how to increase the stimulation at a gradual pace. This is why S & M enthusiasts are coming to describe their experience as intense sensation rather than pain.

least some ambivalence or guilt about their desires, which others see as sick, sinful, debased and disgusting. Their feelings are fostered by the dominant psychological view that S & M is symptomatic of psychopathology. The conviction of most psychologists is that those who enjoy S & M share a common personality structure, e.g., they're angrier, meaner, more self-hating or in deeper psychic conflict than others. Actually, people who like S & M are as different from one another as they are from those who are turned off by it. Enjoyment of S & M is not the result of psychopathology. It is found among severely disturbed *and* exceptionally well-functioning individuals. Of course, the level of one's psychological health can affect the forms that S & M interests take and the ways in which they are expressed.

The human fascination with dominance and submission is expressed in every aspect of our society: at work, in family relationships, in politics and sport. Freud felt that sex was the central driving force in human personality. Alfred Adler, once Freud's friend and later his theoretical rival, felt that the central force was the search for power — an attempt to counteract the powerlessness inherent in the human condition (Adler, 1964). Freud and Adler were both partially correct. If we set aside, for a moment, the revulsion that erotic S & M sometimes elicits, it is easier to understand how some people find that amplified expressions of power and sex enhance each other.

Among those who enjoy S & M roleplaying, many report benefits in addition to the heightening of sexual arousal. For instance, it can provide a symbolic means of balancing the one-sided demands of sex-role socialization. Some people find that by exaggerating or exchanging sex-role stereotypes in S & M scenes they become more aware of, and are better able to understand the power dynamics in their relationships. There are even some couples who discover that acting out the power dynamics of their relationship in an exaggerated form during sex allows them to discharge the emotions invested in non-erotic conflicts that had previously been unexpressed and destructive.

At the same time, there are a number of potentially negative aspects of S & M activities. The ambivalence that usually accompanies a violation of social mores, in addition to intensifying excitement, can also undermine self-esteem. Consequently, some S & M enthusiasts take unnecessary and unwise risks. For example, some act out scenes without clear agreeements, such as how far they wish to go and how to signal the desire to stop (in S & M "no" usually means "yes," so some other signal is necessary). Occasionally, people allow themselves to be tied up by total strangers and are badly mistreated (S & M attracts more than its share of violent people who enjoy sex even more when it's non-consensual). Similarly, the heavy drug use common with S & M can reduce the awareness necessary for self-protection, and also undermine the immune system. Finally, people who practice S & M on a regular basis occasionally become dependent on intense stimulation and desensitized to milder forms of sexual expression. Most people, however, usually have "ordinary" sex regularly too and therefore do not become dependent.

Problems like this have convinced many people that S & M is inherently "bad" and that all S & M fantasies should be suppressed. However, the self-conscious vigilance necessary to maintain the suppression also inhibits the capacity to abandon oneself to a sexual encounter. Sexual desires are, of course, subject to change. After a period of S & M exploration (through fantasy or behavior), some people find that they lose interest. But suppression never has this result, because the more a desire is suppressed, the more persistent it becomes. A better approach is to allow oneself the freedom to explore, but to do it in a self-loving, safe and comfortable way.

POWER AND ANAL INTERCOURSE

Receiving sexual intercourse is commonly viewed as an act of submission, and it is inevitable that some people *want* to feel dominated when they receive anal intercourse. They are very clear about it. In fact, they can be remarkably aggressive in arranging encounters where this need will be met.

Those who clearly want to feel dominated while receiving anal intercourse usually find anal intercourse quite comfortable. Here, playing a submissive, even a subservient ("slave") role does not result in anal tension. In fact, for some people, the excitement of feeling sexually overpowered is necessary for anal relaxation and pleasure.

A few people who become very tense whenever anal intercourse is attempted express fear of being dominated or "taken over" precisely *because* they are attracted to the idea of being dominated *in fantasy*. Usually they are relieved to discover that it is quite common for people to have fantasies they do not choose to act out. Allowing fantasies free reign without feeling that they *have* to be acted out usually clears the way for more comfortable experimentation with partners.

In some instances, however, the fantasies will eventually be acted out in sexual roleplaying, not because they have to be, but because this is what the person really wants. For this roleplaying to be positive, it is necessary that the person do it only when he/she feels ready to do so. People who wish to include anal intercourse in S & M roleplaying should be certain that their anal muscles are relaxed, especially if rectal stimulation is to be vigorous. Those who enjoy intense, perhaps painful, stimulation during anal intercourse greatly increase the risk of damaging rectal tissues. They must carefully weigh the potential risks against the enjoyment they would receive from anal pain. The most self-affirming approach would be to focus the enjoyment of very intense sensation on other body zones that can more easily be monitored for tissue damage.

Most of my clients either do not want to feel dominated (in fantasy *or* sexual roleplaying) or else have mixed feelings about it. For these people, feelings of submission are *not* conducive to sexual arousal and enjoyment. Some of the men are troubled by their own dominance fantasies when they are "on top" during anal or vaginal intercourse. The thought of having the tables turned, of having their partner feel that way toward *them,* causes an instant protective tensing of the anal muscles. On the other hand, some who feel that their role in life is always to be passive, whether they want to or not, find themselves resenting their partner for being "on top" in yet one more way. These are rarely isolated feelings, but reflect basic dynamics operating throughout a relationship, e.g., feeling like the other person always gets his/her way, or is selfish, demanding, insensitive or inconsiderate. Few people can feel receptive with a partner they view this way.

If you think that your enjoyment of anal intercourse is being blocked or limited by interpersonal power dynamics (or if you would like to find out), you have two general options. First, you may be able to divest anal intercourse of some of its symbolic significance, gradually coming to view it less as exchange of power and more as exchange of pleasure. While most people do seem to move in this direction in the course of anal self- exploration, personal symbols of power are quite persistent and can rarely be abandoned altogether.

The second option is to discuss power and powerlessness openly with your partner, asserting your desire to feel secure and powerful in the relationship, and acknowledging that you won't always get your way.

A combination of the two approaches is usually the most effective. Depending on the degree to which you feel that receiving anal intercourse is a symbol of submission, you may need to take direct steps to change your attitude. It is often best to avoid anal intercourse for a while (by *direct* agreement with your partner, *not* with excuses). Instead, give yourself, and ask your partner to give you, lots of anal pleasure in ways that are less emotionally charged. Continue this until you feel more aware of your anus and rectum as sensual organs, quite apart from any symbolic significance you might have associated with anal intercourse.

At the same time, begin experimenting with more direct communication. You can express your anger if you feel resentful about being ''on the bottom,'' or you fear losing what power you do have. You can agree to confront your partner when you feel like the victim of a manipulative ''power play.'' You may also have to be assertive in demanding your right *not* to be in control all of the time. Discuss the ways you go about making decisions, who seems most often to be in control, how you each go about getting your way and how you tend to respond when you do not get your way (e.g., do you give your partner the ''silent treatment'' or tell him/her directly how angry you are). Let each other know about any old resentments you are saving up, whether or not they seem to be related to sex (e.g., "I've always resented the way you expect me to do the things that *you* feel like doing!"). After airing your feelings, make sure your partner has *heard* what you have said (this does not mean he/she is going to *agree*). Then you might be more open to seeing how you have contributed to your own problem (e.g., "It's true you didn't *ask* me what I wanted, but I didn't *tell* you either").

These discussions will not always be comfortable, especially if conflict makes you uneasy. But if you can learn how to fight fairly with your partner(s), you will be better able to love yourself and thus be more open to intimacy. The ability to fight when you need to is basic to a secure sense of autonomy and power in your relationships. From this position you will probably find it easier to be soft and receptive because doing so will in no way be a threat to your self-esteem. Psychologist George Bach insists, "It is not a person's sweet and loving side that shapes his (her) bond with an intimate; it is the talent for airing aggression that counts most (Bach and Wyden, 1968)." For some people, this insight, and the communication skills necessary to put it into practice, can mean the difference between a guarded, angry body and one that is open to pleasure.

15

THE CONTEXT OF ANAL PLEASURE

Integrating New Information and Experiences

Once you have explored various forms of anal stimulation, discovering those you do and do not like (and the factors that make the difference), you may think that your anal exploration is over. Actually, learning to enjoy your anus and rectum is just the beginning. From now on, what role will anal pleasure play in your life?

To some extent, the answers to this question can unfold only as you live them. Yet, conscious consideration of some of the options can be valuable. It is, then, primarily the *future* of your anal pleasure that is the focus of this chapter.

THE PRIVATE SIDE

Much of this book has been devoted to the development of personal awareness and enjoyment of the anus. Some people, however, once they learn how to share anal pleasure with others, begin neglecting private anal experiences. If you do this, you will be missing out on many pleasures that could be part of your daily experience. But even more is at stake. Ignoring the private side of anal enjoyment can result in a reduction of anal awareness and a recurrence of tension. This is especially true for those with a history of chronic anal tension. Conversely, if you continue regular private anal self-pleasuring and exploration you are far more likely to become increasingly comfortable with anal pleasure as time passes. For this reason, *I strongly suggest that you find ways to continue anal self-exploration quite apart from any anal sensuality you might be sharing with others.*

Regular exercise of your anal and pelvic muscles should be continued in order to maintain their tone, elasticity and sensitivity. Likewise, you will want to continue the maintenance of a diet rich in fiber and the avoidance of straining during bowel movements for the rest of your life.

It is especially valuable to continue regular visual examination of your anus. Minor irritations of anal tissue as well as some potential medical problems can often be detected visually more readily than by any other means. By looking at your anus frequently you will be better able to note any signs of irritation and take appropriate steps to discover and eliminate the irritating factors. This is even more important if your anal muscles tend to get tense when you are under stress. During periods of increased stress, you can allow more time for relaxation, perhaps take long, warm baths and do what you can to reduce emotional pressures. At such times, you may want to avoid anal intercourse, concentrating more on gentle stroking of the anal opening.

FINDING A PHYSICIAN

An important aspect of maintaining anal health is arranging for a rectal medical examination about once a year or any other time when you discover an indication of a potential medical problem. It is not easy to find a competent, nonjudgmental physician with whom you can openly discuss what *you* can do for the restoration and maintenance of anal health as well as which forms of anal pleasure (if any) should be avoided during any necessary treatment. Asking friends about their experiences with particular physicians is a good start. Beyond this, I recommend an assertive approach. When you consult a physician, *ask* about his/her attitudes toward anal pleasure. Don't be intimidated. The doctor may know less about it than you. If he/she will not talk about it or is clearly judgmental, find someone else. Many (but by no means all) doctors will relax their professional aloofness somewhat if you make it clear that you *expect* to be treated like an intelligent person who is capable of understanding your body and actively participating in the prevention and treatment of problems. The best doctors already encourage and support self-care, so you will not have to convince them.

Physicians who specialize in anal/rectal problems are called proctologists. However, many physicians in general practice or with other specialties are quite capable of conducting a basic rectal examination. If a problem is discovered which requires a rectal specialist, he/she can refer you. This will give you a wider choice of physicians, hopefully including one with whom you can feel comfortable. Keep in mind that many gay physicians, or those with many gay male patients, are as experienced with common anal problems as most proctologists. And chances are that such a doctor will be considerably more at ease with the subject of anal pleasure. Most of these physicians will welcome female and straight male patients as well. Physicians like this can be found in most urban areas.

With care and self-awareness, chances are very good that medical problems will never be a part of your anal experience, but it is a good idea to have some information about common problems. With this understanding, you can be aware of what to look for so that you can consult a physician as soon as symptoms appear. At one time, I felt that discussing medical problems might frighten people, perhaps making anal sensuality even more threatening and difficult. However, experience suggests that open discussion of the medical aspects of anal pleasure, rather than threatening most people, actually helps demystify the entire subject and tends to *reduce* fear—especially irrational fear based on ignorance.

For this reason, I have compiled basic information on the most common medical problems affecting the anus and rectum (see Appendix A). I hope you will become familiar enough with this material to discuss anal health intelligently with your physician.

WHO, WHEN AND HOW

When you have become comfortable sharing anal pleasure with partners, you are faced with many new choices. With whom do you feel comfortable including your anus in sensual/sexual activities? What sort of activities do you wish to include or exclude? And how will these choices be affected by the circumstances of each encounter? There is a variety of possibilities. Consider and experiment with as many as you choose.

Almost everyone who follows the approach to mutual exploration outlined in Chapters 12 to 14 decides to continue including anal stimulation in at least some sensual and erotic activities with *intimate partners* (people with whom they feel trust, rapport and the desire to communicate honestly). Even those who are not currently involved with such a partner feel that they, too, will want to experience anal stimulation with intimates in the future.

Casual sexaul encounters are sometimes enjoyed by most of the gay and bisexual men, half of straight men and a few of the women with whom I've worked. In the years since the AIDS crisis began, most people, especially gay men, are having far fewer casual sexual encounters. Those who do have casual sex must decide to what extent—if any—they want anal stimulation to be included in these encounters. Many feel that stimulation of the external anal area by a willing casual partner is usually acceptable and enjoyable for them. However, they tend to be much more cautious about the insertion of a finger or anything else into the rectum by a casual partner. Most feel that this depends on the gentleness they sense in their partner. Some are quite assertive about making sure the partner's fingernails are smooth before allowing insertion, a practice I encourage. Generally, people are more apt to enjoy the insertion of a finger if, at the same time, they are willing and able to say "no" if for any reason they do not desire such stimulation.

Clients who learn to enjoy anal intercourse express a wide variety of feelings about the conditions under which they want to share this activity with a partner. Almost all feel that this could be a comfortable part of their sexual activities with an intimate partner. With a casual partner, on the other hand, most feel that the decision to receive anal intercourse is dependent on the level of trust and rapport, and the willingness of the partner to use a condom. About half consider it unlikely that they could feel sufficiently secure with a casual partner to be comfortable receiving anal intercourse.

The feelings expressed by Don are highly representative of the feelings of both men and women who are reluctant to receive anal intercourse from a casual partner: ''I like sex for fun and I don't always have to *know* the person to enjoy it. Sometimes I don't particularly *want* to get to know the person but it still can be good to have the momentary pleasure with them. When it's over, it's over. But with other people I want it to be the *beginning* of something. For me, sex can either be intimate or not. It all depends on the situation and how we feel about each other. I can enjoy oral sex with just about anybody I'm attracted to—or mutual masturbation. And I always like lots of touching and body contact, even with a relative stranger. But it seems to me there's something much more intimate, really personal about anal fucking. I hardly ever feel comfortable with that when I first meet somebody. I have to trust the person and feel close to him and want to know him and have him know me. At first I thought this was a little weird 'cause there are lots of men who want to get fucked by anybody. But that's not me. I accept that now. I just tell the guy I'm not getting fucked until I get to know him better. I sort of feel the same way about me doing the fucking, but I'm more flexible about that. Anyhow, if somebody can't accept how I feel, well, it's too bad. I no longer think it's my duty to satisfy everyone. I'm also not so afraid of being rejected when I say no.''

Other men and women don't feel the same as Don. Instead, they veiw anal intercourse as being inherently no more or less intimate than any other sexual activity. Naturally, they are more open to including it in casual encounters and seem able to do so in most cases, without difficulty (if they are willing to accept a greater risk of disease, or use a condom).

A few people have mixed feelings about it. On the one hand, they want to be able to enjoy casual anal intercourse, but in actual practice, they don't like it. Followup interviews indicate that most continue to feel some conflict about this even several months later. In general, though, most people become more accepting of their need for trust, even if they hope to be more relaxed about it in the future. Paradoxically, those who become most comfortable about saying "no" discover that their willingness to say "yes" increases simultaneously. Obviously, such people learn to rely more on their needs at the moment and pay less attention to what is expected of them.

For many people, decisions about whether to allow anal play in casual encounters are strongly affected by concerns about sexually transmitted diseases, especially AIDS. Because many sexually transmitted diseases can be spread via anal sex with an infected partner, it is important to become familiar with them as part of your decision-making process (see Appendix A).

As you can see, there is quite a range of potential choices. As you go about discovering which are best for you, you will probably discover that the level of enjoyment you receive has very little to do with which choice you make. A far more important factor is your willingness to be assertive about whatever it is you want (or do not want) to do.

ANAL PLEASURE AND EROTIC PREFERENCE

Just as it is helpful to consider the settings and situations in which anal pleasure is desired, the place of anal pleasure among all other erotic activities is important. Of course, some people feel that they shouldn't have any preferences of their own. Instead, they want to be able to respond to whatever their partner desires (the Nice Person Syndrome again). Yet virtually everyone has definite preferences which, while certainly subject to change, tend to become more clearly defined with experience.

As each kind of anal pleasure becomes enjoyable, it must be integrated into a pre-existing set of preferences. For most people, this happens naturally; but this is not always the case. Any new sexual experience may turn out to be different than expected. For example, some people experience varying degrees of *disappointment* with anal stimulation even when it has become comfortable and quite pleasurable. In spite of frequent discussions about expectations in the course of therapy, some persons do not become fully aware of the impact of their expectations until anal stimulation has become a regular occurrence. Mary expressed her disappointment this way: "I guess I thought that having anal sex would perk up my sex life with Frank. But it hasn't changed anything. I *still* don't like the way he makes love to me." Jeremy voiced a different kind of disappointment: "I was hoping it [anal intercourse] would be the greatest sexual trip ever. I mean, it's okay, but I like oral sex much better—just like always. I don't feel anything like my friend, Rob, who thinks getting fucked is the ultimate."

These disappointments, in some instances, result from subtle vestiges of the anal taboo. Just as taboo images can turn anal sex into a negative "big deal," they can also turn hopes into larger-than-life expectations. Discovering that anal sex is not the solution to a dull sex life or a source of "cosmic" intensity understandably may feel like a loss. A few people actually go through anger, depression, grief and other feelings associated with loss before they are able to feel good about their preferences. In the midst of this process, Andy had this insight: "I think this whole thing [disappointment with anal sex] is one reason why I had so much trouble learning to do it. Somewhere inside, I suppose I knew it wasn't going to be everything I had imagined. I lost my tense ass, but I also lost my fantasy."

Feelings like these, at first glance, seem negative and unfortunate. However, with a little support most people are able to accept them quickly. Soon they are able to allow desired forms of anal pleasure to take their place as additional options for enjoyment. It is uncommon for the ability to enjoy anal sex to change one's preferences very much. Of course, for some people, anal erotic activities quickly become favorites. Others decide that they do not like some or any form of anal stimulation much after all. Still others find themselves somewhere between the two extremes. They are happy to have discovered anal stimulation as one more way to please themselves and enjoy their partners.

A

COMMON MEDICAL PROBLEMS OF THE ANUS AND RECTUM

Although many diseases affect the anus and rectum, only the most common are considered here. Information about AIDS (Acquired Immune Deficiency Syndrome) is also included. Even though it is far less common than any of the other diseases discussed in this appendix, it is spreading at an alarming rate. Moreover, the consequences of AIDS are so potentially devastating that any self-affirming person must be aware of this disease and how it can best be prevented.

None of the information in this appendix is a substitute for regular consultation with a competent and sensitive physician. Nonetheless, basic knowledge about these medical problems can help you decide when to consult a physician and what questions to ask. And perhaps most important of all, adequate information is required for you to develop and follow a preventive or self-healing program.

SEXUALLY TRANSMITTED DISEASES (STD's) INVOLVING THE ANUS AND RECTUM

Never before has it been so important that a sexually active person become conscious of the various sexually transmitted diseases, commonly called STD's. The most well-known STD's — syphilis and gonorrhea — account for only a minority of infections that can be spread by sexual contact. Furthermore, many STD's occur without symptoms, or with symptoms too minor to notice. For this reason, regular STD checkups are strongly recommended for people who have more than one partner, whether or not they are bothered by any symptoms. When getting a checkup, be sure that the doctor takes an anal culture, which he/she will do with a cotton swab. Many doctors still do not want to acknowledge the sexual significance of the anus and rectum and will, therefore, ignore them, unless the patient specifically requests this attention.

Until recently, STD's affecting the anal area were rarely suspected by physicians. As a result, symptoms were often incorrectly interpreted. Sometimes anal STD's were discovered incidentally during treatment for some other condition (Catterall, 1975). Awareness that STD's can and do affect the anus is certainly growing, albeit slowly, among physicians. And so many "new" STD's and combinations of STD's are common now among gay men, especially in big cities, that "gay medicine" has, for all practical purposes, become a specialty.*

Contributing to the increasing incidence of STD's is the persistent feeling that they are more embarrassing than other diseases. It is not unusual for a person to feel so guilty about the possibility of having an STD that he/she avoids seeking treatment or is reluctant to be honest with partners. The morally charged character of STD's is further intensified when the anus is involved, because of the anal taboo.

Many clients report being questioned by physicians about anal sexual activities in an accusatory tone. The belief that STD's, particularly AIDS among gays, are punishment for wrongdoing often influences both doctor and patient — and certainly those close to the patient as well. Consequently, precautions necessary to avoid spreading a disease take on the aura of a moral imperative, rather than common sense or basic adult responsibility. Some people become consciously or unconsciously defiant, ignoring precautions as if doing so were an act of liberation or manly recklessness. Meanwhile, some moralists view the steady increase of STD's as evidence of the righteousness of their restrictive attitudes, and the vicious cycle is perpetuated.

RECTAL GONORRHEA

Rectal gonorrhea is an acute infection of the mucous membranes of the rectum caused by the gonococcus bacteria, the same organism that causes urethral, vaginal and throat gonorrhea. Gonococcal infections in the throat are relatively rare, although they certainly do occur. The other forms of gonorrhea are extremely common, rectal gonorrhea being especially prevalent among gay men. Rectal gonorrhea is communicated only by receiving anal intercourse from a male

*See, for example, *Sexually Transmitted Diseases in Homosexual Men* (Ostrow, et al, 1983).

who has urethral gonorrhea.

At least half of the time, rectal gonorrhea produces no symptoms. When there are symptoms, they may include soreness or burning with bowel movements or perhaps a discharge from the anus. If there are going to be symptoms, they will usually be noticed within three to seven days after exposure.

Diagnosis is made by a bacteriological smear and culture taken from the rectum. A smear can be checked immediately, but positive diagnosis requires a rectal culture. Once diagnosed, all types of gonorrhea are treated with penicillin or another antibiotic. Throat and rectal gonorrhea are usually more resistant to treatment than urethral or vaginal gonorrhea. Consequently, an injection *and* oral medication may be required. All sexual activity involving the anus should be avoided until the infection has been eliminated as determined by a follow-up examination. Recent sexual partners should be notified and treated, if possible.

When rectal gonorrhea goes untreated, as it often does, complications such as a rectal abscess may follow. In the meantime, a male who has anal intercourse with this person stands a good chance of developing urethral gonorrhea. In a few cases, when rectal gonorrhea remains untreated for quite a long time, the bacteria may enter the bloodstream, causing symptoms like fever, chills, rashes and painful joints. The proper use of a condom ("rubber") during intercourse and careful washing before and after can virtually eliminate the spread of rectal and vaginal gonorrhea.

At the time of this writing, word has just arrived from Stanford Medical Center that a possible vaccine against gonorrhea looks very promising in laboratory research. Tests on humans are about to begin. This is very good news indeed.

NONGONOCOCCAL URETHRITIS AND PROCTITIS

Other organisms can produce gonorrhea-like symptoms in the urethra, vagina or rectum. Nongonococcal Urethritis (NGU) is more common in males than gonorrhea (Felman and Nikitas, 1981) and can be transmitted to the vagina or rectum during intercourse. Symptoms are similar to those of gonorrhea, but very frequently there are none at all. Nongonococcal infections are usually caused by chlamydia or T-strain mycoplasma. Chlamydia infections can sometimes make their way up the male urethra, causing infections of the prostate or epididymis (part of the sperm-producing apparatus attached to the testicles). In women, chlamydia infections can cause Pelvic Inflamatory Disease (PID).

Diagnosis is made when the tests for gonorrhea are negative or when the specific causative organism can be identified.

Nongonococcal infections are usually treated with tetracycline or erythromycin because penicillin is not effective against these infections.

SYPHILIS

Syphilis is not nearly as common as gonorrhea or nongonococcal infections. Even so, the number of reported cases increased by about one third during the last few years of the 1970's. And since the early stages of the disease are so easily missed or ignored, there are no doubt many thousands of untreated cases. It is caused by a microscopic organism shaped something like a corkscrew, a spirochete called *T. Pallidum* that can survive only in warm, moist areas of the body. During penis-vagina, oral-genital, or penis-anus sexual contact, the spirochetes pass from an infected person through a partner's mucous membranes or perhaps a skin abrasion, usually somewhere on the genitals, mouth or anus.

From ten to ninety days following exposure, a round, dull red ulcer called a *chancre* appears at the point of contact. The chancre is virtually always painless when it occurs in the genital region, but in and around the anus it is sometimes painful (Gluckman, et al, 1974). This is the *primary stage* of the disease. Since a rectal or vaginal chancre probably won't be visible, a person may not know that he/she has been infected. Whether or not the person is treated, the chancre (there may be more than one) becomes hard around the base, eventually heals and disappears. There may be no more symptoms for awhile, but the infection continues to develop in the body.

Two weeks to six months after the appearance of the primary chancre, the *secondary stage* begins. It can produce a general skin rash that usually does not hurt or itch. In the anal or other moist areas, the rash may develop into moist, red or pink growths that can be quite painful. Syphilis is extremely contagious at this stage. In some cases, there are other secondary symptoms such as fever, swollen glands, headaches, nausea or constipation. Most people are motivated to seek treatment during the secondary stage. Without treatment, however, secondary symptoms will also eventually disappear, beginning the *latent stage* (no symptoms) which may last for many years. The *tertiary stage*, extremely rare in North America, can produce serious complications, even death.

Syphilis is diagnosed by examining fluid or scrapings from a chancre or rash with a special microscope. Several types of blood tests are also used, but they tend not to detect the disease very well early in the primary stage. Treatment is with penicillin or another antibiotic. Follow-up examinations are required to assure a complete cure. During treatment, sexual contact should be avoided and recent partners should be notified and examined whenever possible. Because *T. Pallidum* can enter the body at virtually any point, the use of a condom can only reduce, but not eliminate, the risk of infection. Thorough washing after sex may also reduce the risk somewhat.

HERPES

Herpes is a common STD affecting the genital or anal area. It is caused by the *herpes simplex* virus. There are five different types of herpes viruses. Type 1 usually causes fever blisters or cold sores in the mouth. Normally it is type 2 that affects the anus and genitals. According to the National Centers for Disease Control, cases of genital herpes may have increased as much as nine times from the late sixties until the end of the seventies.

Herpes infections produce painful bumps or blisters within a week after exposure. If the blisters rupture, they can become even more painful. In the anal area, herpes usually causes itching or soreness that may develop into severe pain. Wherever the herpes sores occur, they usually heal themselves in one to three weeks, unless there is a secondary infection.

Once a person is infected with herpes, the virus stays in the body. Nonetheless, the first outbreak of herpes symptoms is often the last. This is especially true with anal herpes, which tends not to recur. Some people, however, experience outbreaks of genital herpes with upsetting regularity. Fortunately, the first herpes episode is usually the most severe, with subsequent outbreaks decreasing in severity and healing more quickly, but this is not always the case. For those with frequent recurrences, the physiological distress may be much worse than the physical symptoms.*

No one knows for sure what causes a herpes outbreak or why some people are troubled by them while others are not. Possible factors that might contribute to a herpes outbreak include: physical trauma at the point of original infection, exposure to ultraviolet light (sunbathing), lowered resistance (which often occurs when a person is fighting another disease), psychological stress, or elevated body temperature (e.g., sitting in a hot tub).

Prior to a herpes flareup, some people experience flu-like symptoms or itching at the point of outbreak. This pre-outbreak period is known as the *herpes prodrome* and it appears that a person is infectious during the prodrome as well as during the outbreak itself. At these times, sexual interaction should be avoided, especially ac-

* A good book for those with recurrent herpes is *Herpes: What to Do When You Have It* (Gillespie, 1982).

tivities that involve the infected area. It is also a good idea not to share toilet articles and/or towels during the infectious period.

Treatments for herpes are currently aimed at reducing the severity, duration and frequency of outbreaks. Acyclovir (Zovirax) in the form of an ointment is now standard treatment for initial herpes outbreaks but does not appear to be nearly as helpful for recurrences. Recent research suggests that acyclovir taken orally greatly reduces the frequency of outbreaks and shortens their duration (Reichman et al, 1984). As we go to press, the Food and Drug Administration has just approved the use of oral acyclovir for the treatment of initial and subsequent herpes outbreaks. The FDA considers it safe for those who suffer very frequent and severe outbreaks to take oral acyclovir on an ongoing basis for up to six months. This approach should be used very cautiously, however, since there is concern about the possible long-term effects of the drug (Whittington, et al, 1984).

ANAL WARTS

Anal warts are caused by a virus which is spread through sexual contact. Warts can also result from non-sexual exposure to the virus. Beginning as tiny, pink swellings, anal warts can spread, sometimes rapidly around the anus and into the anal canal. As they spread, they form clumps that, if on the surface, are readily detectable by sight and touch. Anal warts are not painful unless irritated by friction or if they become the site for a secondary infection, although they may cause some itching. Some people have a few anal warts, even for long periods of time, without any spreading or discomfort. But even these non-troublesome warts should be removed when they are discovered to prevent future spreading or transmission to sexual partners.

Warts are treated in one of three ways: by applying chemicals, usually acids, to each wart or clump of warts; by burning the warts through electrocautery (electric needle); or by freezing the warts with liquid nitrogen (cryotherapy). If discovered early, or if they have not spread too extensively, warts can be treated in the doctor's office. However, if spreading has been extreme, a few days' hospitalization may be necessary so that the warts can be removed all at once under anesthesia. Recovery can be uncomfortable, especially during bowel movements.

Anal warts sometimes recur, even after they appear to have cleared up. For this reason, the anal area should be examined periodically after treatment. Most people — even those with the most persistent warts — eventually establish resistance to the wart virus, but never any too soon.

HEPATITIS

Hepatitis is an inflammation of the liver. Types A and B, the best known, are each caused by a different virus. Non-A, Non-B hepatitis is caused by yet another virus, probably a retrovirus. Delta hepatitis can occur only in those who already have active type B hepatitis. The mononucleosis virus or cytomegalovirus (CMV) may also cause hepatitis. Chemical abuse, alcohol, other street drugs, mushroom poisoning, general anesthesia and syphilis are also possible causes of hepatitis.

All forms of hepatitis have similar symptoms which can be too mild to notice or extremely severe. They may include: loss of energy and/or appetite, depression, body or joint aches, nausea, diarrhea, abdominal pain, rash or itching of the skin, swollen glands, fever, chills, sweats, reduction in tolerance for alcohol, dark urine or clay-colored bowel movements. In more serious cases, there may be jaundice, in which the skin and/or eyes become yellow. Even though there is no medical treatment, the vast majority recover completely with no permanent liver damage. During the course of the disease, it is important to get plenty of rest, have a healthy diet and avoid alcohol or other recreational drugs.

Hepatitis A (formerly called infectious hepatitis) can be transmitted through sexual contact as well as other forms of close contact. Since the hepatitis A virus is shed in stool, fecal-oral contact is the most common mode of transmission. Obviously, a very effective means of making oral contact with infected feces—only a microscopic amount is required — is through oral-anal contact (rimming). Hepatitis A has an incubation period of 15-45 days. Once a person has the disease, he/she may be sick from one to six weeks, remaining infectious until about ten days after symptoms begin.

Hepatitis B (formerly called serum hepatitis) can be much more serious than hepatitis A. When a person is infected, the virus is present in all body fluids, including semen (particularly high concentration of the virus), saliva, vaginal secretions, tears, blood, feces and sweat. It is most commonly transmitted by infected needles (among intravenous drug users) and by taking contaminated semen into the body during oral, vaginal or anal sex. Being exposed to infected semen during anal intercourse is an especially effective mode of sexual transmission because microscopic breaks in rectal tissue offer the virus direct access to the bloodstream (Villarejos, 1974). Since fisting is even more likely than intercourse to cause rectal abrasions, it is also a high-risk activity for contracting hepatitis B, particularly if the fisting is followed by anal intercourse with ejaculation. The incubation period for hepatitis B ranges from 1.5 to 5.5 months. Once the disease is contracted, symptoms usually persist

212

for 5-13 weeks. The person remains infectious throughout this period, sometimes even longer.

Approximately 200,000 new cases of hepatitis B occur each year in the U.S., with about half of these cases never being diagnosed. More cases occur among gay men than any other group. In fact, as many as two thirds of the most sexually active gay men in large urban areas have antibodies to the hepatitis B virus, although the vast majority of them never experience any symptoms.

About 4% of those who actually contract hepatitis B will develop the chronic form of the disease. A person with chronic hepatitis B can be sick for many months. In a small percentage of cases, the disease persists for years, sometimes leading to cirrhosis of the liver, which can be fatal. Those who do develop cirrhosis also face a much higher risk of liver cancer.

Some people become hepatitis B carriers, remaining infectious to others long after their own symptoms have disappeared. By some estimates, there are as many as a million hepatitis B carriers in the U.S. It has also been suggested that about five percent of sexually active gay men may be carriers (D'Eramo, 1983).

Once a person recovers from hepatitis A or B, he/she will develop immunity and won't get that form of the disease again. However, it is still possible to contract whatever forms of hepatitis one has not already had. The good news is that there is now a vaccine available which can provide immunity against hepatitis B for those who have never had the disease. The vaccine is 85-95% effective, is extremely pure (so it won't cause any other disease) and produces very minimal side effects (Szmuness, et al, 1980). *All sexually active gay men should be tested to see if they have ever had hepatitis B and, if not, they should be vaccinated.* Six months later, they should be tested again to be certain that immunity has been established (as indicated by the presence of antibodies in the blood).

INTESTINAL INFECTIONS

A variety of organisms make their home in the gastro-intestinal tract. Most of these are normally present and cause no problems. A few, however, can be quite troublesome should they enter your system. *Amoebas* and *giardia* are parasitic infections caused by protozoa (single-cell animals). *Shigella* and *salmonella* and *campylobacter* are bacterial infections. Technically speaking, these intestinal infections are not diseases of the anus and rectum. The infecting organisms settle higher up in the intestinal tract. However, when someone is infected, the bacteria or the protozoan cysts (eggs) are carried in feces.

Intestinal infections are very widespread in underdeveloped countries where the infecting organisms may contaminate the water supply. It is also possible, though probably rare, for infected food handlers to pass along the disease by contaminating food. In the U.S., however, these intestinal infections are, for all practical purposes, sexually transmitted diseases. Especially in New York, Los Angeles and San Francisco, intestinal infections have become extremely common among gay men. Experts estimate that anywhere from 40% to 80% of sexually active gay men in these cities may have amoeba or giardia parasites, making them by far the most prevalent of the intestinal infections.

Sexual activities provide many opportunities for tiny amounts of contaminated feces to find their way into the mouth of a sexual partner. The most direct transmission route is oral-anal contact (rimming). But oral-genital contact with a penis that has recently had contact with infected feces can have the same effect. There have been some reports of the protozoa surviving outside of the body for many days. Therefore, it is conceivable that sharing sex toys, or even towels, could spread these diseases. It is also possible for protozoa to be passed along by anal lubricants in open containers into which fingers are repeatedly dipped following anal contact. Keep in mind, though, that sexual activities, not contaminated objects, account for virtually all parasite transmission.

About 50% of the time, parasitic infections produce no symptoms at all, or the symptoms may be too mild to notice. Nonetheless, the disease can still be transmitted. When there are symptoms, they range from vague abdominal discomfort or bloating, gas and/or loss of appetite to severe cramping, nausea, intense diarrhea (sometimes containing blood and mucous), fever and chills. Fever and *bloody* diarrhea are more likely to be symptoms of bacterial rather than parasitic infections.

Diagnosis is made by examining stool samples in the laboratory. One sample will reveal the disease only 45-60% of the time. To get the accuracy up to around 90%, three samples, tested several days apart, are normally used. Giardia infections may never show up in stool tests. In spite of the difficulties, accurate identification of the infecting organism is necessary for effective treatment. Medications that work against one organism may be totally or only partially effective against another. Sometimes, inexperienced physicians treat suspected intestinal infections with general antibiotics that only temporarily suppress some of the symptoms, creating an illusion of being cured. Salmonella, for example, usually should not be treated at all, since drugs may actually prolong the infection. Therefore, it is important that diagnosis and treatment be directed by a physician who is very experienced with intestinal infections. Newer medications or combinations of drugs can now be used in some cases with far fewer side effects than older treatments.

It is especially important that parasitc infections be brought under control because these diseases may suppress the immune system. They also can damage the intestines and allow foreign particles to enter the bloodstream (Asher, 1984). There is considerable speculation that parasites might play a role in making a person susceptible to AIDS. Whether or not this turns out to be the case, every gay and bisexual man would be wise to inform himself about intestinal infections and develop sexual behavior patterns that reduce the risk of contracting them. At minimum, rimming should be practiced *very* selectively, following careful washing of the anal area, or else avoided altogether. The "safe sex" practices that I will discuss shortly for the prevention of AIDS will also greatly reduce or eliminate the risk of intestinal infections.

MULTIPLE INTESTINAL INFECTIONS

Sometimes more than one STD can affect a person simultaneously or one right after the other (e.g., one or more intestinal parasites combined with rectal gonorrhea or a herpes infection). Since these combinations are most often seen among gay men with many casual sexual contacts, the term "gay bowel syndrome" has been proposed (Sohn, 1977). However, multiple infections are also seen among heterosexual men and women who have casual sex with many different partners. Obviously, multiple infections can complicate diagnosis and treatment, so physicians need to be alert to this possibility.

AIDS (Acquired Immune Deficiency Syndrome)

AIDS is a disease that suppresses and, in the worst cases, ultimately destroys crucial disease-fighting capabilities of the immune system, leaving its victims vulnerable to a host of common and exotic infections and cancers. The first cases of AIDS in the U.S. were diagnosed in the middle of 1981. However, the disease has been around for much longer than that. For one thing, it can take as long as five years (apparently even longer in a few cases) for the virus to incubate before serious symptoms appear. In Central Africa, where AIDS probably first got its foothold, some cases have been traced as far back as 1975. There are also increasing numbers of cases in Europe.

So far, there are many more cases in the U.S. than anywhere else. More than 14,000 cases have been reported at the time of this writing (October, 1985). And nearly half of them have already died. Although the *rate of increase* in the number of new cases appears to be slowing somewhat, the total number of cases is still doubling approximately every twelve months. Clearly, we are faced with a health crisis of staggering proportions.

Thus far, the disease is primarily confined to members of just a few groups. The vast majority of the cases — approximately 73% — are among gay and bisexual men, especially in large urban areas.*

An additional 17% of the patients are heterosexual intravenous drug users. A significant percentage of the gay and bisexual men, 12% at least, also have histories of intravenous drug use. About 1% of all AIDS patients are hemophiliacs. Another 2% have contracted the disease through blood transfusions. About 6% do not fit into any of these high-risk groups.

It is now certain that the primary cause of AIDS is a virus identified by French investigators at the Pasteur Institute in Paris in May of 1983. A very similar, if not identical, virus was discovered by American researchers at the National Institutes of Health one year later. The French call the virus LAV (Lymphadenopathy Associated Virus) while the Americans call it HTLV-III (Human T-cell Lymphotropic Virus). Another American investigator has named the virus ARV (AIDS Related Virus). For the sake of simplicity, I will refer to LAV/HTLV-III/ARV as the "AIDS virus."

The AIDS virus can be transmitted when blood contaminated with the virus gains direct access to a person's bloodstream. There are several ways that this can occur. When intravenous drug users share needles, they may also be sharing the AIDS virus. Pregnant mothers infected with the AIDS virus — mostly intravenous drug users — may also transmit the virus to their unborn children because the blood supplies of mother and fetus are intricately connected. So far, most of the children with AIDS have contracted the disease this way.

The virus can be carried in blood products. Some hemophiliacs, including a few children, have contracted the disease apparently via the blood clotting protein, Factor VIII, they receive to help control bleeding. Factor VIII concentrate may be prepared from the blood of up to 20,000 donors. Others have been exposed to the virus

---

* Official figures showing extremely high concentrations of AIDS cases in New York, Los Angeles, San Francisco and other urban areas with large gay populations are somewhat misleading. Gay and bisexual men from smaller cities and towns commonly move to these large cities when they are diagnosed with AIDS (or fear that they might have it) because of the vastly superior services available to them. Consequently, they are included in the statistics of the larger cities. This statistical quirk can contribute to a dangerous illusion of safety among those who live in smaller cities. AIDS awareness is equally important no matter where one lives.

through routine blood transfusions involving contaminated blood. Fortunately, blood transfusions will become less and less significant as source of transmission — and eventually disappear — now that an accurate test exists for antibodies to the AIDS virus. Currently, all donated blood is routinely screened. I will discuss this test further shortly.

The vast majority of AIDS patients have been exposed to the virus through sexual contact, especially sexual activities that may produce tiny breaks in the skin, providing a way for the AIDS virus to enter the blood stream. Anal and vaginal intercourse can have this effect. And since a male infected with the AIDS virus is likely to have significant concentrations of the virus in his semen, all sexual activities that involve taking semen into the body are currently considered risky. Other types of sexual behavior (e.g., tongue kissing) may also provide a means of transmission in some instances, but this seems unlikely.

There is no indication that the AIDS virus has ever been transmitted in any way other than through contaminated blood products or intimate sexual contact. The AIDS virus is *not* transmitted by routine forms of contact, such as touching, expressions of affection (including kissing), sharing food or eating utensils, living together, coughing, sneezing, etc. Health workers intimately involved with AIDS patients, even those who have accidentally had contaminated blood splashed in their faces, do not show any signs of exposure to the virus. Discrimination against AIDS patients or those considered at risk for exposure, although widespread and growing, is totally unjustified.

So far at least, gay and bisexual men seem to be particularly at risk for exposure to the AIDS virus. One reason is that gay and bisexual men are more likely than other groups to have had many casual sexual encounters. In fact, the early AIDS cases tended to occur among gay men with hundreds, or even thousands, of sexual partners, especially those who used a lot of recreational drugs and were the most sexually experimental. Most of these men were in the "fast lane," chemically and sexually speaking. When the AIDS virus was first introduced into the U.S., one had to have a lot of contacts in order to be exposed to it. Unfortunately, this is no longer the case. However, the number of different sexual partners one has is still a strong factor increasing the risk of contracting AIDS.

While gay and bisexual men are currently suffering the most from AIDS and the fears associated with it, heterosexuals are by no means immune. In actuality, gays and straights are not distinct groups at all. Many straights have gay sexual contacts and vice versa; experimentation is a hallmark of human sexual behavior. The number of heterosexuals contracting AIDS through sexual contact is still quite small, but these numbers will inevitably grow. After all, heterosexual intercourse appears to be the most common mode of transmission of AIDS in Europe and Africa. So it is crucial that men and women, regardless of their sexual orientation, familiarize themselves with the facts about AIDS, especially how it can be prevented.

All sexually active people have a potential interest in the test that is now available for identifying antibodies to the AIDS virus. The development of this test has made it clear just how rapidly the AIDS virus can be spread. For example, an early study of San Francisco's most sexually active gay men — those who sought treatment at an STD clinic — showed that two-thirds had antibodies to the AIDS virus. A more recent study of a much more representative cross section of San Francisco gays suggests that slightly over a third have the antibodies. A test of frozen blood samples taken from gay men back in 1978 found that only one percent had been exposed. But by 1980, the figure had risen to one quarter.

But what does the presence of antibodies to the AIDS virus mean? Certainly it indicates exposure to the virus, except in those few tests that show ''false positives,'' i.e., the test indicates the presence of the antibodies when they don't actually exist. Beyond this, however, the antibody tests have raised many disturbing questions. How many of those exposed to the virus will actually develop AIDS? No one really knows, but it is virtually certain that the majority will not. Hepatitis-B virus is even more widespread among gay men, but only a small minority actually get sick. Does the presence of antibodies to the AIDS virus indicate immunity to the disease? Perhaps, but not necessarily. These may be ''non-protective'' antibodies, which means that their presence simply indicates exposure, not protection from the disease. Until the meaning of these antibodies becomes much clearer, most physicians are recommending that people *not* get tested. Doing so provides little, if any, useful information at this time — just something else to worry about.

In my work as a psychotherapist, I have come across two types of situations where the AIDS antibody test *can* be of value. Some people are totally obsessed about getting AIDS, even though their sexual behavior suggests that their chances of exposure are very low. A number of these people have decided to be tested, received a negative result (no antibodies were found) and, of course, were tremendously relieved. I have also worked with gay and straight monogamous couples who were restricting their sexual activities because of concern over possible past exposure to the AIDS virus. Some were so concerned that they had lost interest in sex altogether.

Some of these couples decided to take the antibody test and a negative (good news!) result for both of them allowed for greater sexual freedom. Obviously, they trusted that the monogamous agreement would not be broken without prior discussion.

Whenever a person considers being tested for antibodies to the AIDS virus, two points are crucial to consider, regardless of the reason for taking the test. First, the person should imagine his/her reaction if the test were positive (antibodies present). If, for example, such a result would throw the person into chronic, intense anxiety about what might happen in the future, then the test should be avoided. If both partners in a relationship are tested, what if one of them tests positive and the other negative? What effect might this have on the relationship? Such questions, as difficult as they are, must be faced and discussed.

Secondly, any person tested should be certain that the results are absolutely confidential, which is by no means automatically the case! California's testing system is a good model. Blood samples are assigned a number by the person being tested; names are not used. Results, whether positive or negative, are given by a trained counselor who can help the person understand what they do and do not mean. The counselor can also help the person make health-promoting decisions. This system, when properly run, assures confidentiality much better than having the test via private physicians and laboratories. Remember, your medical records are not completely confidential. They are available to others under many different circumstances (e.g., when filing insurance claims, during some legal proceedings).

The more that AIDS is studied, the more complex this disease appears to be. The AIDS virus seems to attack the part of the immune system known as *cellular immunity*. This part of the immune system fights viruses, parasites, suppresses the growth of cancer cells and also protects against yeast, fungal and mycobacterial infections. So these are the kinds of diseases that people start to develop when their immune systems are compromised by the AIDS virus. The virus attacks and kills "helper cells" that activate cellular immunity. When this happens, "suppressor cells" take over. Too many suppressor cells are dangerous because they inhibit the functioning of the immune system.

It is possible — perhaps probable — that to be vulnerable to the AIDS virus, the immune system may have to be suppressed to begin with. Conceivably, some people are more susceptible to the virus because of a genetic predisposition. More likely, repeated exposure to other diseases, especially STD's, weakens immunity so that it cannot fight off the AIDS virus. It is known that most, if not all, popular recreational drugs suppress immunity — at least temporarily. Could frequent and heavy drug use leave a person more vulnerable to the AIDS virus?*

The last two possible co-factors in the development of AIDS — repeated exposure to disease and heavy recreational drug use — have certainly been very common among gay men in general, and especially AIDS patients in particular. I have already noted that the majority of the most sexually active gay men in urban settings exhibit signs of exposure to diseases like hepatitis-B, cytomegalovirus (CMV) and intestinal infections. Virtually all AIDS patients have an active CMV infection. And the vast majority have had hepatitis-B. Does this mean that these infections suppressed the immune system to some extent, or is it just that these other viruses are transmitted the same way as the AIDS virus? All of these diseases no doubt take their toll on the immune system. But is the toll serious enough to make any of them major co-factors for AIDS?

Whatever co-factors turn out to be most significant in the development of AIDS, it is already painfully evident that a significant percentage of those exposed to the AIDS virus (current estimates range from 5% to 20%) will become sick, at least to some degree. These people may experience one or more symptoms including: chronic fatigue, swollen lymph glands, fever, drenching night sweats, recurrent diarrhea not related to parasites, chronic sore throats, and sometimes a lowered sex drive. There may also be bacterial infections, herpes outbreaks, eruptions of shingles or recurrent yeast or fungus infections such as thrush — white spots in the mouth followed by shallow ulcers — caused by the candida fungus.

Symptoms such as these, persisting over time, are diagnosed as *AIDS Related Conditions* (ARC). The relationship between ARC and possible later development of AIDS is not understood very well. Some experts now predict — but no one really knows — that as many as a quarter of those with ARC may eventually develop AIDS. Since most of the symptoms of ARC are also frequently associated with many kinds of common diseases, it is not surprising that many people, especially gay men, often become anxious and/or depressed whenever they get any symptoms at all. As one man put it, "You

---

* Volatile nitrite inhalants—"poppers"—have been the focus of some particularly disturbing research in the last few years. Preliminary, but convincing, evidence, suggests that heavy popper use may indeed increase a person's vulnerability to the AIDS virus (D'Eramo, 1984; Mathur-Wagh, et al, 1984). Popper use may also be associated with the development of Kaposi's Sarcoma among those who do get AIDS (Newel, 1984).

can't even enjoy getting a cold and missing work any more!''

What stands out most about the symptoms of ARC is their persistence. It is not unusual for someone with ARC to be sick with one thing after another, or to feel generally under-the-weather for six months to a year — or even longer. The only positive thing about it is that most appear eventually to recover. Recovery seems to be especially likely for those who immediately begin a health-promoting campaign which includes: abstinence from all but the very safest forms of partner sex (some choose total abstinence for a while), a healthy diet free of drugs, plenty of rest and reduction of emotional and physical stress in every way possible. In addition, many find it extremely beneficial to enter psychotherapy to explore their deepest feelings toward themselves and their attitudes toward life and death.

The diagnosis of AIDS is made when a person not only shows signs of suppressed immunity, but also develops one of the primary *opportunistic infections* or malignancies associated with AIDS. The most common AIDS diseases are *pneumocystis carinii pneumonia* (PCP) and *Kaposi's Sarcoma* (KS). Both of these diseases are very rare in the general population and occur only when a person's immune system has essentially collapsed. In fact, it appears that once a person succumbs to one of these infections, he/she will probably die from some future infection, within a few years. Treatments for each opportunistic infection are becoming increasingly effective, especially if diagnosed early. But until and unless a cure is found for the underlying immune deficiency, it is only a matter of time until the next infection hits.

PCP is a protozoan infection of the lungs. It produces few symptoms. And symptoms that do occur — shortness of breath, fever and chronic dry cough — are common with other, much less serious diseases. Diagnosis is made with an X-ray and lung biopsy. It used to be that 50-60% of AIDS patients died from their first PCP infection. More effective treatments and early diagnosis now mean that about 70-75% survive their first infection. Usually, long-term preventive medication is continued even after an apparent recovery — just in case a remnant of the disease remains.

KS is a rare form of skin cancer that can occur anywhere on the surface of the body as well as on internal organs. This disease appears to be virtually always associated with a persistent CMV infection. KS lesions begin as pink or red spots on the skin. The spot usually starts out flat but after a few days, it rises slightly above the level of the skin. As the lesion develops, it not only gets larger, but it turns purple and eventually becomes purplish-black. The lesions may look like bruises, but they are not painful. Although KS lesions sometimes cluster in the same area, they are not tumors that spread like some other cancers. Instead, the lesions can occur in many places simultaneously. Therefore, removing one KS lesion is of no value in preventing others. The lesions may fade slightly, but they don't go away. These days, 75% of KS patients respond, at least somewhat, to treatment and 25% have total remission. When a person dies from KS, it is because the lesions have occurred on vital organs like the lungs, liver, etc. For those who may know someone with KS, it is important to realize that there is no evidence that KS lesions are contagious.

People with AIDS are also susceptible to many other diseases, some of which are life-threatening. Included are many viral infections, parasitic infections besides PCP, TB-like bacterial infections and lymphomas. At the time of this writing, the effects of the AIDS virus on the central nervous system — including the brain — are receiving particular attention. Impairment of neurological functioning now appears common among AIDS patients.

At this point, nothing can be done to restore basic immune functioning in a person with AIDS. At this writing, however, a number of immune-boosting and anti-viral agents are being tested. A few of these show some promise. As the slow process of testing these drugs unfolds, it may turn out that one or a combination of drugs will be able to prevent the development of AIDS when given to people with ARC. For now, we can only hope — and make certain that we take advantage of every possible resource available to us.

COPING WITH THE AIDS CRISIS

The devastating diseases that will afflict and eventually kill those whose immune systems have collapsed are, of course, the most dramatic and frightening manifestations of AIDS. However, tens of thousands of other people who will never get AIDS are nonetheless affected by this health crisis. Fear of being exposed to AIDS can, for some, be debilitating, making it impossible for them to enjoy sex without a cloud of worry disrupting their pleasure. Consequently, "AIDS anxiety" has now taken its place alongside "performance anxiety" as a significant factor contributing to sexual problems.

Gay men — especially those with a history of multiple sexual contacts — face special worries. Might they have been exposed to the AIDS virus in the past and be incubating it now? As you might imagine, questions like this have become the major source of panic attacks among gay men. Some are so overcome with fear that they can hardly carry out their day-to-day responsibilities. And as awareness of AIDS cases increases among heterosexuals, the same kinds of fears that afflict gay men will spread at a much more alarming rate than the disease itself.

Not-yet-gay men who are in the process of coming to terms with their sexuality now face a difficult complication. AIDS can easily become the focal point for a whole range of fears about being gay. For example, those who must deal with strong religious prohibitions may be tempted to adopt the all-too-common view that AIDS is punishment from God. There are no doubt thousands of gays who will simply suppress their sexual urges much longer than they would have only a few years ago.

Coping with all of this is difficult at best. But there are many things to do that can be very helpful. Some suggestions:

Stay informed. Information usually reduces fear, even if that information is incomplete. And now that AIDS research is progressing at a rapid pace (after a slow start), new discoveries are being reported all the time. It is almost certain that some of the information presented here will be outdated by the time you read it. Find a source of information that you trust. In general, the gay press has done a good job of reporting research findings to its readers. To my knowledge, the best source of accurate, clearly-presented information about AIDS is *The New York Native,* * a bi-weekly newsmagazine oriented toward gay readers.

Those who have become obsessed with AIDS may not be calmed by information. Instead, their concentration on media stories about AIDS only serves to heighten their preoccupation and fear. People like this often do better when they avoid reading anything about AIDS, perhaps asking an informed friend occasionally to report significant information to them.

Develop clear guidelines for AIDS risk reduction. How will you reduce your chances of being exposed to the AIDS virus? Although you may prefer not to think about it, it is wise to develop a clear policy for yourself. The guidelines you choose must make sense to you, otherwise you are unlikely to follow them — especially in the heat of passion. Decide what sexual behaviors you will and will not engage in and with whom — and then stick to your decision, no matter how persistently a partner may attempt to change your mind. You may also need to avoid certain situations and circumstances that might undermine your decisions (e.g., going to sex clubs and baths, having sex when intoxicated).

It is best to agree on safe sex guidelines with a new partner *before* having sex. The purpose of a safe-sex policy is not just to restrict

---

* *The New York Native,* 249 West Broadway, New York, NY 10013.

your behavior (although that may be necessary), but also to allow you to let yourself fully enjoy the things you choose to do, without having to worry about it. In this sense, a safe sex policy can be a source of freedom.

At the time of this writing, most of the organizations dedicated to AIDS prevention suggest similar guidelines. Currently, sexual behaviors are placed in categories, according to the degree of risk. Three categories are most commonly used. Subsequent research discoveries may make some changes necessary.

Safe Sex. Sexual activities that involve only skin-to-skin contact, without the exchange of any body fluids, make it virtually impossible for the AIDS virus to be transmitted. These activities include: hugging, cuddling, stroking, massaging (including gentle massage in and around the anal opening), rubbing, wrestling, masturbating yourself and/or your partner, mutual masturbation, dry kissing (lips only) and tongue kissing anywhere on the body except the mouth, genitals and anus. These activities can be enjoyed without concern about being exposed. AIDS transmission with these activities is only possible if there are breaks in the skin at points where contact might occur with body fluids.

Probably Low Risk Sexual Activities. This category of sexual behavior is the focus of some controversy because of conflicts between what might happen (theoretically possible) and what appears to occur in actual practice. Which body fluids contain the AIDS virus in sufficient concentrations to allow for transmission? Can the AIDS virus enter a person's body through mucous membranes or must there be direct access to the bloodstream? There are no definitive answers as yet. However, it now appears that the AIDS virus probably *does* have to gain direct access to the blood in order to cause infection. Currently, sexual activities are considered to be relatively low risk when only saliva is exchanged or when there is only a slight chance of exchanging very small amounts of semen, blood or feces. Possible risk increases with the number of different partners one has.

Anal or vaginal intercourse practiced with a condom are probably low risk activities unless the condom breaks allowing ejaculation into the vagina or rectum.

Fellatio (mouth-penis contact) is probably safe as long as ejaculation does not occur in the mouth. The person receiving fellatio should let his partner know before he is about to ejaculate; manual stimulation can then be used. There is a concern over pre-ejaculatory fluid whch might contain the AIDS virus in an infected person, but the risk of exposure this way is probably low. The same is probably true for cunnilingus (oral-vaginal stimulation). Oral-vaginal contact during menstruation may increase the risk somewhat.

French (tongue) kissing is a subject of particular controversy. Among those infected with the AIDS virus, the virus may be present in saliva, although in much lower concentrations than in semen or blood. Still, it is conceivable that exposure could occur through tongue kissing. However, if AIDS were transmitted this way, there would clearly be many, many more cases than there are. For this reason, most researchers currently consider tongue kissing to be probably safe. However, tongue kissing should be avoided if either partner has bleeding gums or any open sores in the mouth or on the lips, since these could allow direct access to the bloodstream for any virus that might be in the saliva.

These activities, although probably safe, are still in the "gray zone" because there are many unanswered questions. Scientists discuss probabilities; regular people want definite answers. It is here that an individual's own judgment must be exercised. Life is filled with a never-ending array of risks and dangers. And some people are naturally more cautious than others. If a particular activity produces fear, then it will be difficult to enjoy — even if other people think that activity is completely safe.

High Risk Sexual Activities. Sexual behaviors with the highest risk of AIDS exposure involve the exchange of semen, blood or feces. These activities include all forms of intercourse, anal or vaginal, giving or receiving, when practiced without a condom.

When receiving intercourse, microscopic breaks in rectal or vaginal tissue can create a point of entry into the bloodstream if the AIDS virus is present in the semen of the insertor. This appears to be more likely during anal intercourse, probably because there is usually more friction than there is with vaginal intercourse due to muscular contractions and/or lack of lubrication.

There is also a risk of exposure for insertive partners during anal or vaginal intercourse. This risk is probably less than for the receiver, since the insertor is not exposed to semen. However, the mucous membranes around the urinary opening of the penis may be exposed to small amounts of blood during either anal or vaginal intercourse, and to feces during anal intercourse, or vaginal secretions during vaginal intercourse. Very vigorous intercourse can cause tiny breaks in the surface of the penis, allowing another conceivable route for exposure. Since insertors are regularly exposed to other STD's during intercourse, the chance that AIDS may be transmitted this way as well must be taken seriously.

A similar potential for exposure to semen, blood and feces exists with "fisting," since the chance of breaks in rectal tissue is particularly high during this activity. This risk can be reduced by using a glove during fisting and not allowing semen to be introduced into the rectum.

Oral-anal contact (rimming) involves the possible exchange of saliva, feces and blood. Therefore, it is considered a high-risk activity. Rimming is clearly responsible for a great many (perhaps most) cases of intestinal infections and hepatitis A, both of which take their toll on the immune system. Rimming should be practiced *very* selectively, if at all, and only after thorough washing of the anal area.

It is clear that most people, especially gay and bisexual men, are making significant changes in their sexual behavior. Spared from this challenge are those in monogamous, long-term relationships as well as more recent monogamous partners who both test negative on the AIDS antibody test. Those who must change are often unprepared for the process of sexual transition. What if you decide to give up or restrict a favorite sexual activity? Understandably, you may experience a sexual "limbo state" in which all of the fun seems to have gone out of sex. The feeling of loss (and anger) may be intense for a while and new patterns have not yet emerged to take the place of the old. When this occurs, it can be tempting to abandon the change process and cling to familiar behavior patterns, perhaps denying — or trying not to think about — the risks. Understand that sexual change takes time. Gradually, you will discover the potential excitement in low-risk sex, even if you thought you never could.

Begin or Expand Your Health-Promoting Campaign. The above guidelines may create the false impression that getting AIDS is simply a matter of being unlucky or careless enough to become exposed to the AIDS virus. Avoiding exposure is, of course, the goal of safe sex guidelines. But the AIDS mystery is much more complex. Safe sex practices reduce the risk of exposure to *all* STD's, some of which may turn out to be implicated in making the body more susceptible to AIDS. Exposure to the AIDs virus is not a death sentence — far from it. Most people who are exposed never become seriously ill. Their bodies appear to be able to fight off the disease.

It is very important that you do everything you can to maximize your overall health and, therefore, your capacity to fight disease. Give more attention than ever to your diet. Make sure you are getting adequate sleep. Consider ways of reducing all forms of stress. Find at least one form of relaxation that you enjoy and practice it every day.

Take an honest look at your patterns of use for all drugs (including alcohol, caffeine and tobacco). Consider conducting this test: stop using all recreational drugs for two months. If you cannot do this, or if you experience strong discomfort, this is a sign of dependence, or perhaps addiction. Seek professional help if this is your experience. People who use recreational drugs in a healthy way often structure such periods of abstinence on a regular basis as a means of avoiding dependency. Be aware that an inevitable aspect of strong dependence or addiction is *denial* — the refusal to acknowledge how intensely one is attached to a drug. Therefore, facing the truth about your own drug use can be an extremely difficult challenge. Be fiercely honest with yourself. And ask one or more close friends to express what they have observed about you (the unedited version). This can be difficult to hear, but it's worth it!

Think about your psychological health. How much time do you spend in a state of alarm: worried, anxious or angry? When your physical defenses are chronically ''revved up,'' this can suppress your body's ability to fight off disease.

Most important, how do you *really* feel about yourself? Anyone can have self-esteem problems. But gay men in particular experience more than their share of self-hate. For some, the AIDS crisis intensifies their negative feelings toward themselves. Some harbor a secret, deep-seated belief — never expressed and rarely thought — that they share with the most avid homosexual-haters: the belief that they somehow *deserve* to get AIDS. It is a good time to explore these questions, perhaps with a close friend. Or you might schedule a meeting with a supportive psychotherapist.

If you decide to make any health-promoting changes in your life, be patient with yourself. Over-zealous attempts to change too much, too quickly can cause more stress. If you hope to make several different changes, select just one to start with — perhaps the easiest one. This approach will increase your chances of success which, in turn, will bolster your confidence that you can make self-affirming changes.

OTHER DISEASES OF
THE ANUS AND RECTUM

A variety of diseases which are usually not related to anal sexual activities affect the anus and rectum. Although some physicians believe that these diseases are more frequent among people who participate in anal sex (especially intercourse), there is no hard evidence that it is true. It is no doubt true that reckless anal stimulation, like any other bodily mistreatment, can result in medical problems. In fact, everyone I have talked to with anal medical problems related to or aggravated by anal intercourse, had simply ignored the pain warning him/her to stop. Sensitive, gentle anal stimulation, without pain, can actually contribute to anal health by promoting relaxation, muscle control and awareness.

The medical problems discussed here commonly affect the anus. A self-aware person should have a basic knowledge of them so that treatment can be sought as quickly as possible should any symptoms be noticed.

CONSTIPATION

Constipation refers to difficulty in having bowel movements or an inability to have them regularly. Two primary factors contribute to constipation: improper diet and chronic anal, rectal and intestinal muscle tension. Without adequate fiber in the diet, which adds bulk and moisture to feces, stools are likely to be small and hard. These tiny stools are unable to create the pressure necessary to trigger the ''rectal reflex'' (relaxation of the internal anal sphincter). Secondly, chronic muscular tension can inhibit the natural muscle waves (peristalsis) which move fecal material through the digestive system.

An indication of the large number of people affected by constipation is the steady stream of advertisements for laxatives. Ironically, the regular use of laxatives is itself a major factor contributing to constipation (Darlington, 1973). Many people become dependent on laxatives and, as a result, are even less aware of the body's natural urges and functions. Stimulant laxatives (such as Ex-Lax) actually cause the muscles of the colon to contract, intensifying the basic cause of constipation (i.e., muscular tension) even further (Plaut, 1982).

The only real cure for constipation is a diet rich in fiber and a reduction of excess muscular tension throughout the whole body, especially in the digestive system. Regular exercise is also important because it improves circulation, muscular tone and elasticity, and helps to discharge emotional stress.

HEMORRHOIDS

Hemorrhoids are one of the most common persistent medical problems in all Western industrialized societies. Hemorrhoids are a disease of the anal cushions which run the length of the short anal canal (see Chapter 7). Again, chronic muscular tension is the culprit. With hemorrhoids, the central focus of tension is the internal anal sphincter. Tension here keeps the anal cushions engorged with blood and the anal opening closed much more tightly than is necessary or desirable. Consequently, bowel movements must be forced over the anal cushions. In time, the connective tissue which anchors the cushions begins to break down. The cushions become distended. Sometimes hemorrhoids are too small to notice although they often cause itching and irritation. Other hemorrhoids protrude beyond the anal opening and must be gently pushed back inside the anus after bowel movements. When hemorrhoids are this severe, they may bleed and are usually very painful.

The relationship between hemorrhoids and excess tension has been noted since the 1940's (Turell, 1949). More recently, studies of non-industrialized societies have shown that hemorrhoids are extremely rare (Hyams, 1970). No doubt, both increased emotional stress and reduced physical exercise are factors in this discrepancy. However, the most important factor appears to be the level of fiber in the diet. The more affluent we become, the more refined foods we eat. Highly refined foods provide little or no bulk so that straining is required to initiate bowel movements. The more straining, the better the chance of developing hemorrhoids. From this perspective, it is clear why constipation and hemorrhoids so often occur together. They are part of the same problem.

The marketing of preparations for hemorrhoids is a multi-million dollar industry. In spite of advertising claims, these preparations have been shown to be of no value in the treatment of hemorrhoids (Grosicki and Knoll, 1973). Swelling is not reduced by these preparations and the greasiness of the products makes anal cleansing more difficult, often resulting in increased irritation.

There are several treatments for hemorrhoids. In many cases, frequent warm baths (especially after bowel movements) and an improvement in diet and toilet habits are sufficient. In more severe cases, the hemorrhoids may be injected with a vegetable oil solution. As the body absorbs the oil, the hemorrhoids usually shrink. If neither of these techniques work, more drastic action is required. Traditionally, surgical excision (hemorrhoidectomy) has been used. This always requires hospitalization. Recovery is a painful, drawn-out affair. In my view, hemorrhoidectomies should virtually never be performed. In severe cases, the trend in treatment is to use cryotherapy, which involves freezing the hemorrhoids with liquid nitrogen. It is far less expensive (it is usually done in the doctor's office) and less painful than traditional surgery. Many physicians are still not familiar with cryotherapy procedures, so patients may have to do a little ''shopping around.''*

* For more information about hemorrhoids and cryotherapy read Robert Holt's *Hemorrhoids: a cure and preventive* (1977).

The movement of stool over constricted, engorged anal cushions leads to the development of hemorrhoids. The forcing of an object (or a penis) into a constricted anal canal can have the same destructive effect. This is one reason to avoid ever using force during anal sexual activity. However, when rectal entry is accomplished through *relaxation*, the results are beneficial, even for the hemorrhoid sufferer. Among my clients, learning to relax the anal muscles, in conjunction with improved diet, always results in an improvement of hemorrhoid conditions, and often the elimination of hemorrhoids altogether.

BLOOD CLOTS

The passage of hard stools through a constricted anal canal can cause tiny blood vessels to rupture forming a clot inside a hemorrhoid or in surrounding tissues. The clot may be very painful and sometimes reaches the size of a grape. Blood clots are often mistaken for hemorrhoids. They are not the same as hemorrhoids, though they are often a complication of hemorrhoids and are caused by the same factors.

Blood clots usually dissolve on their own in one or two weeks. This fact is exploited by the advertisers of hemorrhoid preparations. The blood clot sufferer thinks he/she is having a ''hemorrhoid attack,'' buys the product and applies it. Soon the clot shrinks and disappears. He/she then feels the product has been effective. However, this has nothing to do with the use of the preparation, since the clot would have gone away by itself. Occasionally, a persistent blood clot needs to be removed by a physician, a simple procedure.

FISSURES

A fissure is a scrape or tear in the anal canal which does not heal. This tear usually results in burning or pain and may bleed. Fissures, like many other anal problems, are often caused by straining to pass hard stools through a constricted anal opening. In some cases, fissures are caused by rough anal sexual activities, but usually only when pain warnings are ignored.

Treatment for fissures includes a bland, non-irritating diet, the use of stool softeners and warm baths several times daily. Fissures which do not heal readily are sometimes cauterized chemically or with an electric needle to stimulate healing. Medicated ointments are sometimes applied. In some cases, underlying conditions (such as intestinal parasites or rectal gonorrhea) prevent a fissure from healing.

FISTULA

A fistula is a tiny passageway which leads away from an abscess in the deeper rectal tissues. This passageway opens into the rectum near the anus. Occasionally, the passageway also leads into the urethra or vagina. Fistulas often go unnoticed unless drainage is detected or unless drainage is blocked, producing pain. Treatment of the fistula involves looking for and treating problems which may be preventing healing, the application of antiseptic solutions, and the use of stool softeners. Warm baths can ease discomfort and speed healing. If the fistula still does not heal, surgery may be necessary.

PAPILLITIS AND CRYPTITIS

The tissue of the lower rectum near the internal anal sphincter naturally has protrusions called *papillae* and depressions called *crypts*. Papillitis and cryptitis refer to inflammation of the papillae and crypts respectively. They may be accompanied by mild or sharp pain. Treatment usually includes the application of medicated ointments. Warm baths help to relieve the discomfort, reduce tension and improve circulation. In severe cases of hypertrophied (enlarged) papillae, the papillae may be removed by electrocautery or surgery. Enlarged papillae are often mistaken for hemorrhoids.

GUIDELINES FOR SELF-HEALING

When the anal-rectal tissues become irritated, or if you should ever develop an anal medical problem, there are steps you can take to soothe the discomfort and increase your body's capacity for healing itself. Usually, minor irritations will disappear within a few days. If not, consult a physician and ask him/her to discuss the examination in detail with you. Inform your doctor that you plan to participate actively in the treatment. Ask for suggestions and comments on the things you're already doing or plan to do. If he/she discourages self-healing, it would be in your interest to find a more supportive physician.

If you are told that you need anal-rectal surgery, it is wise to seek a second opinion. A great deal of needless anal surgery is regularly performed, resulting in trauma to the anal area as well as the psyche. If you become convinced that you do require anal surgery, discuss with your doctor how long you can reasonably postpone it in order to allow your self-healing program to do what it can. In many instances, focused attention and deep relaxation in the anal area can improve anal medical problems sufficiently to eliminate the need for surgery. This is particularly likely with the anal problems which are clearly tension-related (such as hemorrhoids).

If and when you actually have anal surgery, follow the outline below before and after surgery. Your recovery will be faster if you actively mobilize your body's healing resources. In addition, focusing on anal relaxation following surgery can help to counteract the tendency of the anal muscles to go into spasm, sometimes for a long time or even permanently, as a response to the trauma of surgery.

At the first sensation or appearance of anal irritation or pain, initiate the following self-healing program and continue it until all discomfort disappears:

1. Examine your anus visually and, unless it is too tender to touch, *gently* explore your anal opening with your fingers. Is the discomfort focused at a particular spot (if so, where does it hurt?) or is the entire area uncomfortable? Examine your anal area visually and tactilly at least once a day until you feel better (see Chapter 4).

2. Suspend all anal sexual activity until your anus feels completely comfortable. There are two possible exceptions to this suggestion: (a) gentle stroking around the anal opening by yourself or a partner might feel soothing. But ask your partner *not* to insert his/her finger, or anything else, into your anus. (b) gentle insertion of your own finger into your anus may help you relax, as long as there is no discomfort. Use a water-soluble lubricant because greasy or oily lubricants may increase the irritation.

3. Increase the number and duration of warm baths, especially after bowel movements. The warm water contributes to muscular relaxation, increases blood flow and removes irritants from the area. Gentle stroking of the anus during baths is also recommended.

4. Pay special attention to your diet and "toilet habits" to make sure they are as healthy as you can make them (see Chapter 7). Remove items from your diet which you have found to be anal irritants. Since the digestive system responds to various foods differently from person to person, past experience is the best guide. However, common anal irritants include: (a) nuts and other foods which may not digest completely, leaving

rough edges to irritate anal tissue during bowel movements; (b) spices which irritate mucous membranes in the mouth (they probably have the same effect on the anus and rectum); (c) any foods or liquids (alcohol, for example) which you suspect are associated with constipation or diarrhea.

5. Set aside at least two fifteen-minute periods each day (preferably three or four such periods) to practice deep, slow breathing combined with any other relaxation technique(s) you have found useful in the past, such as meditation or progressive relaxation. If you have never tried any relaxation techniques, now is a good time to begin. During deep breathing and warm baths, visualize your anal muscles relaxing, pain and irritation receding and the anal tissues becoming warm and healthy (see Chapter 6).

B

RESEARCH PROCESS AND FINDINGS

This appendix will provide researchers, clinicians and interested lay readers with detailed information about the research process of which this book is a result.

The purpose of the research was to evaluate the effectiveness of the short-term therapy process that I had developed for reducing anal spasm and enhancing the capacity for anal pleasure. While reports of participants in an earlier pilot study had been highly encouraging, there was a need to examine the effects of therapy on a larger and more varied population. I felt that it was especially important for women to be involved because they had not been a part of the pilot study.

I expected that *short-term therapeutic intervention (eight weeks) would effectively reduce anal spasm and enchance the capacity for anal pleasure* with an overall effectiveness in the range of 70-90%.

In addition, I wanted to look for any measurable variables that might have significantly influenced the impact of therapy. It was my hope that an awareness of such variables would maximize the effectiveness of therapy. At the least, a clearer understanding of variables that tend to block progress in therapy could help future clients avoid unnecessary discouragement during the course of therapy.

Preliminary observation during the pilot study suggested three specific variables that appeared to affect the course of therapy. First, both observation and common sense supported the expectation that a *general* pattern of anal tension would be more resistant to change than a *situational* pattern. When anal spasm occurs only in certain situations, it seems reasonable to expect that removing or reducing the anxiety associated with those situations will allow the anal muscles to return to their normal "baseline" state of tonicity. On the other hand, with anal muscles that are always or almost always tense, there is no baseline state of relaxed tonicity to which the muscles may return. Consequently, I expected that *reserach participants manifesting general anal tension would respond to therapy more slowly and with less overall success than participants manifesting situational anal tension.*

The pilot study also suggested that a person's motivation for entering therapy was a crucial variable influencing the effectiveness of therapy. Some research participants sought therapy for anal spasm not because of their own hope of enjoying anal stimulation, but because of pressure from their sexual partners. Such people frequently resisted change by not doing "homework," missing sessions or dropping out of therapy altogether. Those who stayed in therapy seemed emotionally less involved or even bored. Therefore, I expected that *therapy would be significantly more effective with participants who were primarily motivated by their own desire for pleasure rather than by a desire to meet the demands of others.*

Finally, there was some indication during the pilot study that participants who were involved in ongoing sexual relationships would progress through therapy more easily. Presumably, such a relationship could provide support for anal exploration. In addition, an ongoing sexual partner would be available on a regular basis for homework assignments which required the participation of another person. It is also possible that people in ongoing relationships are more likely to be comfortable relating intimately to others. Therefore, I expected that *participants involved in ongoing sexual relationships would respond to therapy more quickly and with more overall success than participants who were not involved in such partnerships.*

Although a variety of more subtle factors appeared to affect the course of therapy, no other measurable variables appeared, in the pilot study, consistently to influence the outcome of therapy. I decided, however, to collect data that would allow me to look for relationships among therapeutic effectiveness and the variables of sex, age, sexual orientation, race, onset and duration of concerns about anal spasm, and sexual relationship patterns. In addition, I hoped to make a variety of clinical observations about the nature of anal tension, relaxation and pleasure.

RESEARCH DESIGN
PARTICIPANTS

Over a two-year period, 164 people participated in my research. Twenty-one of these people did not complete the therapy process. I consider this "drop-out rate" (13%) to be somewhat low given the highly charged nature of anal exploration. It is interesting to note, however, that over 20% of the men and women who expressed interest in therapy dropped out, as it were, before they even started. While many reasons were given, it is reasonable to assume that most became too threatened as the start of therapy approached. In no case did a man or woman report that his/her concerns about anal spasm had disappeared. Some people did eventually enter therapy several months, and even as much as two years, later.

Of those who dropped out of therapy, 16 were men and five were women, which is close to the same ratio of men and women who completed therapy. Of the 21, five left therapy without notice or comment. The remaining 16 offered the following reasons for stopping:

Therapy too threatening — 4
Moved out of town — 3
Serious anal medical problems discovered — 3
Financial constraints — 2
Conflicts with other group members — 2
Depressed over breakup of relationship — 1
Thought the group was "stupid" —1

One hundred forty-three people completed therapy. One hundred fourteen were men, ranging in age from 21 to 62, with a median age of 30. Twenty-nine of the participants were women, ranging in age from 25 to 44, with a median of 32.

The fact that the study involved so many fewer women than men raises some important questions. Why was there such a discrepancy? First, because of frequent presentations about my work to gay male groups, there was more awareness of my work among gay men. Second, gay men as a group seem to be more open to anal sexuality; they hear about it more often from friends and acquaintances, perhaps see anal sexual activity in bath houses, read about it in gay publications, etc. Overall, anal intercourse is more likely to be viewed as a primary sexual activity in the gay community. Reports from women participants suggest that they are far less likely to discuss anal sensuality/sexuality with friends than are gay men. Finally, it seems likely that some women are reluctant to consult a male therapist, understandably fearing male bias.

Does the smaller number of women limit the usefulness of this research for women? Perhaps, in some ways, it does. However, the therapy process is, by design, open-ended, emphasizing personal preferences and values and de-emphasizing notions about what clients "should" do or feel. In addition, to help neutralize any male bias, I stressed the importance of women participants talking with other women as an integral part of their anal exploration process.

Because the research sample was self-selected, the participants, although they probably share a great deal with all people troubled by anal spasm, should only be considered representative of those who (1) have been unable to solve problems of anal spasm on their own and (2) are inclined to seek professional help for such concerns.

Of the 143 participants, 62 responded to workshop announcements that appeared in a San Francisco-based "open university" catalogue directed toward gay men and lesbians. Another 43 were referred by medical and mental health professionals who were aware of my work. Eighteen had heard me lecture on the subject of "Anal Awareness and Relaxation." The remaining 20 were friends or acquaintances of men and women who had previously participated in therapy.

DATA GATHERING: RESEARCH PARTICIPANTS

The following information was recorded for each participant during the first therapy session.

Sexual Orientation. In categorizing sexual orientation, I used the seven-point "Kinsey Scale" (Kinsey, et al., 1948), taking into account both internal responses (attraction and desire) and behavior. There was rarely any discrepancy between desired and actual sex partners in this group.

For simplification, I refer to points 0 and 1 on the scale as "straight." I refer to points 2, 3, and 4 as "bisexual." I refer to points 5 and 6 as "gay" or "lesbian." I was concerned only with the last five years of participants' experience. Following is the sexual orientation of the research participants according to their biological sex (percentages, in parentheses, are of the total research sample):

	men	women	totals
straight	9 (6%)	17 (12%)	26 (18%)
bisexual	27 (19%)	10 (7%)	37 (26%)
gay	78 (55%)	2 (1%)	80 (56%)
			143 (100%)

Clearly, gay and bisexual men and straight and bisexual women were far more represented than straight men or lesbian women. The reasons of this have most to do with the goals of the participants.

Goals. During the first session, I asked each participant what he/she hoped to get out of therapy. The specific ways in which goals were stated were as unique as the individuals themselves. Some wanted to be able to enjoy receiving anal intercourse. Others did not. However, all were clear that they wanted to experience more pleasure from anal stimulation. Toward the middle of therapy (usually the fifth session) I asked participants to reevaluate and restate their goals. I believed that new information and experience might result in clarification or goal changes.

The table below shows the percentages of those who expressed each of the two major goals at the beginning and at the middle of therapy. Those who expressed serious ambivalent feelings toward anal intercourse were placed in the non-intercourse category. Percentages are also shown according to sex and sexual orientation. (All percentages are rounded off to the nearest point.)

Goal:	Session:	overall (n = 143)	straight men (n = 9)	straight women (n = 17)	bisexual men (n = 27)	bisexual women (n = 10)	gay men (n = 78)	lesbians (n = 2)
less pain and more pleasure from anal stimulation *other than intercourse*	1	27	89	41	15	20	19	100
	5	20	78	29	11	20	13	100
less pain and more pleasure from anal stimulation *including intercourse*	1	73	11	59	85	80	81	0
	5	80	22	71	89	80	87	0

By the middle of therapy, 80% expressed a desire to be able to enjoy receiving anal intercourse. The lesbians had no such desire, nor did the straight men except for two who felt that this would be an interesting experience that they hoped to have at least once in their lives. Obviously, a strong, persistent desire to receive anal intercourse would have made it impossible to be rated a straight man or lesbian on the Kinsey sexual orientation scale.

During the first half of the therapy process, there was some increase in the percentage of those who expressed a desire to be able to enjoy receiving intercourse. This was no doubt due to personal goal clarification as well as the general supportive attitude conveyed throughout therapy. This shift, however, was quite small (7%), suggesting that particpants usually began therapy with a clear idea of what they hoped to gain. During the course of therapy, no one who originally wanted to explore anal intercourse changed his/her mind. However, there was a tendency for all participants to become far less *urgent* about their desire to enjoy anal intercourse, i.e., they became more gentle with themselves and less self-demanding.

The stated goals of the participants suggest that the desire to be able to enjoy anal intercourse is most likely to bring a person into therapy. There is no way of knowing how representative this is of the general population of people affected by anal spasm or people who desire to enjoy pleasurable anal stimulation. Many people who would like to enjoy other forms of anal stimulation (but *not* intercourse) may be considerably less motivated to seek therapy. These people, however, might seek information and permission in a book like this or from other sources.

In addition, most participants mentioned the obvious: The ability to enjoy receiving anal intercourse is more directly dependent on the release of anal tension than are other forms of anal stimulation that can be enjoyed, or at least tolerated, in spite of anal tension.

Gender Identity. All but four participants were clearly and positively self-identified as their anatomical sex. Three men were considering entering the pre-operative phase (living as a woman and hormone treatments) of gender reassignment (sex change). Because they were still living as men, these three were counted as males. One anatomical male who had been living as a woman for nearly a year and was preparing for gender reassignment surgery was counted as female.

Race. Among the women, 27 (93%) were white and 2 (7%) were black. Among the men, 91 (80%) were white, 11 (10%) were black, 7 (6%) were Asian, and 5 (4%) were Latino.

Sexual Relationships. Thirty-two percent of the men and 54% of the women lived with a lover or spouse. An addiitonal 25% of the men and 32% of the women were involved in primary, non-living-together sexual relationships. Almost 80% of the gay and bisexual men regularly or occasionally enjoyed casual sexual encounters. This was true for slightly less than half of the straight men. While almost half of the women considered their sexual relationships "open," i.e. non-monogamous, only one-fifth said they had any more than incidental experiences with casual sex.

Past Anal Sexual Experience. All participants had experienced some anal stimulation in sexual situations, finding it anxiety-provoking and almost always uncomfortable. Ninety-five percent of the gay men had attempted receiving anal intercourse. Of these, 80% said their experiences were always or nearly always unpleasant; 20% had had some positive anal sex experiences, but said they were infrequent and unpredictable. Among the women, slightly less than 60% had tried anal intercourse; all found it unpleasant. Eighteen men and four women had actually been forced or strongly pressured into anal intercourse (anally raped). Over half of the participants reported any anal touching by another to be anxiety-provoking or uncomfortable, often so much so that sexual response was inhibited, usually because the touching was feared to be a prelude to a request (or demand) for anal intercourse.

Patterns of Anal Tension. Anal spasm manifests itself differently in different people. First, anal tension may be either "general" (chronic) or "situational." When the tension is *general* it is present all or most of the time and is not strongly dependent on the situation (although particularly stressful situations make it worse).

Situational anal tension occurs only under circumstances such as moments of anxiety or emotional stress. In some people, situations of potential and desired anal pleasure trigger anal muscular spasm. The specific situations are highly variable. For example, a person might be quite relaxed while touching his/her own anus but become tense when touched by someone else. Others may remain relaxed when touched by a partner, becoming tense only when the insertion of a finger or other object is attempted. In still others, spasm results only when the insertion of a penis is attempted. A few others become tense only when receiving anal stimulation from specific people or in specific positions.

In addition to this distinction between general and situational tension, anal spasm may be either "primary" or "secondary." And tension is *primary* when it has always or almost always been a problem to the person. Anal tension is *secondary* when it occurs, either gradually or all at once, after a period of not having been a problem.

There are four possible tension problems:

> Primary, general anal spasm—always been tense in all or most situations
>
> Primary, situational anal spasm—always been tense in only some situations
>
> Secondary, situational anal spasm—used to be relaxed, but now tense in some situations
>
> Secondary general anal spasm—used to be relaxed, but now tense in all or most situations

During the first session, I described these four possible anal tension patterns. Once they understood the distinctions, over 60% were easily able to determine which pattern most accurately described their experience. The remaining 40% had to make self-observations outside of the therapy sessions. Within two weeks, all were able to discern their own tension patterns except for five men and one woman who were unable to see how these distinctions could be important and, for varying periods of time, resisted looking more closely at their anal response. They said things like, "I don't care what my anus does. I just want to have anal sex, that's all!" It took as long as six weeks for some of these people to understand their anal response patterns.

The frequency with which each of the four tension patterns occurred was as follows:

> primary, general anal tension (49%, n = 70)
> primary, situational anal tension (34%, n = 49)
> secondary, situational anal tension (12%, n = 17)
> secondary, general anal tension (5%, n = 7)
>
> totals: 100% (n = 143)

Both forms of secondary tension were relatively rare among participants in this research. I think this reflects the fact that there is virtually no support—or accurate information—available in our society for people who want to enjoy their anuses either sensually or sexually. Therefore, the earliest anal experiences are likely to be clouded by guilt and uncertainty, and a pattern of negative expectations is set from the start.

It could also be that relatively few people with secondary anal tension seek therapy because they can work through their concerns on their own. This explanation for the low frequency of secondary patterns in this group of therapy-seekers seems highly unlikely because there is no indication that secondary tension patterns are, in fact, easier to change.

Onset and Duration of Concerns. The existence of any of the four anal tension patterns does not necessarily constitute a personal concern. For example, even those participants with primary, general anal tension did not always consider it a problem, though some remember vague anal discomfort since adolescence or even earlier. With a few exceptions, participants reported that they first became concerned about anal tension under one (or occasionally both) of two conditions. Attempted or considered anal intercourse motivated almost 90% of participants to think about the negative effects of anal tension. The remainder began to think seriously about anal tension as a result of pain (not related to anal intercourse) or medical problems (anal touching by another often made them aware of the pain).

The length of time participants had been concerned about anal spasm varied from less than six months to more than five years. A higher percentage of men than women had been concerned about anal spasm for longer periods of time. One explanation is that there is (and has been in the past) more awareness of, desire for and pressure to be able to enjoy anal sexual activities among gay and bisexual men. Only recently has it become more acceptable for women to talk about and experiment with anal stimulation. On the other hand, gay and bisexual men, because of their sexual orientation, have always tended to be seen, by themselves and others, as sexual "outsiders." Once having broken the bounds of convention, gay and bisexual men have probably been more open to sexual experimentation. In addition, the tendency to equate "real sex" with (vaginal) intercourse has left some gay and bisexual men feeling that anal intercourse is the only "real sex" available to them. Taken together, these two factors adequately account for the fact that more men than women have been concerned about anal tension for longer periods of time.

Before seeking therapy, most participants had seriously and persistently attempted to reduce anal tension on their own through a variety of means, including anal exploration with fingers, repeated attempts at anal intercourse (if intercourse was desired) or practice with the insertion of objects such as dildos or vibrators. Many had finally given up until deciding to enter therapy. While no data is available on the experience of men and women who do *not* enter therapy, informal discussions with dozens of these people suggest that attempts at anal intercourse often *are* successful (eventually, if not initially). This was definitely not the case with the research participants, almost all of whom viewed therapy as a last resort. A similar attitude is usually expressed by men and women entering sex therapy for other concerns.

In short, pleasure-limiting anal tension is highly stable over time and resistant to efforts to change it. This was particularly evident among those who had to (or chose to) wait, sometimes as long as six months, before beginning therapy. With only one exception, their conerns were not alleviated either by the passage of time or through continued personal effort.

Medical Problems. Fourteen percent of the women and 20% of the men had anal-rectal medical problems serious enough to require professional treatment. Of these, almost half did not know for certain that they had these problems (although they had often suspected ''something isn't right back there'') until a proctologic examination was scheduled early in therapy. The fact that a smaller percentage of the women had anal-rectal medical problems may be simply coincidental. However, it appears that men are more likely than women to receive anal intercourse in spite of persistent pain warnings. This may be yet another manifestation of the extreme pressure that some gay and bisexual men feel to be able to receive anal intercourse whether they like it or not. While women often express the same intensity of desire to please their partners, even at their own expense, women are obviously able to initiate an alternative similar to anal intercourse—vaginal intercourse—when anal stimulation is uncomfortable:

Following is a list of the most common anal-rectal medical problems and with the number of participants affected by each:

	men	women
hemorrhoids	13	2
fissures	3	1
anal infections	2	1
anal warts	5	1
anal gonorrhea	2	—
fistula	1	—
herpes	1	—
total:	27	5
percent:	24%	17%

Interestingly, *all* of these medical problems, except for two cases of anal warts, and one case of anal gonorrhea, were found among men and women with *primary, general* anal tension. In addition, all 14 men and five women who said they were frequently bothered by constipation (but did not requrire medical treatment) were also in this primary, general tension group. Of course, the correlation between persistent, long standing anal tension and these medical problems does not, in itself, warrant an assertion that tension "causes" the medical problems.

There were only five instances in which medical problems appeared to be in any way related to anal sexual activities (two fissures and three cases of hemorrhoids that were apparently aggravated by anal intercourse). In each case, there were clear pain warnings that the person ignored or tolerated or, in two cases of anal rape, was forced to endure.

Motivation for Entering Therapy. In the pilot study, it was obvious that some people sought therapy in order to expand the ways in which they could give pleasure to themselves or share it with others. Others, though they may have wanted these things, were primarily concerned about "being prepared" to meet their partner's expectations.

During the first session, I asked each participant about his/her motivation for entering therapy. Distinguishing pleasure from performance motivations was less difficult than I had anticipated. Most were quite willing to state candidly why they had sought therapy *and for whom*. In cases where there was doubt, I found that motivation could quickly be clarified by asking: "If your partner really wanted to stimulate your anus and you were not in the mood, would you rather (a) be able to say 'no' comfortably or (b) be able to go ahead and please him/her as long as it didn't actually hurt you?" This question translated the respondent's motivational stance into behavioral terms.

As therapy progressed, there was an unmistakable shift among many participants *away* from a performance orientation and *toward* a pleasure orientation. In many instances, this was clearly due to their discovery that anal stimulation actually could feel very good, whereas they had originally felt that neutral toleration was the best they could reasonably expect, given their past experiences.

I recorded those changes in motivation when I believed they were authentic. However, I was extremely cautious in recording such changes because I soon discovered that those people who were the most eager to please their sex partners were also the most eager to please me by insisting that their motives had "changed."

Consequently, I considered motivation change to be authentic only when the change was reflected in reported behavior. This determination can most readily be made as clients discuss their experiences doing homework. Those oriented toward performance discuss their "progress" (or lack of it) while those focused on pleasure discuss their level of enjoyment (or the fears that seem to block it).

At the beginning of therapy, 54% (n = 77) of the participants expressed more concern about satisfying their partners than they did about discovering new options for pleasure. During the course of therapy, 22% (n = 31) made a clear shift in emphasis. They spoke less and less about how they would to be able to "measure up" to what their partners wanted and more about how good they were feeling. However, 32% (n = 46) retained an unmistakable performance orientation throughout therapy and followup. I used this performance-oriented group for my later analysis of the relationship between motivation for seeking therapy and therapy effectiveness.

There was little or no relationship between a person's motivation for seeking therapy and sex or sexual orientation, indicating that issues of motivation apparently reflect an aspect of personality that functions independently of these considerations. There was a slight (and understandable) tendency for those who wanted to receive anal intercourse to be more performance oriented.

DATA GATHERING DURING THE THERAPY PROCESS

All participants completed a therapy process that included all of the information and practical suggestions contained in this book. In addition, of course, there were regular dialogues with the therapist, individualized suggestions and additional therapeutic interventions as needed. Almost 90% (n = 94) of the gay and bisexual men and one straight man were in an "Anal Exploration and Relaxation Workshop." Each of these groups consisted of 8-12 participants who met for two hours each week for eight weeks. The groups offered the added benefit of interaction with a variety of people with similar concerns.

The other participants, including all of the women and all but one of the straight men experienced the same process in the context of individual or couple therapy. Fourteen of the straight and bisexual women were in couple therapy with a lover or spouse who, in many cases, was also intersted in anal exploration. Nearly 20% of those who saw me in individual or couple therapy were concurrently concerned about other sexual problems in addition to anal spasm.

Individual and couple therapy followed the same eight-session format with once-a-week sessions, except when other concerns required more sessions.

In order to monitor the movement of participants toward or away from their goals, I relied on weekly verbal self-reports. During the last session, each person was asked to evaluate, in detail, his/her current experiences in light of earlier-stated goals.

In spite of the difficulties inherent in self-reports, they are the best mechanism available for evaluating therapy effectiveness. It would have been possible, with medical assistance, to make objective measures of anal tension levels at various points during therapy. But participants' self-evaluations, while clearly related to anal tension levels, are primarily concerned with the *subjective* experience of pleasure while receiving anal stimulation. Only the participant can provide data about the perception of pleasure or, conversely, discomfort or pain. These are not quantifiable phenomena.

How can we be certain that participants' reports are valid? Are the reports accurate descriptions of what they actually experienced? Absolute certainty, of course, is impossible. However, several factors contribute to a high *probability* of validity. An *in*accurate self-report could either be a *sub*conscious attempt to fool both therapist and self, or a conscious attempt to fool only the therapist (presumably to please him by telling him that the therapy was successful when, in fact, it was not). The first possibility—self-delusion—is highly unlikely in this instance given the participants' intense awareness of not being able to have the kind of pleasure experiences they wanted. In every case, talking about their dissatisfaction in therapy served to intensify the desire for change.

Similarly, consciously falsifying self-reports in order to please the therapist would require abandoning the very goal that brought the person to therapy in the first place. Furthermore, motivation to please the therapist would likely be strongest among "performance oriented" participants. Consequently, to the extent that participants sought to please the therapist, we would expect *more* positive reports from the performance-oriented group than from the pleasure-oriented group. In fact, the performance-oriented group reported fewer positive results.

Finally, an attempt (whether conscious or unconscious) to falsify or exaggerate self-reports would require a concerted effort on the part of the participant, not only during the evaluation session but throughout the entire therapy process. Any discrepancy between the final evaluation and earlier reports would have

246

been immediately noticed and challenged by the therapist and, in the small groups, by other participants as well. The continuity of self-reports, however, gives them high validity.

SUCCESS CRITERIA

In order to determine the effectiveness of therapy, some guidelines are necessary for interpreting and evaluating self-reports from participants. How thoroughly does a client have to meet his/her goals in order for therapy to be considered successful? What if, for example, a person wants to be able to enjoy receiving anal intercourse and, as a result of therapy, learns to do this, but only under certain conditions? For this research I established, somewhat arbitrarily, this standard: *A participant was considered to have reached his/her goal when anal stimulation—of the type desired—was experienced positively at least 75% of the time when the individual wanted that experience.*

It should be noted that this standard is not as clear-cut as it may appear. Even though it is widely assumed that Masters and Johnson led the way in solving criteria problems in evaluating sex therapy success, this is not the case.* Nor have these problems been resolved in this research. In fact, the desire for quantifiable indices of sex therapy success (or failure) will probably never be fully satisfied. This is true, to a large extent, because successful sex therapy (and other psychotherapies) virtually always combine increased self-acceptance with actual behavior change. Many sexual problems are solved easily and effectively when the client redefines his/her experience in a less performance-oriented way.

One of the research participants, Valerie, expressed this phenomenon perfectly. In a follow-up interview, I asked if she felt she had reached her goals. As we discussed her experiences, she explained: ''I guess it all depends on how you—or I, more importantly—look at it. Take last night. Pete (her husband) wanted me to try anal sex but I wasn't really in the mood, so I knew I couldn't enjoy it. I *wished* I was in the mood, but only because he seemed so turned on by the idea. I have a tendency to think of this as a failure on my part, even though I know it's not. So I would say that I've reached my goals in the sense that I enjoy anal sex a lot when I feel ready for it. Pete wishes I could do something to want it more often.''

Valerie and I agreed, though others may not, that she had reached her stated goals, but not necessarily her unstated desire to be able to ''deliver'' her anus, on demand, for the pleasure of

* For a criticism of Masters and Johnson's lack of clear success criteria and other methodological problems, see Zilbergeld and Evans(1980).

her husband. She estimated that she enjoyed anal sex, including anal intercourse, over 90% of the time when *she* wanted it.

In addition to the problem that success criteria pose to the researcher, the entire issue is often troublesome for therapists and clients. This is because success criteria, whatever they are, tend to fit better into a performance-oriented model of sexual health—precisely the model that many sex therapists view as the most important contributor to sexual problems. Thus, while clear, sensible criteria are needed to evaluate therapy effectiveness, care is required to avoid codifying old performance ideals or generating a new set of performance demands.

DATA GATHERING AFTER THE THERAPY PROCESS

During the final evaluation session, participants discussed plans for continuing the anal exploration process on their own. They were encouraged to proceed at their own pace and to avoid, whenever possible, both self-imposed and external pressures to "hurry up" or do anything they did not feel ready to do. This emphasis on individual timing, including reassurances that they did not have to accomplish everything in just eight weeks, was incorporated throughout therapy.

Those who did not reach their goals by the end of therapy were contacted by telephone between two and four months after the end of therapy. Each was asked these questions:

1. Do you still have the same goals that you stated during therapy?
2. Have you continued anal exploration since therapy ended? In what ways?
3. How close do you now feel you are to reaching your goals?

They also were given an opportunity to discuss, in retrospect, feelings and thoughts about the therapy process.

CLINICAL OBSERVATIONS

To help me in making clinical observations, almost half of the small group sessions were recorded in their entirety on audio tape. Nearly one quarter of the individual and couple sessions were also recorded. I reviewed the tapes, made notes on the exchanges I considered most significant, and transcribed verbatim representative statements of participants. The tapes were then erased according to agreements I had made with participants.

In addition, 20 participants (14 men and six women) who *had* reached their goals by the end of therapy were contacted by telephone between two and six months after the end of therapy. They were asked if they were still satisfied with their experiences of anal stimulation. Their retrospective comments on the therapy process were also invited.

ANALYSIS OF DATA

Participants' reports were tabulated according to whether or not they reached their goals by the end of therapy or within four months after therapy.

Frequency distributions were tabulated for each variable for which data was available (sex, age, sexual orientation, race, onset and duration of concerns, and sexual relationships) showing the relationship, if any, of that variable to therapy outcome as well as the *timing* of therapy outcome (i.e., whether participants reached their goals by the end of therapy or within four months after the end of therapy). A chi-square test was performed on each of these frequency distributions to determine the statistical significance of the relationship between each variable and therapy outcome.

Only bi-variant calculations were made (i.e., the relationship of each variable to therapy outcome or the timing of therapy outcome was tested independently of other variables). Although a multi-variant analysis might have revealed significant relationships between two or more variables and therapy outcome, multivariant analyses were not performed in this study for two reasons: (1) the relatively small sample size; and (2) the fact that the discovery of interacting variables would have been of limited value in the evaluation of the therapy process—the major purpose of this research.

Frequency distributions were considered significant if the chi-square test resulted in a probability of less than 5% ($p < .05$) of that distribution being tested could have occurred randomly.

RESULTS

OVERALL THERAPY OUTCOME

During the final evaluation session, 71% of the participants (n = 101) reported that they had reached their goals. In follow-up telephone interviews with 20 (14 men and six women) of these participants, conducted between two and six months after the completion of therapy, all of the women and all but one of the men reported that they continued to enjoy anal stimulation of the kind they had originally desired.

Of the 40 participants who had *not* reached their goals by the end of therapy, I interviewed 33 by telephone between two and four months after they had completed therapy. Seven participants could not be reached and were presumed *not* to have reached their goals even though some may, in actuality, have done so. My personal knowledge of these seven participants, however, suggests a low probability that any of them continued anal exploration after therapy.

Of the 33 participants who were interviewed, 17 reported that they had continued the anal exploration processes which they had begun during therapy and had, by the time of the interview, reached their goals. They represented an additional 12% of the total research population. Therefore, a total of 118 or 83% of all the participants who completed therapy reached their goals within four months of the conclusion of therapy.

ANAL TENSION PATTERNS AND OUTCOME

I had expected that participants who originally manifested either of the two *general* anal tension patterns would be less likely to reach their goals than participants with either of the two *situational* anal tension patterns. Graph 1 shows the number and percent of participants who originally manifested general and situational anal tension (both primary and secondary) according to whether they reached or did not reach their goals.

Seventy-five percent of participants who originally manifested general anal tension reported reaching their goals within four months after the end of therapy versus 91% of participants with situational anus tension. Thus, whether participants originally manifested general or situational anal tension was significantly related to therapy outcome ($p < .02$), confirming my expectation.

I had expected that participants who originally manifested either of the two *general* anal tension patterns would be less likely to reach their goals, but that those who *did* reach their goals would be more likely to reach them sometime *after* therapy than participants who originally manifested either of the two *situational* anal tension patterns. Graph 1 also shows the number and percent of participants who originally manifested general and situational anal tension according to whether they reached their goals by the end of therapy or within four months after therapy.

Among all the participants who *did* reach their goals, 22% of those who originally manifested general anal tension patterns did so sometime *after* therapy as compared with 7% of those who manifested situational anal tension patterns. Thus, whether participants originally manifested general or situational anal tension was significantly related to the timing of therapy outcome ($p < .02$), confirming my expectation.

Whether participants originally manifested *primary* or *secondary* anal tension was *not* significantly related to therapy outcome ($p < .30$).

MOTIVATION FOR SEEKING THERAPY AND OUTCOME

Graph 2 shows the number and percent of participants who were motivated to seek therapy by "pleasure" and "performance" according to whether they reached their goals by the end of therapy or within four months after therapy.

Eighty-nine percent of those motivated by "pleasure" reached their goals as compared to 67% of those motivated by "performance", indicating a significant relationship (p < .01) between motivation an outcome of therapy. Motivation for seeking therapy was *not* significantly related to whether goals were reached by the end of therapy or within four months after therapy (p > .10).

ONGOING SEXUAL RELATIONSHIPS AND OUTCOME

Graph 3 shows the number and percent of participants who were or were not involved in ongoing sexual relationships according to whether they reached their goals by the end of therapy or within four months after therapy.

I had expected that participants involved in ongoing sexual relationships would be more likely to reach their goals than participants not involved in such partnerships. However, whether or not participants were involved in ongoing sexual relationships was *not* significantly related to therapy outcome (p > .70).

I had also expected that participants not involved in ongoing sexual relationships who *did* reach their goals would be more likely to take longer to do so. Among all participants who eventually *did* reach their goals, 8% of those involved in ongoing sexual relationships did so sometime *after* therapy as compared with 26% of those who were not involved in ongoing sexual relationships. Thus, whether or not participants were involved in ongoing sexual relationships was signficantly related to the length of time required for them to reach their goals (p < .02). No other variables for which data were collected proved to be significantly related to therapy outcome.

DISCUSSION

Before evaluating and interpreting the results, it is necessary to consider whether other variables, besides the impact of the therapy experience could have been responsible for the reported changes. Assuming that the changes were not a miraculous occurrence, three major variables other than therapy could conceivably have brought about the changes: (1) the passage of time, (2) something the participants did to or for themselves not related to the therapy experience, or (3) something other people did to or for the participants that was not related to the therapy ex-

Graph 1

ANAL TENSION PATTERNS AND THERAPY OUTCOME

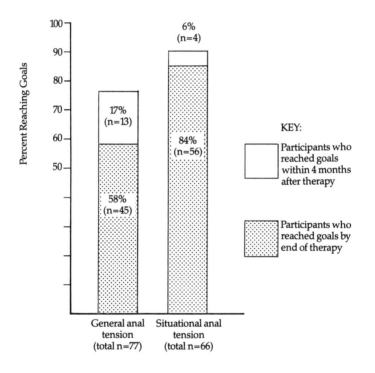

perience. Earlier in this Appendix, I noted that in no case had either the passage of time or the participants' efforts to change proved to be of much value in reducing anal tension or enhancing anal pleasure.

The third possibility—intervention of other people not related to the therapy experience—is also an unlikely explanation for the changes reported by participants. Earlier, I pointed out that all participants had previously experienced anal stimulation by sexual partners and that 95% of the gay men and 60% of the straight women had attempted receiving anal intercourse, often repeatedly. I also noted that these experiences had been uncomfortable far more often than they had been comfortable. That any more than a few research participants, during or after therapy, would have encountered someone with whom their experiences were dramatically different, independent of the influence of therapy, is highly improbable. The most reasonable explanation for the changes reported is that, through the therapy experience, participants learned to use time, personal effort and experiences with others in different and more positive ways than they had previously.

However, no quantitative data were gathered in this study that could help specify *which aspects* of therapy had the most or least impact. My observations suggest that all aspects of therapy contribute to the overall impact with, of course, some aspects being more valuable than others, depending on individual needs.

The fact that all therapy sessions were facilitated by one therapist could be considered an imperfection in the research design. Although it is reasonable to assume that any experienced therapist could facilitate this process just as effectively, such an assumption can not be supported by this research.

Within the limits and probabilities I have just discussed, my central contention—that short-term, active, behavioral-evocative psychotherapy can effectively reduce anal spasm and enhance the capacity for anal pleasure—is strongly supported by the data. Eighty-three percent of participants reported reaching their goals, 71% during the eight weeks of therapy and another 12% during the four months following therapy.

ANAL TENSION PATTERNS AND THERAPY EFFECTIVENESS

In order to understand the full meaning of the findings related to anal tension patterns, it is necessary to look beyond the quantitative data, examining the nature of anal tension. To do so inevitably involves a certain amount of speculation. However, working closely with the research participants as they explored

Graph 2

MOTIVATION FOR SEEKING
THERAPY AND THERAPY OUTCOME

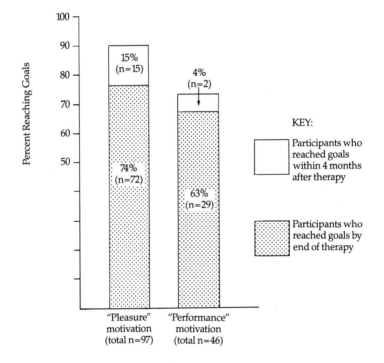

anal tension, relaxation and pleasure has provided me with a unique opportunity for making observations, asking questions and drawing tentative conclusions.

Where does anal tension come from? I have observed a variety of factors that contribute to the development and maintenance of anal tension. In some cases, people are very aware of the factors contributing to their anal tension. In others, the factors exert their disrupting influence largely outside of consciousness until anal exploration brings them into awareness. Following is a list of what I consider to be the most common factors, starting with the most simple and proceeding toward the more complex:

Improper diet. lack of fiber in the diet assures that feces will be of insufficient bulk to trigger the rectal reflex; this results in chronic straining during bowel movements and, eventually, an overall pattern of anal canal constriction.

Physical pain. Anal tension can be a direct response to physical pain.

Fear of pain. The anus tenses to fend off anticipated or feared pain or bodily damage. This reaction is exacerbated by negative experiences.

Learned tension patterns. Families teach their children, usually through "body language," to store excess tension in particular body zones. The anus, negatively charged by the anal taboo, is a popular tension zone. This factor operates particularly in instances of *general* anal tension.

Tension-produced tension. Chronic tension causes irritation and pain, resulting in more tension to cover the pain—a classic vicious cycle.

Performance anxiety. When a person fears that he/she cannot "deliver" what is expected (e.g., anal intercourse), the whole body, including the anus, tenses to meet the threat to self-esteem. Performance anxiety quickly turns a potentially pleasurable experience into hard work.

Unrealistic expectations. Tension is often a response to unrealistic expectations (e.g., the belief that one *should* be able to receive anal intercourse anytime a partner wants it).

Threats to self-image. Any threat to a person's self-image generates protective tension (e.g., fear that enjoying anal pleasure makes a person "bad" or "perverted," fears of not being "manly" or "womanly,' or fear of being homosexual—mostly an issue for men).

The "Nice Person" Syndrome. Performance anxiety and threats to self-image and esteem are often felt most strongly by those who

Graph 3
ONGOING SEXUAL RELATIONSHIPS
AND THERAPY OUTCOME

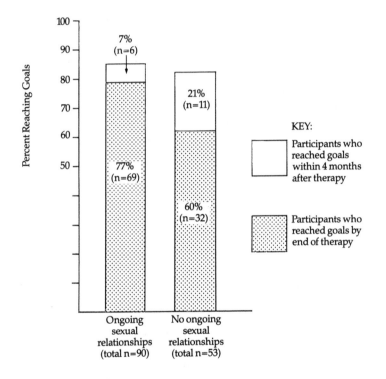

are over-anxious to please other people, putting their own needs in second place.

Interpersonal stress. Fear, anger, frustration or resentment resulting from interpersonal conflict sometimes expresses itself in anal tension.

Concerns about power. Many people associate passivity and loss of control with the muscular receptivity necessary for anal intercourse. Consequently, people who feel this way, especially men, find it difficult to relax, feeling that they *must* always be in charge. On the other hand, some women (and some men) feel anger at always *having* to be receptive whether they want to or not. Either response can be reflected in anal tension. These power dynamics are often reflected in the "sadomasochistic" images that some people associate with anal intercourse.

Conflicts about sexual pleasure. Tension in the anal area is sometimes a means of keeping pleasurable sensations in the entire pelvic area under control. Here, anal tension is merely incidental to a larger conflict about all physical (especially sexual) pleasure.*

Fear of intimacy. Discomfort with emotional or physical closeness or both can be expressed in anal muscular contractions, particularly in situations of real or potential intimacy. This factor seems to be pronounced among those who view anal intercourse as an especially intimate act.

General insecurity and rigidity. If a person does not feel safe in the world, the anus is likely to be tense. Some people specifically describe anal tension as a feeling of grasping for "grounding" or security.

Other factors could be added to this list, and many overlap; rarely is there just one cause of anal spasm. The more complex factors toward the end of the list are more likely to be unconscious and, consequently, less likely to be dealt with directly in short-term therapy. However, it is not uncommon for anal exploration to trigger long-repressed memories and feelings from early in life. For instance, a number of research participants were able to recall specific occasions during early childhood when perceived threats of losing mother's or father's love were accompanied by extreme, sometimes excruciatingly painful, anal tension.

In therapy there appeared to be a tendency for the processes underlying the disruption of anal pleasure to become conscious automatically. Participants who attempted to figure out how they

---

* For a discussion of the relationship between sexual repression and muscular armoring, see Reich (1973) and Lowen (1975).

had become so alienated from their anuses were usually unsuccessful. When, however, they allowed themselves to *experience* the alienation, clear images were likely to emerge, shedding light on the evolution of anal tension.

Among those who did reexperience long-suppressed feelings related to anal tension, I was unable to find a single instance supporting Freud's view about the etiology of chronic anal tension. Freud thought that children learn to save up feces because of the pleasure derived from holding on followed by the release of one big bowel movement. In Freud's own words:

> . . . the retention of fecal masses, which at first is intended in order to utilize them, as it were, for masturbatic excitation of the anal zone, is at least one of the roots of constipation so frequent in neurotics (Freud, 1905).

Although there are obviously many instances in which children and adults use muscular contractions and relaxation to enhance anal pleasure (whether or not feces are involved), no one has ever reported to me that the severe, chronic muscular holding necessary to produce constipation is anything but unpleasant. In fact, my clients who are troubled by constipation (and other tension-related medical problems) invariably report an unusal *lack of feeling* in the anal area. In my view, chronic anal tension initiated in childhood is rarely, if ever, a means of *producing* pleasure. On the contrary, it is one of the most effective means of *avoiding* anal pleasure.

Turning again to the four patterns of anal tension, I found that both forms of *secondary* anal tension are almost always traceable to specific experiences, e.g., one especially painful sexual encounter, a medical problem resulting in pain, a destructive relationship with a lover or spouse. Usually the specific experience was readily recalled when the person felt comfortable and safe. Thereafter, steps could be taken to discharge pent up emotions, reduce fears and resolve the difficult situation. With reassurance and patience, the client usually became responsive to therapy. However, this research suggests that *secondary general* anal tension is the most resistent to therapy of all the anal tension patterns. Although this finding was not *statistically* significant (probably due to the small size of this part of the sample), I believe it to be highly significant. *Secondary general* tension, like secondary situational tension, is usually traceable to a specific experience. However, in every case in which secondary tension was *general*, the specific contributing event was *highly traumatic*. Five of the seven people in this group reported traumatic instances of anal coercion very close to, if not actually, rape. The other two had undergone painful anal surgery from which recovery had been slow and difficult. As a result, these people's anuses were always or almost always tense, as if on guard against further trauma. The lower success rates for those with secondary general anal tension are probably due to the fact that severe trauma is not easily forgotten.

Primary general anal tension appears to be related to many interacting factors, including subtle, longstanding fears and behavioral patterns that are usually not readily brought into awareness. I think this is why participants who manifested this tension pattern were, overall, less successful in therapy than people manifesting either of the two situational patterns. Still, 77% were able to reach their goals, although they were likely to take a little longer. Most cases of anal numbness were found in this group.

Participants who originally manifested *primary, situational* anal tension were, overall, the most successful in therapy (although the difference between primary and secondary situational tension was not statistically significant). This form of anal tension was usually traceable to long-standing fears of specific situations or experiences which, in many instances, had never actually occurred, at least not in the traumatic way feared. These participants were likely to report fears of being hurt or violated during anal intercourse. Overall, participants in this group spoke more about negative associations with anal stimulation than people with any other tension pattern. Most moral concerns about the rightness of anal intercourse or specific medical questions were expressed by participants with primary, situational tension. Accurate information was probably the most important aspect of therapy for these people. Also, giving them permission to stay away from specific tension-producing situations (usually intercourse) allowed them to relax and enjoy other forms of anal pleasure with relative ease.

MOTIVATION FOR
SEEKING THERAPY AND
THERAPY EFFECTIVENESS

My expectation that therapy would be significantly more effective with participants who were primarily motivated by their own desire for pleasure rather than by a desire to please others was supported by the data. I am convinced that the difference between those motivated by pleasure and those motivated by performance would have been even greater if I had discovered a better way of penetrating the facade of sophistication and sexual liberation worn by many of the research participants. I am certain that many participants were reluctant to admit their true motives for being in therapy because of the popularity of the idea that people *should* enjoy sexual activities *for themselves.* Sexual self-sacrifice is ''out'' in theory if not in practice.

Although differences in the percentages of those reporting that they had reached their goals *after* therapy ended were not statistically significant, they do reflect a tendency on the part of those motivated by pleasure to continue their anal exploration after the conclusion of therapy. The performance-oriented group appeared more likely to give up after therapy, perhaps having placated a lover (or themselves) by having given anal exploration a try and failed (many of these people fully intended to fail and therefore really succeeded at what they wanted to do).

It should be noted, however, that 63% of the performance-oriented participants reached their goals in spite of their motivation for seeking therapy. Many of these people genuinely wanted to please their partners and obtained a great deal of pleasure by being able to do so, even though they probably would not have come to therapy just for themselves. Those who did *not* reach their stated goals were not simply motivated by performance, but were probably also *resentful* toward whomever they were trying to please.

SEXUAL RELATIONSHIPS AND THERAPY EFFECTIVENESS

There was very little difference in overall success between participants involved in ongoing sexual relationships and those not involved in such partnerships. However, people with ongoing sexual relationships were more likely to reach their goals, if at all, by the end of therapy. Only 7% reported reaching their goals during the four months after therapy. People without ongoing relationships had essentially the same overall results, *but it took them longer.* Twenty-one percent did not reach their goals until sometime after therapy had ended.

People without ongoing sexual relationships did not always have access to a trusted partner with whom to experiment comfortably, and in a non-demanding way, with anal pleasure. On the other hand, people with ongoing sexual relationships usually *did* have a partner for anal exploration, but this was not always a *trusted and comfortable* partnership. Particularly with participants in couple therapy, it was clear that some of the relationships actually got in the way of positive anal exploration. Many of these relationships were scenes of intense fear, anger and power struggles. Consequently, my expectation was not supported because

I failed to consider that the important factor was not simply the existence of an ongoing relationship, but rather the *quality* of that relationship.

IMPLICATIONS

This research has a variety of implications for clinical practice and research as well as for men and women exploring their own bodies and sexuality. The most important overall implication is that both anal tension and the capacity for the enjoyment of anal pleasure are primarily *learned*. Many people troubled by anal tension and blocked from anal pleasure can, in a relatively short period of time, *un*learn anal tension, even of long duration, and *re*learn or enhance the capacity for anal pleasure.

This finding (which some have no doubt known about for a long time) has important implications for professional helpers, particularly those in the fields of sex education, counseling, therapy and research. I hope that sex educators will eventually begin talking more openly about anal stimulation as a source of sensual and sexual pleasure which is as legitimate and healthy an aspect of personal and interpersonal self-expression as any other form of sexual activity. Likewise, sex counselors and therapists are likely to be called upon with increasing frequency to discuss anal sexuality comfortably with their clients. They will also be asked for specific suggestions by those who wish to explore anal pleasure further. Sex researchers will need to learn more about anal tension and pleasure among people in this country and all over the world. I suspect that other cultures, which have not so thoroughly embraced the anal taboo, have a great deal to teach us about this hidden and feared part of the body. In our own society, a great many people enjoy the anal area as an erogenous zone without requiring therapy to do so. I hope that sensitive and accepting investigators will, at some point, ask these individuals what their experience has taught them.

Physicians—especially those in the field of proctology—have a responsibility to become more informed and at ease about anal sexual behavior so that they can give accurate information and advice to their patients. This is particularly important because virtually everything a proctolgoist does has potential significance for a patient's anal pleasure experiences. Physicians who feel that anal sexual activities are inherently dangerous need to reconsider this belief and understand that the anal awareness necessary for the enjoyment of anal pleasure is also conducive to anal health.

Careful, unbiased research about the medical aspects of anal tension and pleasure is seriously needed. For example, would the correlation between anal tension and anal medical problems, so evident in my research, also be demonstrated among a large population of patients with anal-rectal medical problems? I feel certain that it would. If so, the medical community has an obligation to inform its patients of what they can do to participate in the treatment of their own anal-rectal problems. Part of that treatment might well be pleasurable self-exploration.

BIBLIOGRAPHY

Adler, A. (Ansbacher and Ansbacher, eds.). *Superiority and social interest.* New York: Viking Press, 1964.

Annon, J. *The behavioral treatment of sexual problems. Vol. 1: Brief Therapy.* Honolulu: Enabling Systems, Inc., 1974.

Asher, J. (Interviewed by D'Eramo, J.). All about parasites. *New York Native.* January 16-29, 1984, 19-21.

Bach, G.R. and Wyden, P. *The intimate enemy.* New York: Avon, 1968

_____ and Goldberg, H. *Creative aggression.* New York: Doubleday, 1974.

Barbach, L.G. *For yourself: the fulfillment of female sexuality.* New York: Signet, 1975.

Bell, A.P. and Weinberg, M.S. *Homosexualities.* New York: Simon & Schuster, 1978.

Belliveau, F. and Richter, L. *Understanding human sexual inadequacy.* New York: Bantam, 1970.

Benson, H. *The relaxation response.* New York: Avon, 1975.

Berne, E. *Games people play.* New York: Grove Press, 1964.

Bolling, D.R. Prevalence, goals and complications of heterosexual anal intercourse in a gynecologic population. *Journal of Reproductive Medicine.* 1977, *19,* 120-24.

Brecher, R. and Brecher, E.M. *An analysis of human sexual response.* New York: New American Library, 1966.

Broverman, I. K., et. al. Sex role stereotypes and clinical judgments of mental health. *Journal of Consulting and Clinical Psychology*, 1970, *34*, 1-7.

Brown, B.B. *New mind, new body.* New York: Harper and Row, 1974.

Buie, L.A. *Practical proctology.* 2nd ed. Springfield: Charles C. Thomas, 1960.

Catterall, R.D. Sexually transmitted diseases of the anus and rectum. *Clinics in Gastroenterology.* September, 1975, *4*, 659-69.

Clark, D. *Loving someone gay.* New York: New American Library, 1977.

Comfort, A. *The joy of sex: a gourmet guide to love-making.* New York: Crown, 1972.

Consumer Reports. *The medicine show.* 5th ed. New York: Pantheon, 1980.

Darlington, R.C. Laxatives. *Handbook of non-prescription drugs.* Washington, D.C.: American Pharmaceutical Association, 1973.

Davenport, W. Sexual patterns and their regulation in a society of the Southwest Pacific. In F.A. Beach (Ed.) *Sex and behavior.* New York: John Wiley & Sons, 1965.

Davis, M., Eshelman, E.R., & McKay, M. *The relaxation and stress reduction workbook.* Richmond, CA: New Harbinger, 1980.

Dawson, L.H. (Ed.). *Sexual life in ancient Greece.* New York: Barnes and Noble, 1963.

D'Eramo, J. Hepatitis now. *Christopher Street.* November, 1983, *7*, 22-3.

———. Poppers: the writing on the wall. *New York Native.* June 4-17, 1984, 9.

Dritz, S. K. and Goldsmith, R. S. Sexually transmissible protozoal, bacterial and viral enteric infections. *Comprehensive Therapy.* January, 1980, *5* (13), 34-40.

Edwardes, A. *The jewel in the lotus.* Tandem: London, 1965.

Ellison, C. Vaginismus. *Medical Aspects of Human Sexuality.* August, 1972.

Erikson, E. H. Identity and the life cycle. *Psychological Issues.* Vol. 1. New York: International Universal Press, 1959.

Farina, A. Stigmas: potent behavior and molders. *Behavior Today.* 1972, *2* (25).

Feigen, G.M. Proctologic disorders of sex deviates. *California Medicine*, August, 1954, *81*, 79-83.

Felman, Y. and Nikitas, J. Nongonococcal urethritis. *Journal of the American Medical Association*, 1981, *245*, 381-86.

Ford, C.S. & Beach, F. A. *Patterns of sexual behavior*. New York: Ace, 1951.

Freedman, M. and Mayes, H. *Loving man*. New York: Hark Publishing Co., 1976.

Freud, S. (1900). The interpretation of dreams. *Standard edition of the complete psychological works of Sigmund Freud* (Ed. James Strachey). London: Hogarth Press and the Institute for Psycho-Analysis, Vols. 4 & 5.

_____ (1905). Three essays on the theory of sexuality. *Complete Works*, Vol. 7.

_____ (1913). Totem and taboo. *Complete Works*, Vol. 13.

_____ (1915). Introductory lectures on psychoanalysis. *Complete Works*, Vols. 15 & 16.

Gillespie, O. *Herpes: what to do when you have it*. New York: Grossett and Dunlap, 1982.

Gluckman, J. B., Kleinman, M. & May, A. Primary syphilis of the rectum. *N.Y. State Journal of Medicine*. November, 1974, 2210-11.

Goliger, J.C. *Surgery of the anus, rectum and colon*. 2nd ed. Springfield, IL: Charles C. Thomas, 1967.

Grosicki, T. S. and Knoll, K. R. Hemorrhoidal preparations. In *Handbook of non-prescription drugs*. Washington, D.C.: American Pharmaceutical Association, 1973.

Haley, T.J. Review of the physiological effects of amyl, butyl, and isobutyl nitrites. *Clinical Toxicology*, 1980, *16*, 317-29.

Heiman, J. R. Women's sexual arousal. *Psychology Today*. April, 1975, 91-94.

Henry, G. W. *Sex variants*. New York: Paul B. Hoeber, 1941.

Holmes, G.W. and Dresser, R. The use of amyl nitrite as an anti-spasmodic in roentgen examination of the gastrointestinal tract. *American Journal of Roentgenology*, 1928, *19*, 44.

Holt, R. L. *Hemorrhoids: a cure and preventive*. Laguna Beach: California Health Publications, 1977. (To order from publisher, send $8.50 to P.O. Box 963, Laguna Beach, CA 92652).

266

Hunt, M. *Sexual behavior in the 1970's*. Chicago: Playboy Press, 1974.

Hyams, L. and Philpot, J. An epidemiological investigation of hemorrhoids. *The American Journal of Proctology*. June, 1970, 177.

Jourard, S.M. *The transparent self* (revised). New York: D. Van Nostrand, 1971.

————. *Self disclosure: an experimental analysis of the transparent self*. New York: Wiley, 1971.

Jung, C. G. (1951) *Aion*. Collected works, vol. 9, Part II (translated by R. F. C. Hull). Princeton University Press, 1959.

Kanfer, F. H. and Saslow, G. Behavioral diagnosis. In C. Franks (Ed.), *Behavior therapy: appraisal and status*. New York: McGraw-Hill, 1969.

Kaplan, H.S. *The new sex therapy*. New York: Brunner/Mazel, 1974.

————. *Disorders of sexual desire*. New York: Brunner/Mazel, 1979.

Karkowski, J., Pollock, W. F. & London, C. W. Imperforate anus. *American Journal of Surgery*. August, 1973, *126*, 141-47.

Karlan, A. *Sexuality and homosexuality*. New York: Norton, 1971.

Karr, R. Homosexual labeling and the male role. *Journal of Social Issues*. Summer, 1978, *34* (3).

Katchadourian, H. A. and Lunde, D. T. *Fundamentals of human sexuality*. 3rd ed. New York: Holt, Rinehart and Winston, 1980.

Katz, J. *Gay American History*. New York: Thomas Y. Crowell, 1976.

Kegel, A. H. Sexual functions of the pubococcygeus muscle. *Western Journal of Surgery*, 1952, *60*, 521-24.

Kinsey, A. C., Pomeroy, W. B. & Martin, C. E. *Sexual behavior in the human male*. Philadelphia: W. B. Saunders, 1948.

————, ————, ———— and Gebhard, P. H. *Sexual behavior in the human female*. Philadelphia: W. B. Saunders, 1953.

Kornetsky, C. *Pharmacology: drugs affecting behavior*. New York: Wiley and Sons, 1976.

Lappe, F. M. *Diet for a small planet* (revised). New York: Ballantine, 1975.

Levitt, M.D. Intestinal gas. *Postgraduate Medicine.* January, 1975, *57* (1), 77.

Lief, H. I. (Ed.). *Medical aspects of human sexuality.* Baltimore: Williams and Wilkins, 1975.

Loulan, J. *Lesbian sex.* San Francisco: Spinsters Ink, 1984.

Lowen, A. Bio-energetic group therapy. In H. M. Ruitenbach (Ed.) *Group Therapy Today.* New York: Atherton, 1971.

_____ *Bioenergetics.* New York: Penguin, 1975.

Lowry, T.P. Bracioproctic Eroticism. *British Journal of Sexual Medicine,* January, 1981, *8,* 32-33.

MacDonald, A. P., et. al. Attitudes toward homosexuality; preservation of sex morality or the double standard. *Journal of Consulting and Clinical Psychology.* 1973, *40,* 161.

Marmor, M. et al. Risk factors for kaposi's sarcoma in homosexual men. *The Lancet.* May, 1982, 1083-87.

Marrou, H. I. *A history of education in antiquity.* New York: Sheed and Ward, 1956.

Marshall, D. S. and Suggs, R. C. *Human sexual behavior.* New York: Basic Books, 1971.

Masters, W. H. and Johnson, V. E. *Human sexual response.* Boston: Little, Brown, & Co., 1966.

_____ *Human sexual inadequacy.* Boston: Little, Brown, & Co., 1970.

_____ *Homosexuality in perspective.* Boston: Little, Brown, & Co., 1979.

May, R. *Power and innocence.* New York: Delta, 1972.

McWhirter, D. and Mattison, A. *The male couple.* Englewood Cliffs, NJ: Prentice-Hall, 1984.

Mercer, B.J. *Anal eroticism in women.* Doctoral Dissertation, 1983. Institute for Advanced Study of Human Sexuality, San Francisco.

Morin, J. *Men loving themselves: images of males self-sexuality.* Burlingame, CA: Down There Press, 1980.

Newell, G.R. et al. Toxicity, immunosuppressive effects and carcinogenic potential of volatile nitrites: possible relationship to kaposi's sarcoma. *Pharmacotherapy,* September, 1984, 235-236.

Obler, M. Systematic desensitization in sexual disorders. *Journal of Behavior Therapy and Experimental Psychiatry.* 1973, *4,* 93-101.

Ostrow, D., Sandholzer, T. and Felman, Y., eds. *Sexually transmitted diseases in homosexual men.* New York: Plenum Medical Book Co., 1983.

Owen, R. L. & Hill, J. L. Rectal and pharyngeal gonorrhea in homosexual men. *Journal of the American Medical Association.* June, 1972, *220*, 1315-18.

Painter, N. S. Diverticular disease of the colon. *Geriatrics.* February, 1976, 90.

Peterson, J.R. The playboy reader's sex survey, part I. *Playboy,* January, 1983, *30*, 108.

Plaut, M.E. The doctor's guide to you and your colon. New York: Harper and Row, 1982.

Reich, W. *The function of the orgasm.* New York: Farrar, Strauss & Giroux, 1973.

Reichman, R. et. al. Treatment of recurrent herpes simplex infections with oral acyclovir. *Journal of the American Medical Association,* April 27, 1984, *251*, 2103-7.

Samuels, M. and Samuels, N. *Seeing with the mind's eye: the history, techniques and uses of visualization.* New York: Random House, 1975.

Sigell, L. T., et. al. Popping and snorting volatile nitrites: a current fad for getting high. *American Journal of Psychiatry,* October, 1978, *135* (10), 1216-18.

Silverstein, C. and White, E. *The joy of gay sex.* New York: Crown Publishers, 1977.

Singer, J. *Androgyny.* New York: Anchor Press, 1976.

Sloane, B. The converging paths of behavior therapy and psychotherapy. *American Journal of Psychiatry,* 1969, *125*, 49-57.

Sohn, N. and Robilotti, J. G. Gay bowel syndrome: review of colonic and rectal conditions in 200 male homosexuals. *American Journal of Gastroenterology,* 1969, *125*, 49-57.

Spada, J. *The Spada report.* New York: New American Library, 1979.

Steiner, C. M. *Scripts people live.* New York: Bantam, 1974.

Szmuness, W., et. al. Hepatitis B vaccine: demonstration of efficacy in a controlled clinical trial in a high-risk population in the U.S. *New England Journal of Medicine,* 1980, *303*, 833-41.

Tavris, C. and Sadd, S. *The redbook on female sexuality*. New York: Delacorte Press, 1977.

Tripp, C. A. *The homosexual matrix*. New York: McGraw-Hill, 1975.

Turell, R. *Treatment in proctology*. Baltimore: Williams & Wilkins, 1949.

Ullman, L. P. and Krasner, L. *A psychological approach to abnormal behavior*. Englewood Cliffs, NJ: Prentice-Hall, 1969.

Villarejos, V. M., et. al. Role of saliva, urine and feces in the transmission of type B hepatitis. *New England Journal of Medicine*, 1974, *291*, 1375-78.

Walker, M. *Men loving men*. San Francisco: Gay Sunshine Press, 1977.

Weil, A. *The natural mind*. Boston: Houghton Mifflin, 1972.

Whittington, W., et. al. Acyclovir therapy for genital herpes: enthusiasm and caution in equal doses. *Journal of the American Medical Association*, April 27, 1984, *251*, 2116-17.

Wolfe, L. The sexual profile of that Cosmopolitan girl. *Cosmopolitan*, September, 1980, 254-65.

Wolpe, J. *Psychotherapy by reciprocal inhibition*. Stanford: Stanford University Press, 1958.

Zilbergeld, B. *Male sexuality*. New York: Bantam, 1978.

_____ and Evans, M. The inadequacy of Masters & Johnson. *Psychology Today*. August, 1980, *14*, 29-43.

Zimbardo, P. G. *Shyness*. New York: Jove Publishers, 1977.

INDEX

A

Acyclovir, 210
Adler, Alfred, 191
Age
  and parent-child dynamics, 184
  as symbol of power, 184-185
AIDS (Aquired Immune Deficiency Syndrome), 2, 111, 120, 157, 161, 205-225
AIDS antibody test, 217-218
AIDS anxiety and anal intercourse, 161
AIDS anxiety and sexual problems, 221, 217
AIDS information sources, 222
Alcohol
  effects of, 109
  use in sexual activity, 105-106
  and hepatitis, 211
  and AIDS, 222, 225
Amoebas, 212
Anal cushions
  and hemorrhoids, 229
  blood flow to/from, 76
Anal health
  monitoring and maintaining, 198-199

Anal intercourse
  and attitudes toward homosexuality, 10, 21
  and power dynamics, 192-195, 256
  attempting with partner, 160-163
  cross-cultural attitudes toward, 10-14
  during menstruation, 14
  partner selection for, 200
  diagrams of positions, 164-165
  receiving, as therapy goal, 237-238
  and personal preferences, 166-169
  abstaining from during AIDS crisis, 161
  concerns of "insertors", 169
  as route for hepatitis transmission, 211
  as route for AIDS transmission, 224-225
  condom use with, 2, 161-223
  avoidance during AIDS crisis, 161
Anal pain
  agreement to protect self from, 39
  drug use to tolerate, 110, 119
  initial awareness of, 67-69
  past memories of, 70-71
  myths about inevitibility of, 72

Jack Morin, psychotherapist, sex therapist, researcher and educator, has developed and tested many new sex counseling techniques. The research upon which this book is based was done at *Saybrook Institute* in San Francisco, where he received his Ph.D. in psychology. In addition to his private therapy practice, he teaches Human Sexuality at *Skyline College*. He is currently engaged in a fascinating research project on the psychology of sexual excitement. He is investigating the structure of eroticism, as expressed in both fantasy and actual behavior. If you would like additional information on this research, write Dr. Morin at Yes Press.

ALSO BY JACK MORIN

Men Loving Themselves: Images of Male Self-Sexuality.
Down There Press, 1980. $10.50

Sensitive photographs of twelve men doing what they usually do to pleasure themselves. The book concludes with a groundbreaking discussion of the psychology of male self-sexuality.

SELECTED PUBLICATIONS FROM
DOWN THERE PRESS/YES PRESS

Joani Blank. **The Playbook for Women About Sex.** 1975. $4.00.
Joani Blank. **The Playbook for Men About Sex.** 1976, Second edition. 1981. $4.00.

Sexual self-awareness workbooks (more fun than work) for women and men of all ages and sexual persuasions.

Joani Blank. **Good Vibrations: the Complete Guide to Vibrators.** 1983. $4.50.

Informal guide to the acquisition and enjoyment of vibrators for solo and partner sex play.

Isadora Alman. **Aural Sex and Verbal Intercourse.** 1984. $8.50.

A delightful and informative look at an urban sex information switchboard.

Yes Press is an imprint of Down There Press. Down There Press was founded by Joani Blank in 1975 to publish her Playbook for Women About Sex. Anal Pleasure and Health is the press' ninth title. Down There Press is the only independent publisher specializing in sex education and sexual self-awareness books for adults and children.

ORDERING INFORMATION

The publications of Down There Press/Yes Press
can be ordered direct from :

Down There Press
P.O. Box 2086
Burlingame, CA 94011-2086

Please add $1.25 for the first item and 75¢ for each additional item to cover postage and handling. California residents add 6% sales tax. Enclose payment in full with your order. Contact the publisher for quantity prices.

Raise your consciousness and that of your local bookstore by requesting that they carry the publications of Down There Press.

Qty	Title		Price
_____	Anal Pleasure and Health	$ 9.50	_____
_____	Men Loving Themselves	10.50	_____
_____	Playbook for Women About Sex	4.00	_____
_____	Playbook for Men About Sex	4.00	_____
_____	Good Vibrations	4.50	_____
_____	Aural Sex and Verbal Intercourse	8.50	_____

California residents, add 6½% sales tax _____

Postage and handling $1.25

TOTAL _____

Name _____

Address _____

_____

Mastercard/Visa #_____ Exp. _____